Advance praise for *Making Love Just*

"This excellent book is a must-read for anyone seeking a progressive, principled, and provocative guide to Christian sexual ethics. In moving us from 'just making love' to 'making love just,' Marvin Ellison addresses difficult and complex issues head-on, ranging from polyamory to same-sex domestic abuse. LGBTQ folks will find this book especially helpful, whether in the classroom, congregation, bedroom, or beyond."

Patrick S. Cheng, Assistant Professor of Historical and Systematic Theology
Episcopal Divinity School, Cambridge, Massachusetts
Author of *Radical Love: An Introduction to Queer Theology*

"*Making Love Just* is an eloquent and comprehensive guide to doing liberative sexual ethics for human and planetary good. While Ellison finds the Christian tradition is in many respects a noble tradition to preserve and promote, when it comes to the dynamic processes of sex and sexuality over time, he pursues its spirited critique and transformation. In solidarity with the sexually abused, exploited, and vulnerable, he raises astute moral questions and demonstrates the difficult process of discerning what is just and loving in sex, gender, and family issues—and to delight in taking a stand with others on controversial matters of sexual justice."

Marilyn J. Legge, Associate Professor of Christian Ethics
Emmanuel College of Victoria University and Toronto School of Theology

"Ellison urges a profoundly loving re-call to compassionate conversation to all who would claim to exemplify 'the unfathomable love of Christ.' With courageous intellectual boldness and a gentle pastoral heart, *Making Love Just* readily provides a theologically grounded ethic way beyond perplexity and into the sacred realm of precious and life-giving relational possibility. What a timely scholarly gift this book offers to those ever anxious to doing justice, loving mercy, and walking humbly."

Dr. Jenny Plane Te Paa, Dean
Te Rau Kahikatea, St. John's Theological College, Auckland, New Zealand

"Marvin Ellison weaves many wise voices, including his own, into a 'liberating method of ethical discernment.' This book starts new, necessary conversations. The welcome result is justice-love and a safer world. Read and heed!"

Mary E. Hunt, codirector of the Women's Alliance
for Theology, Ethics and Ritual (WATER)
Editor with Diann L. Neu of *New Feminist Christianity:
Many Voices, Many Views*

"Faith leaders across traditions are calling for a new sexual ethic focused on personal relationships and social justice rather than particular sexual acts. That yearning for a sex-positive and justice-oriented framework is expressed strongly in the Religious Institute's own 'Religious Declaration on Sexual Morality, Justice, and Healing.' That's why I am so pleased with Marvin Ellison's latest book, which provides such a helpful guide for the theologian, seminarian, and person of faith who is seeking to understand and integrate a truly redemptive Christian ethic of sexuality."

Debra Haffner, Executive Director, Religious Institute
Author of *A Time to Build: Creating Sexually Healthy Faith Communities* and *Meditations on the Good News*

"In advocating for a sex-positive transformation of Christian approaches to sexual ethics, Ellison offers here a challenging and much-needed discussion of many of the thorny issues that plague contemporary conversations about sexuality. By helping readers to reframe the questions, Ellison opens up entrenched debates about what is 'right' and 'wrong' to new avenues of discourse that privilege justice, human dignity, and relationships of equality and mutual respect. This book is essential reading for anyone interested in questions of human sexuality."

Rebecca Todd Peters, Associate Professor and Chair,
Department of Religious Studies, Elon University
Author of *In Search of the Good Life:
The Ethics of Globalization*

"A Revolution of Justice! Remarkably written, Ellison gives us a gift of sex-positive approaches to Christian sexual ethics. Weaving the analytic with sincere attention to tears in our communities crying for hope, *Making Love Just* exposes the truth in our traditions that silences sex talk and dishonors bodies and sexualities by breaking forth new streams of thought with liberating clarity, method, and purpose. This book meets us at our point of need with a prophetic tongue and transformative embrace. You must read this book! It paves a brave path of healing grace, wholeness, and safer spirituality for us all!"

Melanie L. Harris, Associate Professor of Religion and Ethics,
Texas Christian University
Author of *Gifts of Virtue: Alice Walker and Womanist Ethics*

MAKING LOVE JUST

SEXUAL ETHICS FOR PERPLEXING TIMES

Marvin M. Ellison

Fortress Press

Minneapolis

MAKING LOVE JUST
Sexual Ethics for Perplexing Times

Cover art: PhotoAlto Photography
Cover design: Alisha Lofgren
Book design: PerfecType, Nashville, TN

Library of Congress Cataloging-in-Publication Data
Ellison, Marvin Mahan.
  Making love just : sexual ethics for perplexing times / Marvin M. Ellison.
     p. cm.
  Includes bibliographical references.
  ISBN 978-0-8006-9884-3 (pbk. : alk. paper) — ISBN 978-1-4514-2440-9
(ebook)
  1. Sex—Religious aspects—Christianity. 2. Sexual ethics. I. Title.
  BT708.E46 2012
  241'.664—dc23
                                    2012005231

Manufactured in the U.S.A.

In gratitude for their courageous witness and
joyful solidarity in the struggle for justice:

Students at Bangor Theological Seminary
and colleagues in the
Maine Interfaith Council for Reproductive Choices
and the
Religious Coalition Against Discrimination

▪ CONTENTS ▪

▪ ACKNOWLEDGMENTS ▪

This book was conceived during the 2009 marriage equality campaign in Maine when it became clear that many people were feeling challenged not only about sexual difference and how to talk publicly about sex and sexuality, but also about ethical values and how to engage publicly in ethical inquiry.

Friends and colleagues helped me early on give shape to this project and have given me ongoing encouragement, including Glenn Miller, Pamela Shellberg, Sylvia Thorson-Smith, and Anne Underwood.

A version of chapter 3 ("Is It Still Adultery if the Spouse Has Alzheimer's?") was presented at the 2008 Schwartz Rounds on Ethics in Health Care at the Maine Medical Center in Portland. An earlier draft of chapter 4 on same-sex marriage was presented as the 2008 Carter Heyward Scholars' Program Lecture at the Episcopal Divinity School in Cambridge, Massachusetts. Nancy A. Foss of Maine's Abortion Access Project did a careful read of chapter 6 on reproductive justice and offered numerous suggestions.

In addition, I am grateful to the Saint Andrew's Trust for the Study of Religion and Society in Wellington, New Zealand, for their kind invitation to give the 2011 Geering Lectures. The timing could not have been better because I was on a sabbatical leave from Bangor Theological Seminary in Maine, working on this manuscript, and was delighted to spend March in a warmer clime. I am very appreciative of the opportunity that my New Zealand hosts, especially the Reverend Dr. Margaret Mayman in Wellington and the Reverend Dr. Sarah Park in Auckland, provided me to "field test" some of this material while enjoying their gracious hospitality.

I also wish to express my appreciation to the Trustees of Bangor Theological Seminary for granting me a sabbatical during 2010–2011 and to my faculty colleagues who carried heavier burdens during my absence. Librarian Laurie McQuarrie has always been generous in helping me locate resources. Moreover, it has been a pleasure to work, once again, with Ulrike Guthrie, a superb editor and treasured friend, and also to carry this project to fruition with Susan Johnson and the fine staff at Fortress Press. Every author should have such a supportive team. And, finally, I am grateful to my life partner, Frank Brooks, my sister, Elizabeth Ellison, and my colleague Mary

Hobgood for reading the manuscript at various stages, making all sorts of fine suggestions, and pushing me to "write big" and reach out to as diverse an audience as possible. After all, many of us are not only sexually perplexed and in need of ethical guidance, but also hungry for a justice-centered spirituality that encourages us to embrace the body as holy and good.

Where Do We Draw Our Lines, and Why?
An Invitation to Ethical Inquiry

Art, like morality, consists in drawing the line somewhere.

GILBERT K. CHESTERTON[1]

Like it or not, today we are all pioneers, picking our way through uncharted and unstable territory. The old rules are no longer reliable guides.

STEPHANIE COONTZ[2]

This book is an invitation to ethical inquiry about sex and sexual values. Given all the personal conflicts and cultural controversies that continue to swirl around human sexuality, an ethical guide for those who find themselves sexually perplexed seems necessary. Who among us is ever surprised to hear people say that they are not well prepared to engage in ethical deliberation about these matters? We might even include ourselves among those who feel both challenged and ill prepared.

Historian Dagmar Herzog, in writing about sex in crisis in contemporary United States culture, comments: "There is much titillating talk about sex in America, yet there is little talk about sex that is morally engaged and affirmative."[3] This book seeks to correct this sorry state of affairs by modeling an alternative discourse that is both sex-positive and ethically principled. I do so because as a Christian ethicist I am persuaded that something far better than "sex in crisis" is possible, but the question remains, how might we get to that better place?

Movement forward requires at least three things from us. First, we must not become so fearful of conflict that we try to avoid it at all costs or rush to settle matters without carefully sorting things out. Second, we must ask the right questions.

Otherwise, despite our best efforts, we are likely to miss the mark. Third, we must engage the rich moral wisdom found not only in the Christian (and other religious) traditions, but also among contemporary feminist, LBGTQ (lesbian, bisexual, gay, transgender, and queer or questioning), and anti-racism scholars and activists. If we disregard alternative voices or dismiss emerging perspectives about contested matters, we risk cutting ourselves off from sources of fresh moral insight. In ethics as in life, *to whom* we pay attention and *what* we notice as important make all the difference.

Because ethics, like art, is about figuring out where to draw one's lines, the process of ethical inquiry takes perseverance and skill. Even with these in evidence, sometimes the effort still goes awry. Whenever that happens, bad ethics, like bad art, must be critiqued, packed up, and discarded. However, good ethics, like good art, requires public display and deserves wide public engagement because of its power to stimulate our imaginations and enrich community life. As artists testify, it is possible to develop into a better artist, but sharpening one's "eye" and refining one's skills take time and practice. The same holds true for those seeking to become more adept as ethical practitioners.

Any ethical guide about human sexuality worth its salt should assist readers in making sense of a broad range of sexual issues and also help them generate effective action responses. My hope is that this guide will promote both sound thinking and sound action. After all, the aim of ethical inquiry is not only to understand, but also to transform the world out of the recognition that not everything is as it should be and out of the belief that change is possible.

My intended audience is people who, like myself, are disquieted about a host of sexuality issues, but find that they have little or no tolerance for moralisms or ethics by taboo. They are ready for the hard work necessary to clarify what is just and loving, and they are committed to act on that moral wisdom even when there may be heated disagreements about the right course to follow. For this reason, ethical inquiry is not for the fainthearted. It takes courage to plunge into and stick with this process of discerning how to enhance the human and planetary good.

When confronted by moral perplexities, including perplexities about sexuality and relational intimacy, philosopher Anthony Weston reminds us that it is seldom enough to "follow our feelings" or "fly by instinct." People "come to ethics," he writes, "to learn how to *live*," or, again, in order to learn to live *mindfully*.[4] Such reflection typically starts when conflict stirs inside us, plays out between us and others, or perhaps does both. Moral ambiguity surfaces when we register that there is more than one credible choice before us, and we must decide which to choose, and why. Moral diversity arises when we recognize that responsible people differ in their moral judgments and can offer good, even compelling reasons for their positions, and we must figure out where we stand, and why. The why is important because ethics asks us to give an accounting of our choices, first, in order to clarify our reasoning to ourselves and, second, so that we might engage others in dialogue, perhaps persuade them to our way of thinking, or even find sufficient reason to change our own minds.

This book invites us, as moral agents who are also sexual persons, to sort out how to live more mindfully in the midst of cultural conflicts about sexuality. Because conflict is unsettling, at various junctures we may be tempted to avoid ethical conflict altogether or, alternatively, be tempted to rush to judgment, all for the sake of putting things to rest quickly. This book proposes a different response. Just as the slow food movement offers a creative alternative to fast food consumption, this book is a project in *slow-down ethics*, asking us to sit with perplexing, even discomforting questions, listen to fresh and sometimes challenging perspectives, and patiently work out matters as best we can. This reflective process is a necessary antidote, on the one hand, to fear of conflict, and, on the other hand, to making snap judgments or indulging in what might be called "moral quickies." As we pause, at least for a while, to focus our minds and consult our hearts, we rightly seek to bring our whole selves to ethical inquiry, both our feelings and our best critical thinking. However, as Weston acknowledges, "when things are really unclear, feelings may even have to wait. Premature clarity is worse than confusion. We may have to live with some questions a long time before we can decide how we ought to feel about them."[5]

When it comes to sex and sexual ethics, people draw their lines all over the place. Some exhibit Weston's "premature clarity" because of their seemingly unshakable confidence that disputed matters can be readily settled by drawing a clear line in the sand or by simply repeating conventional wisdom, though perhaps in an ever-louder voice. Others, confused about Christianity's good news in relation to sex and uncertain about what ethically principled sexual relationships look like, remain silent so that they won't offend others in a postmodern, increasingly diverse church and culture.

The approach I offer here differs from both the shouting and the silence found in Christian circles. Although many presume that the work of Christian ethics is to describe a fixed, noncontestable moral code "for all time" and then call people to compliance, I dissent from following that path. Rather than map out a code of (typically) prohibited sexual acts, I am interested in developing a liberating method of ethical discernment that critiques outdated assumptions about gender, sexual difference, and family patterns and clarifies how "sexual sin" these days is far less about sex and far more about the misuse of power and exploitation of vulnerability.

At present, matters of sex, gender, family, and the social order are under intense scrutiny not only within Christianity but within every religious tradition. The conventional Christian moral framework of "celibacy in singleness, sex only in marriage" is being explicitly contested by many inside and outside the church who no longer abide by that moral code. While some argue that what is most significant here is how human sinfulness and irresponsibility are at play, I find that that reading of social reality misses the mark and fails to account adequately for the widening gap between the conventional moral code and how many, perhaps even most people live their lives and structure their loving. I would argue that the real problem is that the inherited moral code can no longer be presumed adequate. As Catholic ethicist

Christine Gudorf insists, "The entire approach of Christian sexual ethics has been and is grievously flawed, [and] gradual, piecemeal revision is not sufficient."[6]

To begin, a rule-based sexual morality has been rigid, legalistic, and punitive, relying on fear and shame to keep people compliant and on the "straight and narrow." A more relationally focused ethical framework is called for, one that appreciates how the presumed ideal of lifelong, procreative heterosexual marriage no longer fits with, or speaks adequately to, our cultural reality. After all, divorce is not always tragic, but is sometimes the public recognition that an authentic marriage never took hold in the first place or at least has now ended for one or both parties.[7] After all, the normative practice for most heterosexual couples most of the time is now contracepted, not procreative sex. After all, not everyone is heterosexual; some are gay, lesbian, bisexual, transgender, or questioning. After all, most heterosexual couples live together, at least for a time, and postpone tying the knot. Moreover, many single persons, including church-attending older adults in retirement communities, are sexually active and living in ways that appear morally responsible, a situation similar to that of many same-sex couples who manage to sustain mature, committed partnerships. At the same time, there is far more public acknowledgment that not everything in heterosexual marriage is ethical, including emotional neglect, marital rape, and spouse abandonment.

A consensus is emerging about the necessity of redrawing the ethical map, but how should a contemporary Christian ethic of sexuality be formulated? How might we help shift the discourse to emphasize justice and love as the normative expectation for intimate relationships across the boards? Would such a single standard—for both gay and nongay and for both the married and nonmarried—raise or lower the ethical bar?[8] Above all, how might we break with a sex-negative, patriarchal religious framework and instead embrace the vitality of a justice-centered spirituality that is women-friendly, gay-affirming, and multiracial and welcomes a diversity of perspectives with the power to name, invoke, and represent the sacred?

Throughout much church history, Christian teachings have been highly negative about the human body (and especially women's bodies), sensuality, sexual intimacy, and the right ordering of sexual and gender relations. The watchwords in Christian moral discourse about sexuality have been suspicion, avoidance, and restriction. From Augustine on, characteristic motifs have been repeated in Christian responses to sex. In the popular mind of a Christian-based culture, sex is an alien and dangerous force to be contained. Sin is defined essentially in sexual terms, above all as loss of control over the body and capitulation to sexual desire. Because women are associated with the body, emotionality, and "lower" nature, they must be supervised and kept under control for men's safety as well as "for their own good." Sex itself is morally suspect and redeemable only if it serves a higher purpose outside itself, namely, procreation. And (male) homosexuality is condemned, in part, because it is non-procreative and, in part, because in the sexual act one partner is supposedly passive (the female) and the other active (the male), and it is demeaning for a man to act womanish or to be treated as a subordinate. Lesbians, bisexuals, and transgender as well as intersexed persons rarely appear on the moral radar (a mixed blessing).

This solemn and joyless moral legacy is both fear-based and exceedingly wary of sex, women, and sexual difference. In the patriarchal Christian imagination, sex is cast as a problem, typically precipitated by the female or gay Other. The fear response to otherness is couched in terms of protecting orthodoxy, reasserting control, and punishing nonconformity to (patriarchal) Christian norms of celibacy and heterosexual procreative monogamy. Guilt, shame, and repression mark the dominant Christian tradition's moral response to sexuality.

Catholic theologian Daniel Maguire speaks of a regrettable turn in the history of the church, beginning with the Constantinian establishment, toward "pelvic theology" and an obsession with sexual control. In the third and fourth centuries CE, as the church shifted from prophetic to establishment status, it no longer defined religious identity and spiritual integrity in terms of resistance to the imperial state and its cult. Increasingly, the church hierarchy asserted power by controlling the sexual behavior of believers and by creating a heightened clerical image for itself. Citing Samuel Laeuchli's historical investigation of the Council of Elvira (309), Maguire observes that the church turned increasingly to sex in order to define both orthodoxy and clerical authority. This "Elvira syndrome" continues to operate today whenever church elites project a narrowly clerical image of the church and rely on sexual control as a primary tool for that project. As Maguire conjectures, "Contrary to popular myth, Constantine did not convert to Christianity. Christianity converted to Constantine, and Elvira signals the first symptoms of this perversion."[9]

This dominant imperial approach to Christian sexual morals is shaped by three assumptions. First, moral truth is located in the past, in a tradition defined by patriarchal authority. Second, theological discourse about sexuality proceeds in a highly abstract, ahistorical, and largely deductive manner. Third, there is a deep suspicion of "advocates" speaking out of their particular moral struggles, especially anyone who appears self-interested in making moral claims. Religious elites proceed on the assumption that they are offering a disinterested, "pure" ethic above the rancor of social divisions and untainted by particular biases or interests.

In contrast, this book follows the logic of a liberating ethic, which operates with quite different assumptions that are born out of a participatory, communal mode of ethical inquiry. First, moral truth is found in the past, but also grasped anew as communities of conscientious people encounter new circumstances and inquire whether and how the past offers insight and direction. We "read" and appropriate the past not for its own sake, but for the sake of present needs and struggles. Second, appropriation of the past is never a simple matter of applying past truths to present issues, but rather a creative, dynamic, and even messy and jarring process of engaging (and being engaged by) a living, pluriform tradition involved in its own continual change and adaptation. Third, although a liberating ethic is aware of the fact that the past makes claims on the present, the present also makes claims on the past. Insight from the past is dependent upon and filtered through the interests and limitations of present communities as they recognize and value the past. Therefore, we may engage the past freely and critically, claiming our responsibility as authoritative interpreters and "ethical artists" to reshape the Christian tradition as needed, in company with many others.

Above all else, the imperial and patriarchalized Christian tradition has obscured the central place of justice in biblical faith. It has also downplayed how justice making restores the vitality of communities, including faith communities. Pursuing a comprehensive justice includes critiquing sexual injustice with its interlocking components of sex-negativity, compulsory heterosexuality, and sexualized violence. Beyond critique, justice making also involves the constructive movement to create the conditions of respect and well-being that would make it possible for all people to thrive, especially those now on the margins. Therefore, actualizing sexual justice means, first, in light of Christian sex-negativity, honoring the goodness of human bodies and recognizing sexuality as a spiritual power for expressing care and respect through touch. Second, in the face of compulsory heterosexuality, sexual justice requires recognition of and respect for sexual difference, including diversity of body shape and size, sexual orientation, gender identity and expression, and marriage and family patterns. Third, in the face of sexual violence, abuse, and exploitation, sexual justice calls for respect and compassionate care between persons and groups. Fair distribution of social power and goods is also required along with safety, health, and empowerment, especially for the vulnerable, so all may participate in shaping social arrangements and developing cultural expectations.

This book seeks to increase the reader's skills and confidence for engaging in ethical deliberation about sexuality and, in particular, to explore the demands as well as the opportunities for embodying sexual justice. Each chapter offers a way into Christian ethical inquiry by first posing a question and then offering a response, all the while inviting readers to take the plunge, explore their own questions, and enrich the conversation in ways that will prove useful and even revelatory to themselves and others. For as New Testament scholar Luke Timothy Johnson suggests, "Revelation is not exclusively biblical but occurs in the continuing experience of God in the structures of human freedom."[10]

CHAPTER 1

Why Do We Have to Keep Talking about Sex All the Time?

Serious talk about sexuality is inevitably about society.

Thomas Laqueur[1]

As a Christian ethicist, my short answer to this question of why we must keep talking about sex, sexuality, and sexual ethics is because harm is being done. This harm burdens both individuals and the community, and it causes suffering. Moreover, this harm is caused by injustice. In order to bring healing and hope, we must pursue a broad social justice agenda that embraces a passionate commitment to sexual justice.

To begin with, in cultures strongly influenced by traditional Christian norms about purity, women, and sexuality, as one social theorist has quipped, sex is "presumed guilty until proven innocent."[2] Given this negativity, it is hardly surprising that many people try to avoid this topic altogether, or when they do manage to talk about sex, they often become defensive, reactive, and judgmental. As many people attest, fearful and shaming messages about sex have had all sorts of negative consequences in their lives, but silence about these matters can be just as debilitating if not more so. For this reason, Peggy Brick, a sexuality educator, has dedicated her book to adolescents and young adults this way: "To the young people of this nation who must find their way to sexual health in a world of contradictions—where media scream, 'Always say yes,' where many adults admonish, 'Just say no,' but the majority just say . . . nothing."[3]

That we keep talking matters. But why?

■ Because a cultural crisis is disrupting sexuality and conventional mores

Remaining silent or becoming speechless does little to curb the mindless chatter about sex and sexuality, much less stop the negative messages, because these tend only to escalate during times of disruptive cultural change when moral panics surface about loss of moral certainty, sexual immorality, and the disintegration of family life. Currently, as we witness a worldwide crisis of literally global proportions, we are encountering not only a tumultuous time of rapid change, but more significantly a protracted and very difficult period of structural transformation in which social relations at every level are being altered, from economic arrangements in a global-izing economy to the reordering of power between men and women in the family and throughout the social order. In the midst of this historic restructuring, cultural battles over sexuality, gender, and family are raging everywhere as deeply contested personal and social struggles about the human good, normative patterns for family life, and the legitimacy of cultural authority.

What are the rules for sexual intimacy, and who gets to define and enforce them? These questions are at once highly personal and highly political. As sociologist James Davison Hunter explains, "Cultural conflict is about power—a struggle to achieve or maintain the power to define reality."[4] Therefore, sex and sexuality are far from frivolous or inconsequential matters that only detract attention from the so-called weightier matters of poverty, racism, war, and ecological degradation. Rather, these "intimate matters," far from being sealed off from larger sociocultural dynamics, are embedded in, and reflective of, these more global transformations.

For this reason, at a time when human suffering nearly exceeds our moral imagination's ability to grasp, we must regain moral perspective about our lives-in-relation from the global to the intimate, especially at a time when many people, out of pain and fear, are either turning inward and blaming themselves for their suffering and bewilderment or turning outward to look for enemies and scapegoats who can serve as the culprits for their upset and misery. Attending to sexuality has become morally imperative these days because, as Gayle Rubin puts it, it is at times like this when "people are likely to become dangerously crazy about sexuality." Therefore, she cautions, "sexuality should be treated with special respect in times of great social stress."[5]

■ Because the way we talk about sex, sexuality, and sexual ethics can lead to justice or injustice

While it is imperative that we speak, we must exercise great care about what we actually say about these tender matters. Making a compelling case that harm is being done and that the appropriate response is sexual justice requires us to "change the subject" in two distinctive ways. First, we need to change *what* is being talked about by shifting the topic of conversation away from the misplaced preoccupation with homosexuality and sexual difference and focusing instead on race, gender, sexual, and economic oppression and the pervasive patterns of sexualized violence in this society. Second, we need to change *who* the subject is that is speaking and listened to. What is shaking the foundations is a global power shift as women and LBGT persons of all colors and classes claim the right to be the subjects of their own lives and participants in the renewal of their spiritual traditions. Morally speaking, constructive critique and alternative visions emerge only as persons are no longer silenced or positioned as objects of other people's discourse (as if aliens or merely abstractions) and when, instead, they become self-defining subjects, real persons with whom to enter into dialogue. When the participants at the table change, so does the conversation.

Sexuality is a justice issue. As biblical scholar Walter Brueggemann emphasizes, "In biblical faith the doing of justice is the primary expectation of God."[6] To be sure, justice is multidimensional, but by all accounts sexual or erotic justice is one of the most neglected, trivialized, and even feared dimensions of a comprehensive social justice agenda. Claiming a passion for erotic justice just doesn't sound very Christian, does it? There lies the crux of the problem. It is an understatement to say that faith communities—and here I mean Christian churches—have difficulties dealing with sex. Although much attention continues to be directed toward women's changing roles, nonmarital sex, and the "sin of homosexuality," the reality is that Christians struggle not only with these particular issues but with sexuality as a whole. Massive cultural change, declining denominational influence, and internal dissension do not ease matters.

In trying to gain our bearings in the midst of these swirling dynamics, my wager is that acquiring fresh moral insight about these concerns will depend on three things: first, our facing conflict and working through it rather than evading it; second, our listening to and learning from people who have been hurt, silenced, and rendered invisible by church teaching and practice; and third, speaking up about gender, sexual, and other forms of injustice and calling the community and ourselves to account for reordering relationships so that all may thrive. In this grand project, survivors of sexual and domestic abuse, LBGTQ persons, sexually active divorced and single people, people living with physical and mental disabilities, elders as well as youth, people living with HIV/AIDS, and many others have stories of faith and struggle that can amplify, correct, and revitalize the church's inherited wisdom about sexuality and sexual ethics. If moving forward requires engaging people's lived questions and discovering fresh moral insight, it will also require courageous leadership to foster the kind of hospitality, mutual respect, and safety that will actually enable us, in Nelle Morton's felicitous phrase, "to hear one another into speech."[7]

■ Because sexuality is indispensable to our humanity

Novelist May Sarton in her book *At Seventy* wrote, "This is the best time of my life. I love being old." Someone asked Sarton, "Why is it good being old?" She replied, "Because I am more myself than I have ever been. There is less conflict. I am happier, more balanced, and . . . more powerful. I felt it was an odd word, 'powerful,'" Sarton said, "but I think it's true. I am surer of what my life is all about, have less self-doubt to conquer."[8] If I may paraphrase Sarton, I would say, "This is the best time of my life. I love being gay." I agree with her that in claiming one's self-respect, including one's self-respect as a sexual person, one stands to become happier, more balanced, and, yes, more powerful. Whenever people honor the goodness of their lives, including their sexualities, and whenever they touch that place within them where their passion and spiritual hunger meet, they often discover sources of personal integrity and spiritual empowerment.

Despite all the disquietude about this topic of sex and sexuality, the truth of the matter is that sexuality remains an indispensable component of our humanity. No doubt we humans would be something without our sexualities, but we would surely not be fully recognizable as humans if we could not experience the delight, and sometimes the pain, of living relationally as friends, lovers, and life companions or if we did not feel strong desire for entering into communion with others through tender touching. By sexuality, I mean not only genital sex, but more broadly our embodied capacity for intimate connection. Erotic desire seeks physical, emotional, and spiritual embrace of others, the world, and God, the sacred source of life. By spirituality, I mean our response to the movement of the sacred in our midst. Any spirituality worth having these days will have at its center a desire for justice as communal right-relatedness. Justice making pays attention to how people's well-being is enhanced or diminished by prevailing patterns of social power and vulnerability. The work of justice is an ongoing, never-ending process of remaking community by strengthening relationships and correcting whatever harms people, other earth creatures, and the earth itself.

A progressive Christian framework appreciates how justice, as communally secured respect and care for persons and the earth, is foundational to good loving. Moreover, a just society and a just church will foster the moral freedom of persons, without distinction, to love and be loved and responsibly express their desire for intimate, respectful connection.[9] This is not to say that everyone must be sexually active, genitally speaking, much less married or partnered, to be complete as persons, but it is to recognize that if we deny whole segments of the community the right (and responsibility) to *be* sexual persons and to *do* love in and through their bodies, then we have denied them their full humanity. In other words, we dehumanize persons by oversexualizing or desexualizing them.

Spiritually empowered justice advocates find the courage to say no to apathy, abuse, and injustice, as well as strength to say an equally resounding yes to joy, creativity, and compassion. That's the good news. The bad news is that so few religious people live comfortably with their bodies or at ease with sexual difference. Fear of sexuality and deep suspicion of the erotic are pervasive in the church. No wonder Christians are often viewed as lifeless and devoid of passion! When people fear sensuous touch and become repressive about sexuality, they risk becoming controlling, rigid, and unfeeling. In the process, they lose touch with what brings joy as well as sorrow to themselves and others and often become disconnected from, and therefore unresponsive to, the world around them. Put humorously, they earn the appellation of "God's frozen people."

■ Because it is time to stop injustices from being sexualized

A fearful people are also likely to project their fear and discomfort about sex and sexuality onto others. In our time the overlapping communities of LBGTQ people, people of color, and people living with disabilities have become the cultural repositories or moral dumping ground for other people's dis-ease about sensuality and the body. People with disabilities are dehumanized whenever they are desexualized as "imperfect bodies" for whom sex and embodied intimacy are considered unseemly. As sociologist Thomas Gerschick explains, "People with less-normative bodies, such as people with disabilities, are engaged in an asymmetrical power relationship with their more-normative bodied counterparts, who have the power to validate their bodies and their identities."[10] He then illustrates this social power dynamic by citing a teenager living with a chronic, body-crippling condition who remarked, "I think [others' conception of what defines a man] is very important because if they don't think of you as one, it is hard to think of yourself as one or it doesn't really matter if you think of yourself as one if no one else does."[11] Our social interactions not only validate our identities (or not), they also provide occasions for approval or sanctioning, depending on our conformity to cultural norms and values. Failure to comply with prevailing codes of normalcy can lead to judgments not only about our (mis) behavior, but also about our "realness" as persons who measure up or not.

Because of white racism, the institutionalized belief in the superiority of one racial group over all others and its right to dominance, black sexuality is subject to relentless stereotyping and projections of white fear onto black bodies. Womanist theologian Delores Williams observes that white culture "considers black frightening, dangerous and/or repulsive—especially when this is the color of human bodies."[12] White fear of and suspicion toward black sexuality give racism an energy and edge, constructed on the degradation of black bodies and on white determination to control them. People of color are caricatured as hypersexual and, therefore, less rational and more prone to be "out of control." As ethicist Miguel De La Torre explains, "Whites [have] projected their own forbidden desires onto darker bodies." This eroticization of race has been used to justify white control and exploitation, including sexual exploitation, of people of color. This cultural construction is, in fact, "so woven into white America's identity that it has become normalized in the way many whites have been taught by their culture to see bodies of color."[13]

Until people get honest and take responsibility for their own confusions and struggles, non-normative communities will continue to be used as moral scapegoats and disenfranchised as "inferior outsiders," which is historian John Boswell's term for LBGTQ persons, whom he regards as "the most obvious 'outsiders' in the modern West." Socially defined outsiders stand in contrast, on the one hand, to "distinguishable insiders," such as blue-eyed and brown-eyed people or, say, Presbyterians and Lutherans, whose differences are noticeable and noted but whose difference does not render them unequal, nor are they socially disadvantaged or segregated because of it. On the other hand, outsiders are also treated differently from "inferior insiders," whose divergence from the social norm is tolerated even while they are relegated to an inferior social status. Boswell cites the caste system in India as an illustration of "inferior insiders," but also the experience of women as a social group within patriarchal society. As he explains, "Although few would argue that it is 'wrong' to be female, being a woman renders one liable to a lower place in the socioeconomic structure of many Western states." Similarly, within certain religious traditions, women are not excluded from the spiritual life of the community, but they are barred from ordination to religious leadership because they " 'lack' some aspect of the norm of 'maleness' presumed to be requisite for sacerdotal functions."[14]

In contrast to both distinguishable and inferior insiders, socially defined outsiders are "either not tolerated at all (they are killed, or banished, or incarcerated) or are relegated to nonexistence conceptually." Their difference, viewed as pathological and threatening to the normative social order, is regarded as a controlling "master trait" that determines their total personality and conduct and makes them into objects without redeeming qualities, either to pity or to punish. As Boswell argues, "In the case of a 'normal' person, heterosexuality is assumed to be one part of his or her personality," but "in the case of a 'homosexual' person, sexuality is thought to be the primary constituent of his or her (abnormal) personality." In other words, "the controlling influence in the lives of gay people is assumed to be overt, abnormal sexuality," and, therefore, "gay people are not a permitted category."[15] To be perceived as nonheterosexual is to be viewed as both different and wrong, a mistake that should be corrected or eliminated. Moreover, from a religiously fundamentalist or absolutist worldview, sexual intimacy between two men or two women is judged morally objectionable without exception, "regardless of how loving or how committed the relationship in which it takes place."[16]

The vilification of bodies, including disabled bodies, bodies of color, and queer bodies, is a moral scandal of the highest order. To correct this injustice, a first step is to stop trashing LBGTQ and other non-normative people. A second step is to stop asking the wrong questions. For example, the moral problem is not homosexuality, same-sex love, or sexual difference. *The moral problem is sexual injustice and the eroticizing of power inequalities to bolster the social privilege of some at the disadvantage of others.* In this culture erotic desire is in trouble because sexuality has been conditioned by or, perhaps better said, annexed to sexism, racism, ableism, and other injustices. In a social order marked by male gender supremacy in which men as a social group feel entitled to social power and privilege and women as a social group are socialized to show deference, many men are turned on by female powerlessness and turned off by strong, assertive female partners. Through such skewed eroticism, people accept in their bodies, as well as in their psyches, that sexism feels right and good. When many men have sex, the power and control they feel in the when, the how, and the "to whom" they feel sexual are all matters that confirm—or fail to confirm—their socially constructed, gendered identity as social superiors. Sexuality conditioned by patriarchy eroticizes gender inequities as something that feels good and right, even natural as the "way things are."

As patriarchal dynamics are played out in and through the body, power as sexualized domination or power-as-control becomes naturalized and somatized, as Patricia Hill Collins conjectures, "precisely because it is felt and not conceptualized."[17] Male gender supremacy, white racial supremacy, and ableism are acquired at the feeling, somatic level of our being. Therefore, male gender supremacy is *sensed* rather than only thought about, through actions giving rise to feelings of being a "real man," the person in charge, and the one who's normal and, therefore, entitled to deference from women and other social subordinates. Real men dominate and take pleasure in controlling women, and "normal" women are expected to be sexually submissive and socially compliant. Anyone who visibly deviates from sexism risks being labeled queer and punished for their nonconformity to patriarchal norms. Named accurately, therefore, the moral problematic is a gendered and racialized social order in which sex is utilized as a means to confirm not only our gender and race identities, but more tellingly, our social status as superiors and subordinates. Engaging in the "right" kind of sex with the "right" kind of person becomes proof of our authenticity as "real men" and "real women" with certain social standing and privilege (or lack thereof).

■ Because talking about it makes it more likely we'll redress moral wrong

Why must we talk about these things? In order to redress a moral wrong, the devaluing of women and LBGTQ persons of all colors along with the distortion of sexuality and its misuse to dehumanize and discredit the moral standing of social groups. At the same time, it is true, as theologian John Cobb reports, that in a post-Freudian era "most Christians acknowledge that humans are sexual beings and that the desire for sexual contact with others is natural and inevitable."[18] Nonetheless, Christians among others are deeply divided over whether expression should be limited to heterosexual (and procreative) marriage and how the church should respond to sexually active single persons, including gay, lesbian, and bisexual persons. Dealing with these and other sexual questions is further complicated by the fact that the dominant Christian tradition has long reflected a fear of and negativity toward sexuality. This negativity has been reinforced over the centuries by two interlocking dualisms, a body-spirit dualism and a male-female dualism. The spiritualistic dualism elevates the superior spirit over the inferior body, which must be disciplined and kept under control. Gender dualism reflects a patriarchal hierarchy of value, status, and power in which good order is understood to require male control of women's lives, bodies, and labor, including their procreative power.[19]

Under the influence of these dualisms, Christianity has given credence to the notion that sex is unclean and should be avoided or at least restricted as a necessary evil. As a contemporary sexologist has observed, "In sum, the Christian Church brought an overlay of sinfulness to almost every aspect of human sexuality. Masturbation, fornication outside marriage, homosexuality, transvestitism, adultery, and in fact almost any aspect of sexual behavior was sinful and ultimately against church law." Even though church authorities may not have been particularly effective in curtailing such activity, Christians have helped "breed a deep feeling of guilt about sexual activity which remains one of the more troubling aspects of the Christian heritage. Though there were modifications of the basic teachings by various Protestant writers, and a general weakening of religious influence in the nineteenth and twentieth centuries, the guilt feelings remain."[20]

Given this Christian sex-negativity, in the process of developing ethically principled speech about sexuality and sexual difference, we will run up against varying degrees of religious ambivalence, if not outright hostility, toward eroticism, as well as a long-standing negative legacy of "managing" this hostility by defaming some persons and groups. If this were not trouble enough, several other factors further impede constructive discourse about these matters. First, we lack a ready language to communicate sexual meanings positively and forthrightly. In this culture, where sex is both feared and fixated upon as both taboo and titillating, "sex talk" falls into certain genres of patterned speech: the highly objectified, clinical jargon of the medical sciences, the whispered disclosures of the confessional, or the breathless utterances of the pornographic. Therefore, as philosopher Mariana Valverde rightly concludes, "talking about sex is not a straightforward matter at all, and this difficulty is not only because of modesty and moral dictates."[21] Moreover, language about sexuality is seldom exempt from ideological taint, including sexism, racism, and heterosexism. Therefore, the categories we typically rely on do not readily express what is most important in our connections with others. For example, the terms *heterosexuality* and *homosexuality* are medicalized categories, but, more telling, these are patriarchal classifications that mystify rather than highlight the qualities of authentic relationship that matter within human intimacy. In a nonpatriarchal society, the gender of the person to whom we are attracted would hardly be of consequence ethically; what would matter, instead, is the character of the relationship itself and whether the parties are treated with respect and care and experience genuine affirmation of their shared humanity.

In addition to the struggle to find appropriate language, a second difficulty involves developing an adequate methodological framework for critical inquiry about sex and sexuality. At present, there are two distinctive approaches. Essentialism, in defining sex as natural and unchanging, emphasizes "what comes naturally" and the biological imperatives that supposedly determine the "normal" course of things. Accordingly, both nature and nature's Divinity have been blamed for such oppressive notions as women's subordination, the presumption that procreative sex alone is healthy and sound, and the pathologizing of same-sex eroticism. In contrast, social constructionism contends that sexuality is more complex, more fluid, and more amenable to cultural molding than essentialists admit. This historical-cultural approach emphasizes that humans develop their sexualities and sexual identities only within institutions and systems, never independently of society or history. Therefore, sexuality's purpose and meaning cannot be grasped by biology alone. A historical, contextualized method is needed to analyze sexuality within social power relations.

This alternative approach argues, to begin with, that sexuality is not a static thing, but rather a dynamic process, constantly being reshaped and reassigned value and meaning in the midst of conflicting social interests. Moreover, sexuality has a history, some of which is oppressive. Because sexuality is political and cultural and not only personal, a *social* ethic is needed to examine how social structures and belief systems affect sexualities for good or ill. Finally, transformations have occurred in social practice and in the meanings attached to sex, gender, and social power, but such shifts require social as well as personal struggle and are not accomplished at will. Theologian John Cobb cites, for example, the rethinking of divorce and remarriage to illustrate the dramatic character of such transformations within Protestant Christianity. "Protestants are becoming so accustomed to this acceptance of divorce and remarriage as the best response in many circumstances," Cobb points out, "that they might forget how drastic a change this is from past Christian teaching." Since Protestants often rely on biblical guidance on moral issues, this more open stance regarding divorce is "particularly noteworthy since it is the acceptance of a practice that is rejected explicitly in the Bible." In fact, Cobb underscores, "it is Jesus himself who opposed divorce!"[22] The fact that a reversal on divorce has taken place demonstrates how a religious tradition may be dynamically subject to revision and renewal.

■ Because the crisis of sexuality lies in the dominant social order and its ideology of sexualized power and control

That said, it is also true that, by and large, faith communities have failed to grasp the scope and depth of the cultural crisis in sexuality. In this culture, the kind of sex scripted as normative is racist patriarchal sex. Eroticism is often about having someone under your control or feeling safe by being placed under another's power. Power as control is erotically charged. Compliance to authority becomes titillating. Above all, a patriarchal ethic grants permission only for those erotic exchanges in private that uphold the social hierarchies of male gender supremacy and white racial dominance. No wonder erotic desire is in trouble!

These insights about the cultural construction of sexuality within patriarchal social relations should help us properly locate the crisis of sexuality. The crisis lies not, first and foremost, in LBGTQ and other marginalized communities, but rather in the dominant social order and its ideology of sexualized power and control. More specifically, the cultural crisis is a crisis within heterosexuality and, more pointedly, within male heterosexuality with its patriarchal macho ethos and distorted power dynamics that encourage men to "lord it over" women and other, less powerful men. In the dominant culture, sex is imagined as an unequal social exchange between a social superior and a social inferior. It ceases to be about love or the sharing of mutual pleasure between willing partners. Sex becomes instrumentalized as a control dynamic between a powerful subject and "his" submissive object.

Unfortunately, the traditional Christian sexual ethic is implicated in this mess because it has legitimated an ethic of male entitlement over women and female bodies. A patriarchal sex ethic has traditionally differentiated "good" from "bad" sex by the particular use that men make of women.[23] Good sex is when a man uses a woman for procreation. Bad sex is when a man uses a woman only for pleasure. The patriarchal religious imagination fails altogether to envision sex as mutually desired, pleasurable touch between peers who are sexual subjects, one to the other. Patriarchy doesn't get it. If it did, it wouldn't be patriarchy.

If we are to move beyond racist patriarchal morality, we must break with this eroticized power-and-control paradigm. The hopeful message in this regard, as Valverde contends, is that "our bodies and our lives are not hopelessly determined by patriarchal oppression—but neither are they capable of complete individual autonomy. . . . The exercise of power, in the sexual as well as in the political realm, always generates some acquiescence and some resistance on the part of those who are the objects of that exercise. The point is to maximize the resistance and minimize the acquiescence, while being aware of the powers over us."[24] Therefore, we must find creative ways to enter into genuine solidarity with women, LBGTQ people of all colors, and survivors of sexual and domestic abuse, all of whom are rising up in resistance to erotic injustice in this culture. But here's the rub. Most people associated with institutionalized religion have been taught to fear difference. Therefore, they avoid flesh-and-blood contact with people "not like them," especially with respect to sexuality. However, when people lack real-life connection with those harmed by the prevailing sex/gender, class, and racial systems, they fail to comprehend the real world. They also have trouble discerning injustice in their own lives. Because many middle-strata white people are woefully out of touch with their own pain, they are sadly in no position to perceive the pain of others. Confused about the cultural crisis around them, they become frightened, susceptible to ideological manipulation, and increasingly dangerous to themselves and others.

The way forward is narrow and demanding. It requires a lifelong commitment to listen to, and learn from, those on the margins. It further requires a willingness to join them in rebuilding the kind of community in which no one is excluded and no one devalued. As one component of that larger movement of community reformation, the feminist, LBGTQ, anti-racism, and anti-abuse movements are calling for a reordering of human sexual relations toward erotic justice. Each of these broad-based, grassroots movements is founded on solidarity, lived out as concrete accountability to those actively resisting oppression. From these movements, fresh moral wisdom is emerging about ethics and eroticism. An ethical eroticism, at odds with racist patriarchal norms and values, aims at enhancing the safety, respect, pleasure, and freedom of persons, especially those who are most vulnerable. It is, at one and the same time, strongly anti-abuse and strongly sex-positive.

Fortunately, the task before faith communities is never simply to repeat the Christian past and apply it, but rather to critique the distortions within the faith tradition and help transform it in more life-enhancing directions. Despite the difficulties of "talking sex," there is urgency about speaking about sexual injustice because so many people are being harmed and because the Christian tradition is implicated in this harm. As Catholic ethicist Christine Gudorf argues, churches must "risk abandoning a familiar but unworkable sexual ethic," and her historical analogy is the challenge to the Dutch Reformed Church of South Africa when it was confronted with its complicity in white racism and was called on to repent and renounce its teachings and practice with respect to apartheid. "The same kind of renunciation of traditional [Christian] teaching in sexuality, followed by repentance," Gudorf proposes, "is necessary on the part of all Christian churches today in response to the suffering and victimization it has long supported and legitimated."[25] Otherwise stated, a theological ethic constructed on the basis of gender and sexual injustice is not a noble tradition to defend, but rather a legacy to critique and transform.

My own Protestant Reformed theological tradition taught me that justice making is central to the life of faith, but this tradition runs into problems whenever it splits off the personal and relational aspects of life from the social-structural and political. When that happens, justice is reserved for public matters relating to political and economic power. Love is reserved for "private" concerns among intimates. This split renders sexuality, reproduction, the care of children, and women's lives less important than the supposedly "really" serious issues of politics and empire-building among powerful, propertied men. Even Christian liberalism has failed to recognize family and sexuality as matters of justice as well as love. It has left unquestioned the power hierarchies of husbands over wives and parents over children. It has not adequately addressed the abuse of power among intimates. Theological liberalism minimizes or ignores oppression in the so-called private sphere and fails to recognize how power, conflict, and injustice exist in the bedroom. Therefore, the Reformed tradition is being challenged to enlarge its theological vision and relocate matters of justice for women, people of color, and LBGTQ persons from the margin to the center.

Granted, the reframing of sexuality as a justice concern requires a conceptual and political shift. "It is not easy to think about [sexuality], marriage, and the family in terms of justice," Susan Moller Okin acknowledges, in part because "we do not readily associate justice with intimacy" and in part because the romanticizing of family life has allowed us to sidestep power, abuse, exploitation, and oppression among intimates. However, Okin argues, "in the real world, justice is a virtue of fundamental importance for families [and friendships], as for other basic social institutions." Justice in intimate relationships and in family life involves a fair distribution of material goods, but also of intangible goods, such as respect and care. In addition, family life is a primary developmental context for forming human identity and for deepening sociability. "If justice cannot at least begin to be learned from our day-to-day experience within [intimate relationships], it seems futile to expect that it can be developed anywhere else. Without [just friendships], just families, [and just marriages]," Okin asks, "how can we expect to have a just society?"[26]

■ Because our expanding scientific knowledge demands we change the conversation

To be candid, the impetus for reforming Christian sexual ethics has come not from inside the tradition, but from two outside sources: first, from the social and natural sciences with their fresh insights about human diversity and psycho-sexual development and, second, from social justice movements and the moral wisdom emerging especially from the feminist, LBGTQ, and anti-racism movements, but also the disability rights movement, the anti-violence movement among survivors of sexual and domestic abuse, and the ecological movement with its nondualistic framework and holistic appreciation of relational systems.

In relation to expanding scientific knowledge, at its best the Christian tradition has encouraged openness to new empirical knowledge, demonstrated a nondefensive engagement with changing cultural patterns, shown adaptability to new conditions, and emphasized human freedom, creativity, and responsibility for promoting personal and communal well-being and the care of the earth. Scientific and medical developments, such as effective and inexpensive contraceptives, medically safe and legalized abortion, and the emergence of assisted reproductive technologies, have greatly affected sexual practices. So, too, have health concerns around sexually transmitted disease, including HIV/AIDS, the rise in nonmarital births among Euro-American and other women, and greater public awareness of pervasive patterns of domestic abuse and child sexual abuse. Moreover, by the mid-1960s, the marital family of two adults with dependent children, the post–World War II cultural icon, became no longer statistically normative.

Of particular significance has been the broad scientific study of sexuality, which has had a significant influence on modern discourse about sex and sexual diversity, in part through the exploration of sex differences between men and women; in part through the cataloguing of varieties of sexual orientations and practices, including homosexuality, bisexuality, transsexuality, and intersexuality; and in part through the promotion of sexual research, sexual health, and sexual therapy. In many respects religionists welcome such developments in the science of sexuality. The natural sciences, by authorizing the body and, in particular, sexuality as legitimate objects for investigation, intervention, and treatment, have encouraged the development of sexology and related disciplines and thereby expanded knowledge about, and public awareness of, a range of topics that might otherwise be shrouded in moralisms, secrecy, and shame.

Science has been particularly helpful in dispelling myths and correcting misinformation that have caused untold grief and suffering. It matters to individual and community health whether syphilis and other sexually transmitted infections, including HIV/AIDS, are seen primarily as diseases or punishment for sin, whether masturbation is thought to cause insanity, whether women are regarded as insatiable in sexual desire, as merely passive, or as self-directing moral agents, and whether homosexuality is judged a pathological or benign variation. It is also important to recognize the limits of biomedical science as, for example, in its treatment of aggressive sex offenders (only modest results), its inability to redirect sexual orientation (not effective in the long term), and its uncertainty about the causes of sexual desire among humans, including heterosexual erotic attraction.

At the same time, the science of sexuality is not exempt from ideological distortion and therefore must be critically assessed. Scientific explorations of human sexuality are historically situated and therefore dependent on the intelligibility of reigning scientific paradigms that help organize complex data and create a plausibility structure of meaning and interpretation. Even a brief review of the history of sexology indicates that socially constructed paradigms about human sexuality are themselves subject to critique, emendation, and even replacement if a competing paradigm emerges that gains the loyalty of a critical mass of adherents.

With regard to the biology of sex, prior to the eighteenth century, the reigning paradigm about the human body held a one-sex view. Men and women were thought to share a common physique even as women's bodies were regarded as less developed versions of men's bodies. The vagina was observed to be an inverted penis, the two more similar than dissimilar in form and function. Subsequent to the eighteenth century, this paradigm was replaced by a modernist paradigm of the two-sex body, which emphasizes that men and women possess highly differentiated bodies and are, therefore, to be regarded as more dissimilar than similar to one another. The power of this schema on the social imagination is reflected in popular discourse that speaks of men and women as "opposites" though supposedly complementary in nature.[27]

This modernist paradigm is currently being called into question by biologists and medical researchers, as well as by feminist, queer, and other social theorists, for fostering a binary theory of sexual identity that posits two and only two sexes (male and female) and represents them as opposites. Sexual dimorphism assumes that biological sex, viewed essentially in terms of reproductive function, determines not only psychological identity (genderized identity of femininity or masculinity), but also a person's preferred social role and, importantly, object of sexual desire. This paradigm naturalizes reproductive heterosexuality and presumes that if human sexual development proceeds on track, then a "normal" adult person will be sexually attracted to an adult of the "opposite" sex. Paradoxically, this naturalized pattern of human sexual development is also regarded as precarious, especially for males. Because successful development of a functioning heterosexual male cannot be guaranteed (homosexuality is considered sexual deviance resulting from, or at least correlated with, gender confusion and nonconformity), medical science and psychological theories have sought to account for, and provide medical interventions in response to, perceived abnormalities, including nonheterosexual erotic attraction, transsexuality, and other gender-identity "disorders."

In contrast, a postmodern paradigm has emerged that emphasizes human sexuality as polymorphous, both more complex and more diversified than conventional categories allow. This alternative paradigm challenges the dichotomous gender assumptions at the core of the reigning paradigm and argues that the biological distinctions between male and female have been overdrawn, are matters of degree, not kind, and are not always clear-cut; that the various indicators (chromosomal, hormonal, anatomical, psychological, social) employed to differentiate sexual identity are sometimes ambiguous and, even when clear, do not necessarily cohere in a single developmental pattern; that social roles and erotic attractions are diverse and not predictable by sex/gender (psychology does not follow biology lock-step); and that the distinctions between normality and deviance (perversion) are cultural and moral judgments, not scientific.[28] Religious traditions, already under pressure to reconsider teachings about gender and sexual orientation, are being further challenged insofar as their foundational stories and moral codes presuppose a strict sexual dimorphism (Gen 1:27, "So God created humankind in his image, in the image of God he created them, male and female he created them") that can no longer be taken for granted as empirically accurate.[29]

■ Because social justice movements prod us to change our entrenched views

The second impetus for rethinking sexuality among progressive religionists is the global feminist and LBGTQ movements. Their advocacy on behalf of gender and sexual justice for persons of all colors has precipitated a shift toward a justice-centered theological approach that seeks not to control but rather to empower women and men alike to live more freely in their bodies and more compassionately in their relationships and communities. *Religious feminists insist on mutuality between coequals as the normative relational expectation.* In doing so, they have sparked a quiet and not-so-quiet revolution in the bedroom and throughout the social order. What is shaking the foundations even further is a power shift as nonheterosexual people claim their right to be the subjects of their own lives. Fresh insight emerges as sexually minoritized people are no longer positioned as abstract objects of other people's discourse, but rather become self-defining subjects with whom to engage in dialogue.

From their vantage point, LBGTQ religionists argue that it is sexual injustice rather than sexual diversity that is dividing religious communities and causing enormous personal and societal suffering. One aspect of the challenge launched by survivors of sex/gender oppression is claiming an appropriate sense of pride by securing a positive sense of self-regard as nonheterosexual persons. Members of various faith communities have joined the Open and Affirming, Welcoming Congregation, More Light, and Reconciling Congregation movements to critique sexual exclusivism; challenge discrimination on the basis of gender, sexual difference, and family patterns; and affirm that same-gender loving persons can also model a fully human way to live and love as sexual-spiritual persons.

Progressive religionists seek to actualize three interrelated components of sexual justice: a strong affirmation of the goodness of sensuality and embodiment; a genuine honoring of sexual difference, including respect for sexual minorities; and attentiveness to both pleasure and pain, including the personal and political dimensions of sexual oppression and exploitation. A progressive Christian social ethic of sexuality aims not at controlling persons and inhibiting erotic power, but rather at empowering each person to claim the goodness of his or her own body and be equipped to understand and direct its use. At the same time, each person has a responsibility to respect the bodily integrity and self-direction of others. In sum, progressives argue that the central norm for intimate relationships is justice-love, understood as mutual respect, commitment, and care and a fair sharing of power, for gay and nongay, marital and nonmarital relationships alike.

In urging the development of a justice-centered discourse about sex and sexuality, progressive Christians make a wager that religious traditions remain open to renewal and their own transformation. Protestant theologian Robert McAfee Brown puts the matter succinctly: "A shift of perspective is not unfamiliar in Christian history; it is called conversion."[30] When such a shift takes place, its signs will likely include the following: increased candor about the tradition's complicity in sexual injustice; a readiness to embrace the body as a privileged site for encountering the sacred in the midst of everyday life; a determination to investigate how "sexism, heterosexism, racism, ethnocentrism, and classism [function] not as separate categories, but as a single unifying framework designed to privilege one group over all others"[31]; deepening respect for women's full moral standing and their empowerment in their families, faith communities, and social and economic institutions; a greater willingness by men to be held accountable for sharing power equitably and engaging with women as allies and partners in leadership; and the lifting up of gay, lesbian, bisexual, and transgender persons as exemplary models of living and loving humanly. A final, most welcome sign will be when the Christian and other religious traditions no longer fixate on the "sin of sex," but rather commit to challenging gender and sexual injustice, along with race and class oppression, as their fervent spiritual calling.

Becoming passionately engaged in this justice agenda for personal and social renewal gives us good reason to keep talking, as well as plenty to talk about.

CHAPTER 2

What Makes "Good Sex" Good?

*Most people cannot quite rid themselves of the sense that controlling
the sex of others . . . is where morality begins.*

MICHAEL WARNER[1]

For persons interested in sex, or perhaps more to the point, in how to have really good sex, the Christian tradition offers little help. If by good sex we mean sex that is pleasurable and powerful to the senses, the Christian tradition will disappoint because it has by and large promulgated a highly restrictive and often quite punitive moral code that warns incessantly about the dangers of illicit pleasures, places severe limits on almost all sexual expression, and teaches people to fear, not relish, their desire for intimate connection. If by good sex we also mean sex that is not only pleasurable but also ethically principled and builds up self-respect in persons and justice within the community, there will be more disappointment because over the centuries, despite the considerable attention given to these matters, the church has never managed to produce a reliable tradition of ethical wisdom about gender and sexual justice. While it has failed to provide guidance about enhancing the delights of erotic power, it has also failed to teach people the delights of pursuing sexual justice in community with others. The Christian tradition, in many respects a noble tradition to preserve and promote, nonetheless requires critique and transformation when it comes to sex and sexuality.

■ Why a major overhaul of Christian sexual teaching is necessary

With respect to sexual pleasure, church historian Mark Jordan notes that "the suspicion of an impure pleasure is the most radical and comprehensive principle in Christian sexual ethics, the one with the greatest power to exclude acts, desires, and dispositions." Even for married couples, he contends, "we do not find advice . . . on how to have more pleasurable sex. Christian theology does not offer anything like an *ars erotica*, a teaching on the cultivation of sexual acts." The final disappointment may well be, Jordan explains, that "the sex that Christians are permitted in marriage—and it is the only sex they are permitted—is defined chiefly by negations. It is [to be] not unnatural, not deliberately sterile, not unchaste, and so on. 'Good' sex is defined as not being one of the many kinds of 'bad' sex."[2]

In terms of contemporary repercussions, historian Dagmar Herzog observes that as a consequence of Christian sex-negativity, "discussions about sex in America center less and less on joy, pleasure, and self-determination and more and more [on] peril and danger."[3] In fact, popular culture has been so profoundly shaped by Christian sex-negativity that sex is commonly associated with sin, danger, and taboo. Moreover, many people simply equate morals with prohibitions against sex. Is it any surprise, then, that in a culture at once fearful and fixated about all things sexual, sex is treated with suspicion, cast perennially as a "problem," and "burdened with an excess of significance"?[4]

With respect to developing a positive sexual ethic, there is a further complication. Many people confuse sexual *mores*, the conventional patterns of the day, with genuine *morals* or critically reflective ethical insight. As ethicist Beverly Harrison points out, it is false to assume "that earlier patterns of practice continue to have value for their own sake, quite apart from our need as rational beings continuously to justify past norms and practices in light of new conditions."[5] In the first decades of the twenty-first century, some of the new conditions pressing for a revision of the conventional Christian ethic include the emergence of a world—and worldview—in which women no longer accept inferiority, in which there is widespread insistence that human intimacy be consensual, nonexploitative, and mutually pleasurable, and where gay, lesbian, bisexual, and transgender persons of all colors insist on public recognition as persons deserving of human dignity and full civil and human rights.

Because religious traditions remain dynamic and meaningful only by staying open to cultural change, adapting to altered conditions, and revising their assumptions as warranted, a major overhaul of Christian sexual teaching is necessary insofar as the traditional Christian framework has been constructed on the basis of devaluing the body, women, and nonheterosexual persons. Above all, this tradition is weighted down by an underlying suspicion that pleasure is at odds with what is genuinely ethical. At the outset of exploring the ethical meaning of sex, we should, therefore, acknowledge that our contemporary appreciation of sex, along with the healthy desire to promote good sex, already places us in considerable tension with the vast bulk of the Christian tradition's persistent bias in favor of sexual abstinence and celibacy. As New Testament scholar Dale Martin writes, "Though many people nowadays—even Christians—don't know this, most early Christianity was strongly ascetic: the majority of Christians for the first many centuries of Christianity, apparently, assumed that God required the severe control, preferably the complete renunciation, of sexual relations."[6] For most Christians during most of Christian history, discipleship has meant the avoidance of sex. In other words, the best sex for Christians has been no sex.

The conviction that sex is a dangerous, chaotic force requiring constraint and controls has supported celibacy and only one other lifestyle option within the Christian moral life. A permissible but always second-best choice for Christians has been marriage. The apostle Paul's admonishment to the Christian communities in Corinth is often cited in support of marriage as the appropriate "safe container" to keep sexual desire restrained: "To the unmarried and the widows I say that it is well for them to remain unmarried as I do. But if they are not practicing self-control, they should marry. For it is better to marry than to be aflame with passion" (1 Cor. 7:8-9 NRSV).

Given the ongoing fear that sexual pleasure tends to excess and threatens to overwhelm reason, early theologians were willing, but only with reluctance, to carve out a narrowly defined space for sex within the confines of heterosexual marriage. Although Christians were permitted to have sex, they were permitted to have sex only within marriage, and even within marriage the purpose of sex was limited to procreation. No justification was given for the enjoyment of sexual pleasure between intimates. Sex was regarded as "good enough" or at least "not bad" to the extent that it was both marital and exclusively procreative.

■ The Augustinian link of sex, sin, and marriage

In the fourth century Augustine expressed strong convictions about the link between sex and sin, and his views have arguably remained more influential than those of any other theologian in the Western Christian tradition. In addressing the good of marriage, Augustine insists rather generously that marriage is not entirely sinful even as he argues that even marital sex will be tainted by sin. While husband and wife enjoy a special bond, they are admonished to exercise restraint by bearing in mind that celibacy is the preferred state even for the married. As Augustine expounds, "Conjugal intercourse for the sake of procreation carries no fault," but, once again, "abstention from all intercourse is better even than marital intercourse that takes place for the sake of procreation."[7] In addition, Augustine argues that while the better wisdom is to recognize, along with Paul, that couples owe to one another the "conjugal debt," it is nonetheless best for them to limit sexual intercourse within marriage to what is necessary for procreative purposes. "The intercourse that is necessary for the sake of procreation is without fault," he asserts, but "intercourse that goes beyond the need for procreation follows the dictates of lust (*libido*), not of reason."[8]

While sex within marriage is permitted, marriage is no license for indulging in sexual pleasure. To the contrary, Augustine encourages the Christian husband and wife, once their youthful passions have dissipated, to cease their sexual activity and live together as Christian brother and sister in a properly chaste, that is celibate, marriage. "The earlier they begin to refrain from sexual intercourse, by mutual consent," he explains, "the better they will be. This is not because they will eventually be unable to do what they wish, but because it is praiseworthy not to wish to do what they are able to do."[9]

Historical theologian Mark Jordan, in commenting on Augustine's cautiously pro-marriage but hardly sex-positive stance, observes that "in many ways the theology of Christian marriage has been the effort to promote sex without eroticism." Christian sex is restrained sex that is not only limited to marriage, but also limited to the kind of sex permitted (procreative only) and the duration of permitted sexual activity within marriage (only for the newly married who are young and passionate).[10] As Jordan summarizes, "So [Christian] Husband and Wife are identities for containing and getting beyond sex—to contain it by making it a thing of the past, a shameful and youthful excess. In this sense, they are in much of Christian tradition *anti-erotic identities*."[11] Marriage functions initially as a kind of veil that drops over a couple's "private intimacies" where sex is allowed but not encouraged, but then, if all goes according to theological conviction, marriage becomes more of a "wet blanket," cooling off any lingering ardor.

In light of this Augustinian legacy linking sex with sin, the traditional Christian ethic has been, at worst, a fear-based negative tradition touting sexual abstinence and the eradication of sexual desire altogether or, at best, a highly ambivalent, restrictive marriage ethic that has carefully monitored the sex permitted even to the married. Married persons were instructed to "have babies" and then move "beyond sex" as soon as possible. While it is true that some important reevaluation of marriage and family begins to take place with the Protestant Reformation, the church did not reverse its long-standing bias in favor of sexual abstinence, nor did it develop anything approximating a positive ethic of sexuality. Rather, because the Reformers remained so alert to the power of sin and forever doubtful that a consistent lifestyle of celibacy was likely even for clergy, they continued to urge marriage as a necessary remedy for, and control on, "unbridled" lust.

The Reformers did not reverse the Christian tradition's long-standing sex-negativity, nor did they challenge the second difficulty that pervades Christian discourse about sex and sexuality. Christian sex has also been patriarchal sex. The one and only site in which sex has been permitted is within a male-dominant marriage. In other words, sex is authorized only within a power structure of gendered inequality in which the husband is in control and the wife submits as a "good woman" should. Within the marital zone, husband and wife are spiritual equals, and, accordingly, Protestantism has celebrated a companionate model of marriage in which the unitive or bonding purpose of marital sex is affirmed in addition to its procreative purpose. However, spiritual equality did not translate into social equality between men and women. Marriage was assumed to work harmoniously "only when the wife understood herself as an obedient subordinate and the husband as a beneficent but authoritative patriarch."[12]

In addition, theologians utilized the patriarchal marriage model to provide a compelling theological image of human obedience to God by emphasizing that the wife stands in relation to her husband as humanity stands in relation to God. Under this sacred canopy, good moral order requires the loyalty and faithful obedience of the less powerful party to the more powerful party. Therefore, marriage normalizes gender inequality as right and good and becomes the fundamental building block for an entire social order in which power and status differentials are touted as divinely willed. Isn't it telling, as theologian Rita Brock notes, that "by the end of the twentieth century most Christian churches, Catholic and Protestant, had acknowledged that sexism was a sin," but "they [had] not, however, scrutinized one major social institution perpetuating sexism—marriage"?[13]

While the celibacy/marriage dichotomy is upended within Protestantism and marriage is promoted as a Christian duty, sexuality continued to be viewed as a dangerous force requiring regulatory controls and ongoing discipline. In the Reformers' view, marriage is an "order of creation" designed by God as an institution to serve human well-being, and therefore all persons should marry to fulfill the divine purpose of uniting people in marital union and having them procreate. At the same time, as theologian Rosemary Ruether explains, "Almost all *must* marry because the lustful urges that had arisen from the Fall could be contained without sin only in marriage."[14] In Protestant culture, marriage becomes expected of all, even compulsory, so much so that the onus is placed on those who remain single and become viewed with suspicion as "loose cannons," deficient and probably defective, or at the very least incomplete because they are not (yet) partnered within a normative heterosexual marriage.[15] A marriage culture leaves hardly any room for independent women or other gender-nonconforming people to shape their lives outside the patriarchal family system with its carefully proscribed gender-role expectations and hierarchical power dynamics.

While the Reformers emphasized that marriage served as a hedge against immorality, marriage could also serve other important ends, including the goods of procreation and companionship between married spouses. However, even among the married, sinful lust remains a problem. As Jordan puts the matter, "Lust confined is still lust." Furthermore, the fact that marital sex can serve good ends "does not mean that our sex is now 'intrinsically' good."[16] While Christians can certainly run into trouble by engaging in sex outside of marriage, they can also run into serious problems if they act intemperately within their marriages. "Marriage covers sex only so far," Jordan continues. "Marriage is not to be a bordello. It is not a license for all sorts of sexual activities with one's spouse. On the contrary, its moral protection is constantly threatened, from within and without. At any moment, an act of sexual excess can strip back the covering and show the depravity of human desire."[17]

■ Why Christians view even heterosexual love negatively

The Christian value system regarding sexuality has been marked by such strong sex-negativity that theologian Karen Armstrong concludes that "for most of its history Christianity has had a more negative view of *heterosexual* love than almost any other major faith."[18] Two other characteristics are noteworthy about the conventional Christian approach to sex. First, over the centuries Christian moralists have mapped out an elaborate set of rules and prohibitions and ranked sexual practices in a distinctively hierarchical order. In terms of this sexual hierarchy, Christianity has placed the celibate life and the sexually "pure and innocent" (prepubescent children) at the very top of the social and spiritual pyramid, and then at the next rung are those who are heterosexual, married, and procreative. (As noted earlier, Protestant Christianity, while celebrating procreative marriage as normative, insists on sexual purity and along with Catholicism also maintains a strong bias in favor of celibacy, especially for single adults. Also noteworthy is how the teachings of the Second Vatican Council affirmed the unitive purpose of marital sex alongside the procreative, but in subsequent decades the Vatican has focused once again on the procreative in light of its staunch opposition to abortion.) Below them are sexually active, even cohabitating heterosexual couples who, especially if they are white and middle class, often pay a price for living together "without benefit of clergy," including being ostracized by family and their church community, but insofar as they are perceived as "on their way" to the wedding altar, then often they are at least tacitly acknowledged as legitimate couples. Below them are sexually active single heterosexuals outside committed relationships, and then gay men and lesbians in committed, long-term relationships approximating marriages. At the bottom of the erotic pyramid are the "lowest of the low," the sadomasochists, commercial sex workers, the fetishists, and adults who engage in sexual abuse of children. As Gayle Rubin observes, "Individuals whose behavior stands high in this hierarchy are rewarded with certified mental health, respectability, legality, social and physical mobility, institutional support, and material benefits. As sexual behaviors or occupations fall lower in the scale, the individuals who practice them are subjected to a presumption of mental illness, disreputability, criminality, restricted social and physical mobility, loss of institutional support, and economic sanctions."[19]

In addition to its sex-negativity, patriarchal gender order, and hierarchy of sexual values, the prevailing Christian paradigm about sexuality also seeks to draw a clear and unambiguous line that differentiates good and bad sex. Because only heterosexual, marital, and procreative sex is morally legitimate, monogamous (heterosexual) marriage marks the boundary between, on the one hand, moral order and decency and, on the other hand, moral anarchy and personal as well as social peril. Conventional moral discourse is therefore framed in terms of marriage as the guiding reference point while all other activities are judged—and found deficient—in relation to that normative practice. The questions typically posed ask if premarital, extramarital, or nonmarital sex is permissible while the unexamined presumption maintains that whatever takes place within marriage is sanctioned and right. Furthermore, "only sex acts on the good side of the line are accorded moral complexity," Rubin argues, while "all sex acts on the bad side of the line are considered utterly repulsive and devoid of all emotional nuance."[20] However, because of the power of sexual desire to disrupt and break boundaries apart, there is an ever-present danger that persons may slip and slide (perhaps fall?), cross the line, and risk reputation and even life by sinking further and further into moral degradation.

What is telling about this Christian narrative of ever-impending sexual peril is that people are left in constant doubt and worry about their capacity to live responsibly as sexual persons, given the fact that "sin abounds." They can easily become preoccupied with the need to police themselves, but also to regulate the sex lives of others, especially those whom they suspect may depart even further from the normative ideal of "good Christian sex." Therefore, much more is at work here than simply an effort to demarcate behaviors as good or bad, right or wrong. The ability of some to label others as morally deficient reflects and reinforces prevailing sexual and other kinds of power relations between socially dominant and socially subordinate groups, including unshared power in economic and race relations. It matters greatly who has the power to judge persons and social groups as morally virtuous or not. In societies marked by gender, race, and other power inequalities, negative judgments about "loose women," hypersexual people of color, and promiscuous gays have been enforced through the power of church regulations, state policies, and the medical-psychiatric establishment. At one and the same time, some groups are disenfranchised by being labeled hypersexual and, therefore, "out of control" while other groups claim moral and spiritual superiority and the entitlement to enforce the rules by disciplining others. This kind of sexual hierarchy is powerful glue cementing other unequal social relations and makes a highly polarized and unjust race, class, and sex/gender social order appear to be commonsense.

■ From judging acts to judging persons and groups

Over time there has also been a subtle but noticeable shift in the theological discourse from judging acts to assigning moral status by marking sexual identities, a shift that may be illustrated by the transformation of the sin of sodomy into a preoccupation with the morally dubious character of the sodomite.[21] Historically, sodomy has been an elastic term that has referred to a wide range of sexual behaviors, including oral sex, masturbation, and other forms of nonprocreative heterosexual sexual activity. All these acts have been considered morally corrupting at various moments, but persons could repent of them, recover, and return to the community's good graces. Increasingly, however, moral judgment has come to focus not on the acts committed but rather on the character of the person doing the acts. With this shift in emphasis, the moral and spiritual pathology of the sodomite becomes the focal concern, and the character flaw is considered of such a fixed and intransient nature that remedial efforts give way to more drastic measures of containment and control. As sociologist Nancy Fischer explains, "Sexual behavior came to be seen as indicative of some deep truth about the individual's character. . . . Individuals who engaged in immoral acts were no longer considered as displaying a mere aberration in their behavior. They were considered fundamentally different types of people than those who were 'normal.'"[22]

Those culturally constructed as morally fit and "normal" are those married (white, heterosexual) couples who alone are (relatively) safe from having their sex lives subjected to public scrutiny or their personal character called into question as morally defective. Lacking a category of benign sexual variations, the prevailing norm-deviant model of sexual morality grants normality exclusively to heterosexual persons and confers upon them the right to label others as morally deficient, abnormal, and "beyond the pale." Employing sexuality to define and stigmatize others as defective in their humanity is a powerful social control mechanism, especially insofar as the righteous are also entitled to police and control everyone else "for their own good."[23]

In this patriarchal schema the church plays the role of "moral code enforcer" by granting permission for sex (for the properly married only) and maintaining the rules about what is licit and not. This arrangement generates a moral minimalism insofar as people become focused on compliance to a narrow, rules-based moral framework. Their goal then becomes figuring out how to avoid what is forbidden or at least not getting caught. While moralisms are effective in generating guilt and shame, they are notoriously ineffective at promoting sexual maturity or clarifying the community's obligations for correcting patterns of sexual injustice. Christian moralisms also foster a stunted ethical dependency on external authority (God, the Bible, church authorities), which alone defines what is right. The faithful person is expected to conform and not outwardly complain. Along these lines, a denominational staff person lamented that when her denomination engaged in a major study of human sexuality, what she discovered, time and again, was that there were "only two sentences of the social statement that most people [were] really interested in"—first, whether nonmarital sex is permissible and, second, whether gay sex is sinful. Exploring moral complexities, questioning assumptions about gender and sexual identity, or offering nuanced ethical arguments, she wrote, is "considered by many to be beside the point."[24]

Patriarchal Christianity proceeds on the assumption that maintaining absolute rules and admitting few if any exceptions is the essence of morality. Many people feel uneasy, perhaps even guilty, if they depart—in fantasy or in fact—from the idealized (heterosexual) marital norm, exercise any measure of sexual freedom, or engage in even mild experimentation, including learning through masturbation about one's own bodily responses and capacities for pleasure. By conceptualizing the world through dualistic categories posed as oppositional and mutually exclusive (good and bad, male and female, white and black), people are not expected to stretch their moral imaginations "beyond the rules," much less tolerate in themselves or others the ambiguity and complex messiness of everyday life. Fear of contamination is often invoked around sex and sexuality, such that a purity-pollution dichotomy differentiates the pure, clean, and safe from the spoiled, dirty, and dangerous. As Nancy Fischer points out, the power of this metaphorical logic helps to explain why "at some level people believe that those whose behavior they find distasteful will contaminate and corrupt others" and, therefore, "why many people do not have a 'live and let live' or a 'to each his own' attitude when it comes to judging others' sexual morality."[25]

■ The Christian code of moral purity

In 2000 the conservative Christian organization Focus on the Family commissioned a group of biblical scholars to produce the "Colorado Statement on Biblical Sexual Morality," which calls for a "sexually pure church" and defines sexual intimacy as "the exclusive prerogative of husband and wife within the context of marriage."[26] While acknowledging that "sex is designed to be pleasing," the Colorado Statement also underscores that "not all sexual pleasure is ethical," that "feelings are extremely unreliable as guides to the morality of sex," and that the Bible alone provides adequate guidance by spelling out how "our sex lives are moral only when conducted according to God's standards."[27] Those standards, encouraging "moral purity in every thought about sex, as well as in every act of sex," are two and only two: life-long celibacy and sex within heterosexual, monogamous marriage. The authorization for this celibacy-and-marriage-only code is God, who has "established the moral definition of marriage, and [we affirm] that it should not be changed according to the dictates of culture, tradition, or personal preference. We deny," the authors continue, "that the morality of marriage is a matter of mere custom, or that it should be allowed to shift with the tide of cultural opinion or social practice."[28]

The Colorado Statement presents the Christian sex ethic as a fixed, binding, and absolute code of morality that is not subject to revision even though the authors admit, tellingly, that Christians continue to debate whether divorce is ever justifiable and, if so, under what conditions. In addition, this statement reflects at least a slight nod in the direction of feminist concerns about domestic abuse and marital rape by clarifying that "we reject the morality of any sexual act, even in marriage, that does not express love seasoned by grace. We believe no sexual act can be moral if it is driven by selfishness or ambition for power."[29] At the same time, there is unambiguous condemnation of nonmartial sex ("Sex outside of marriage is never moral") and an equally unambiguous insistence that the only moral sex is "always heterosexual in nature." God is invoked as making "no mistake in prohibiting homosexual sex without qualification or exception." This means that even if the sex between adults is "honest, consenting, or sufficiently committed," as well as "safe," they insist that it is morally wrong. These absolute rules are backed up with enforcement insofar as the authors argue that churches should not "welcome into fellowship any person who willfully refuses to turn away from the sin of living in a sexual relationship outside marriage."[30]

Here outlined in bold relief is a contemporary Christian ethic that defines good sex as either lifelong celibacy ("no sex") or as exclusively heterosexual and marital. However, this statement departs from traditional Christian conviction insofar as it fails to adopt an absolutist prohibition against divorce. "Divorce is never God's ideal," they admit, but they make room for dissent with respect to whether fidelity requires marital permanence or even whether remarriage is permitted after divorce or the death of a spouse. Perhaps this is a small concession to the social reality among conservative Christians insofar as "evangelicals are slightly more likely to divorce even than the rest of American society."[31] Notice too another departure in conventional emphasis. While the procreative purpose of marital sex is acknowledged, the accent is placed far more on the unitive or bonding purpose of sexual intimacy. Moreover, the statement affirms the goodness of pleasure insofar as "sex that honors God's guidelines and standards is pleasurable. [God] designed sexual activity to be physically enjoyable, emotionally satisfying, psychologically fulfilling, and spiritually meaningful because [God] delights in the joys and pleasures" of human beings.[32] While no mention is made of contraception, most Protestants all along the theological spectrum, as well as the majority of United States Catholics, have accepted family planning and contracepted sex as normative practices although some very conservative Christians insist that "holy sex" requires openness always to the possibility of procreation.[33]

■ A contrasting Christian ethic of justice-love

In contrast, a 1991 Presbyterian study document, "Keeping Body and Soul Together: Sexuality, Spirituality, and Social Justice," takes a pro-sex, feminist, and gay-affirming stance and offers a radically different ethical framework about sex and sexuality. Although this document was not formally adopted by the denomination, it provides an alternative perspective by mapping out a progressive Christian ethic of sexuality grounded in the central affirmation that "a gracious God delight[s] in our sexuality and call[s] us to wholeness in community." A life of holiness manifests itself in the promotion of human well-being and justice in community. Faithfulness is exemplified in an ongoing commitment to embody justice-love in all connections. "Such love, such justice, such passion for right-relatedness," the report affirms, "seeks to correct distorted relations between persons and groups and to generate relations of shared respect, shared power, and shared responsibility."[34]

In calling for a justice-love social ethic, the document articulates five value commitments that should guide ethical assessment of human sexuality: (1) honoring the goodness of bodies and of sexuality, "our capacity to give as well as receive pleasure and comfort; and the power of intimacy to build mutual respect and well-being";

(2) gratitude for diversities of age, gender, sexual orientation, and so forth; (3) special concern for the sexually abused, exploited, and violated; and (4) accountability not only to our partners, but also in terms of the well-being of the whole community. A fifth commitment is distinctive to a liberatory ethical methodology: to learn from the marginalized, "those relegated to the underside of history, theology, and ministry [who] have unique angles of vision from which to estimate how faithful, just, and loving the church is in its internal life, as well as in its engagement with the culture."[35]

A primary learning that emerges from solidarity with the overlapping categories of feminists, people of color, LBGTQ persons, and persons living with disabilities is that "the fundamental ethical division in the church has never been between men and women or between heterosexual and homosexual persons. Rather, the great divide is between justice and injustice." The ethical choice facing people of faith is whether to remain loyal to a patriarchal Christian spirituality that fosters an ethic of gender oppression and sexual control or whether to embrace a justice-centered Christian spirituality that affirms women's full equality, the integrity of same-sex love, and a diversity of relational and family patterns.[36]

In proposing a Christian sexual ethic of common decency, the document contends that the problem of sexuality has long been misnamed as the "problem" of nonmarital sex or, again, of homosexuality. To the contrary, the moral problematic is appropriately named as the "Christianized blessing" of a sex-negative, patriarchal construction of sexuality that has incurred guilt and shame about sex, demeaned women, marginalized LBGTQ persons, and deployed sexuality as a social control mechanism to dehumanize people of color and others. As a corrective, the report reaffirms that marriage and celibacy are two options in which persons may live faithful, responsible lives as sexual persons, but there are other possibilities as well. "A reformed Christian ethic of sexuality," the statement reads, "will not condemn, out of hand, any sexual relations in which there are genuine equality and respect. What is ruled out, from the start, are relations in which persons are abused, exploited, and violated." Stated positively, the church is called on to "identify, honor, and celebrate" not only ethical marriages, but also "all sexual relations grounded in mutual respect, genuine care, and justice-love."[37] This more encompassing sexual ethic redraws the boundaries between good and bad sex by sketching the normative value of justice-love as central to an ethically principled intimate relation. "All persons," the report insists, "whether heterosexual or homosexual, whether single or partnered, have a moral right to experience justice-love in their lives and to be sexual persons. . . . The church must actively promote and protect this right for all persons, without distinction."[38]

In a progressive Christian frame, good sex is defined less by the form of the relationship, for example, whether it is a marriage or even a heterosexual coupling, and more by the moral character of the relationship and whether it is constructed on the basis of mutual trust and respect, whether the parties are committed to a fair sharing of power and resources, and whether the relationship and its pleasures, as well as its responsibilities and burdens, are equitably distributed and open to fair renegotiation as needed. In promoting what may be called an ethical eroticism, the church is called upon to *raise, not lower* expectations of what people owe to others in their intimate and social connections, as well as what they, too, deserve. "Good sex," the study suggests, "is good not only because it touches our senses powerfully, but also because it enhances self-worth and the desire to connect more justly with others. In raising our moral expectations, a Christian ethic of common decency will teach us how to demand of ourselves (and of others) what we deserve: to be whole persons to each other and to be deeply, respectfully loved."[39]

Utilizing a progressive theological lens, the moral problematic is no longer the "sin of sex," but rather the eroticization of injustice and the misuse of power to exploit and harm self and others. A justice ethic of sexuality highlights the centrality of a responsible use of power, including erotic power, to enhance personal well-being and strengthen community ties of mutual respect and care across social categories. Progressives within Christianity argue, therefore, that the conventional ethic of "celibacy for singles, sex only in marriage" is no longer adequate for at least two reasons. First, this moral code has failed to affirm the varieties of responsible sexuality, including nonprocreative and nonmarital sexual intimacy between adults. Second, the code has not paid adequate attention to the ethical violations within heterosexual marriage, including domestic abuse, sexual coercion, and partner neglect. A reframing of a theological ethic of human intimacy is needed that focuses on relational justice and addresses ways to enhance the dignity and well-being of persons of diverse sexual identities, both partnered and not.

■ Cultural shifts in the meaning of sex

Two broad cultural changes have prepared the way for an egalitarian, justice-focused social ethic of sexuality. One change is the development of effective, affordable, and widely accessible means of contraception with abortion as a necessary backup. Among other things, this means that for the majority of heterosexual couples, the normative sexual practice is no longer procreative, but rather contracepted sex. Mutually agreed upon sexual intimacies are not engaged in primarily for the purpose of making babies, but for other purposes: to solidify intimate bonding, for the sharing of pleasure, and even for relieving tension and boredom. A second, equally momentous change is the global feminist movement and the reordering of gender relations, in the bedroom and throughout the social order, on the basis of women's full and equal personhood. Although the "longest revolution" is still far from complete, heterosexual couples are now struggling with how best to organize their erotic, family, and work lives in order to enhance women's status and well-being and not just men's.

With these two cultural transformations, the meaning of sex has changed. However, as theologian Dale Martin observes, "the problem is that Christian theology and ethical teaching have not caught up with the radical change in the 'meaning of sex' that we have experienced in the past forty years." One flashpoint among Christians in the sex debates is the moral status of same-gender loving people. As Martin inquires, "If sex isn't for procreation anymore, then why can't two men or two women have sex?" Moreover, the debate is really less about homosexuality and more about sex itself. "Homosexuality is just the tip of the iceberg," Martin points out. "It is just the most obvious site where the older 'meaning' of sex no longer holds and yet many people still assume some of the older 'rules' about sex."[40]

In reflecting on the incompatibility between a traditionalist and progressive framework of sexuality and sexual ethics, William Stayton, an American Baptist clergyperson and leading United States sexologist on the faculty of Morehouse Medical School, shares his experience of working for many years with clients who struggle with issues of sexual identity and relational dysfunction. Because they are often religiously affiliated, they have been deeply socialized to accept conventional views about sex and sexual morality, including the investment in controlling other people, especially those culturally defined as sexually "impure" and socially inferior. Many operate with what he calls a traditional sexual value system that judges specific acts as moral or immoral, has a strongly procreative (and anti-pleasure) bias, is male-centered and focused on maintaining men's entitlement, and claims divine and biblical authorization for this unchangeable code. By way of contrast, he speaks of an alternative value system that is based on the integrity and vitality of relationships. In this second schema, "there is nothing inherently immoral or evil about acts of sex. The important issues regarding sex are the motives and consequences of the act(s)."[41] This value system also claims biblical and theological roots with its fundamental mandate to honor God and "love neighbor as self" in sexual as well as other kinds of relating. The purpose of sexuality is to enable personal growth and development, as well as the development of community life.

What Stayton finds challenging is the discovery that "most people are somewhere between these two theological systems, which becomes the third sexual value system." In this third option, people feel obligated to publicly endorse and teach the conventional act-centered and patriarchal ethos, but when it comes to making their own private and personal decisions, they often discover that "a relation-centered theology is more relevant and 'right.'" However, as Stayton points out, "these theologies are not compatible. As hard as people try, the two sexual theologies cannot be reconciled or integrated."[42] Moreover, he also concludes, from years of clinical experience working with singles and couples, that whether people are helped or hindered in terms of resolving their sexual difficulties "will largely depend upon which theological system the person adheres to."[43]

■ A conflicted Christianity shows internal splits

Religious traditions are neither monolithic nor fixed, but rather are the products of dynamic, evolving communities with multiple voices and perspectives that are sometimes in deep internal conflict about a host of concerns, including sex, the role of women, and diverse relational and family patterns. A Christianity in conflict about these (and other) matters is nothing new. In fact, as Catholic theologian Daniel Maguire notes, "From the beginning there has never been just one Christianity."[44] The divide within contemporary Christianity over conflicting meanings of sex and divergent ethical visions about "good sex" may be illustrated by comparing denominational resolutions on same-sex marriage from the Southern Baptist Convention (SBC) and the United Church of Christ (UCC). As with Stayton's irreconcilable clash between act-centered and relation-centered theologies, the marriage debate demonstrates a deep conflict between traditionalists and progressives when it comes to normative patterns for intimacy and family life.

Opponents of same-sex marriage argue against extending the right to marry to same-sex couples because of their beliefs about marriage and sexuality. An SBC statement on sexuality defines marriage as exclusively heterosexual, the union of "one man, and one woman, for life."[45] In 1998 the SBC amended its "Baptist Faith and Message" to add a section on the family that notes three purposes for marriage: to provide a framework for intimate companionship between a husband and wife, to control sex by channeling sexuality "according to biblical standards," and to provide "the means for procreation of the human race."[46] The SBC has offered additional reasons for opposing same-sex marriage by declaring that homosexuality is "not a 'valid alternative lifestyle,'" but rather a sin.[47] According to this viewpoint, for the church to grant religious affirmation or the state to offer legal standing to same-sex unions would be to sanction immorality. In a 1996 resolution opposing the legalizing of same-sex unions in Hawaii, the SBC further elaborated its objections by describing homoerotic relationships as "always a gross abomination . . . in all circumstances, without exception," as "pathological," and as "always sinful, impure, degrading, shameful, unnatural, indecent, and perverted." Leaving no doubt about its opposition to marriage equality, the SBC concludes by stating that the movement to legalize same-sex unions "is and must be completely and thoroughly wicked."[48]

In opposing same-sex marriage, these traditionalists seek to preserve a model of social relations organized in terms of natural hierarchies of unequal status and power. Although affirming that husband and wife are "of equal worth before God," the SBC describes marriage as an unequal power relation in which the two parties have different roles and expectations. The husband must be the leader; he is "to provide for, to protect, and to lead his family." A wife is expected "to submit herself graciously" to her husband "as the church willingly submits to the headship of Christ."[49]

The heterosexual marriage paradigm espoused by the SBC resonates with, and gains cultural weight from, a set of assumptions about gender, sexuality, and family that emphasizes biological factors ("anatomy is destiny"), views sexuality as naturally determined and unchanging, and operates within a binary sex/gender schema in which biological or anatomical sex is presumed, first, to give rise "to proper" masculine or feminine gender identity and social roles, then to generate "normal" heterosexual desires and interest in the "opposite sex," and finally to lead steadily to procreation in the context of marriage. Traditionalists accept the notions that there are two (and only two) naturally complementary sexes, that "opposites attract," that sexuality is primarily procreative, and that homosexuality signals deviance from the heterosexual norm. In this framework, marriage is as much about gender hierarchy, gender control, and the regulation of sex and property as it is about love and affection.

In contrast, the United Church of Christ became the first mainline Christian denomination to give official support for same-sex marriage by adopting a resolution at its 2005 General Synod that affirms "equal marriage rights for couples regardless of gender." In recognition of the fact that marriage is a changing, ever-evolving institution, the UCC emphasizes its commitment to marriage as a covenant of equals and contends that the biblical call to justice and compassion "provides the mandate for marriage equality."[50] Justice, a value to be embodied in interpersonal relationships as well as institutional structures, should seek the elimination of "marginalization for reasons of race, gender, sexual orientation or economic status" and work to create the conditions for social equality. From this justice perspective, the mandate to pursue marriage equality expresses two interrelated notions of equality. First, marriage is defined as a covenantal relationship based on the "full humanity of each partner, lived out in mutual care and respect for one another."[51] The UCC is, therefore, affirming equality of partnership within marriage. Second, equality refers to an affirmation of the full humanity of persons with differing sexual orientations. "We also recognize and affirm that all humans are made in the image and likeness of God," the marriage pronouncement states, "including people of all sexual orientations." The implication is that, "as created in God's image and gifted by God with human sexuality, all people have the right to lead lives that express love, justice, mutuality, commitment, consent, and pleasure."[52] Equality in this second sense means equal access to marriage, including the moral freedom of same-sex couples to marry, legally and religiously, as well as the freedom not to marry.

The UCC statement affirms marriage but also acknowledges that there are other ways that responsible people live and love. In fact, there are "many biblical models for blessed relationships beyond one man and one woman." Marriage is not the only place in which people "can live fully the gift of love in responsible, faithful, just, committed, covenantal relationships." To underscore this point, the resolution states that "indeed, scripture neither commends a single marriage model nor commands all to marry, but rather calls for love and justice in all relationships."[53]

The United Church of Christ resolution refuses to privilege heterosexual coupling. Same-sex and different-sex partnerships are affirmed as covenantal relationships having comparable worth. Such covenants should be regarded equally within the church and be eligible to receive equal benefits and protection under civil law. At the same time, by calling for full equality between marriage partners, the UCC statement challenges the legacy of patriarchal Christian marriage in which the spiritual equality of spouses has been asserted, but men have remained in charge and enjoyed advantages of unequal power and status. Finally, the UCC position paper makes room for covenantal relationships outside the institution of marriage. While doing so, it encourages a single ethical standard for all intimate (and other) relationships: relationships are ethical only when they are loving, just, and based on mutual respect and care for all persons.

Progressive religionists, including those within the United Church of Christ, increasingly find that they have more in common, in terms of faith and values, with their liberal counterparts in other denominations and traditions than they have with their more conservative co-religionists. Even among Southern Baptists there are dissenting voices, including congregations that have been disaffiliated because of their acceptance of women's leadership and affirmation of committed same-sex unions. Therefore, a massive realignment is taking place within the religious landscape. This realignment may be described as a "new ecumenism," as the progressive wings of various denominations seek ways to link together in order to pursue justice advocacy in both church and society and as a similar realignment is taking place among religious conservatives seeking to forestall further change by reasserting heterosexual monogamy as the exclusive norm for intimate life.

■ What fuels the intensity of the debate about "good sex"?

It is likely that dissension and conflict will characterize Christian (and other religious) responses to sex and sexuality into an indefinite future, in part because religion provides alternative and sometimes incommensurate visions of the good life and, in part, because marriage and family remain such important social institutions in which human psycho-social and psycho-sexual development take place and where most people learn to internalize and abide by their community's value systems. What has sparked the debate over "good sex" is the broad-based LBGTQ grassroots movements for sexual justice claiming that same-sex love can be as ethically sound a way to love as heterosexual coupling may be. However, the social transformation under way is calling for far more than tinkering at the edges or "simply" a reevaluation of homosexuality. Core religious assumptions about sex and sexuality are being tested, and the cultural tectonic plates are shifting though not yet settled.

In the midst of this cultural earthquake, what is causing alarm, even moral panic, among traditionalists is not, first and foremost, the "gay agenda," but rather the fact that the heterosexual majority, their primary constituent, has been adopting the attitudes and behaviors of sexual and gender nonconformists, of those designated pejoratively as queer. First, for increasing numbers of heterosexual couples, the normative practice, as mentioned earlier, is now contracepted, not procreative, sex and therefore the purpose of sex is mutual enjoyment and the sharing of pleasure. Second, increasing numbers of heterosexual couples are committed to equalizing power and responsibilities within the family and throughout the social order. Finally, the cultural majority is exhibiting a fascination with and openness to greater experimentation with ways to organize personal life outside the confines of the biological family or any hierarchical gender pattern. Therefore, the "family values" campaign of the religious right is seeking to do much more than keep the LBGTQ community from joining the mainstream. Their prime political target is to convince the heterosexual majority that "morality" requires pushing everyone back into conformity with conventional gender power roles and once again restricting sex to a male-dominant, that is, patriarchal, marriage structure.

Anti-gay vitriol and violence are a warning to any nonconformist that stepping out of line puts them at risk of being stigmatized and punished. Therefore, the intensity of the debate about "good sex" is about more than clashing worldviews. It is a personal and political contest, as yet unresolved, about the kind of social world we desire to inhabit and about those with whom we are willing to share it.

CHAPTER 3

Is It Still Adultery If the Spouse Has Alzheimer's?

It is not easy to know whether we are asking the right questions.

MARGARET A. FARLEY[1]

Christians have traditionally drawn a hard line between monogamy and non-monogamy and presumed that ethical marriages are marked by monogamy, sexual exclusivity, and permanence. Because of the widespread practice of divorce and remarriage, the ideal of a lifelong intimate partnership may persist, but significant numbers of people practice what may be called serial monogamy. It is not unusual for people, over the course of a lifetime, to have two or more marital partners but, granted, only one at a time. Even with this cultural change, fidelity as sexual exclusivity remains a settled, noncontestable expectation for an ethical marriage. Or does it?

For some, even posing this question sets off alarms about the kind of moral slippage that should be met with stern disapproval and quickly put to a stop. Others disagree, at least to the extent of granting the possibility of a principled debate about marriage and fidelity, but they too are likely troubled by the prospect of lowering ethical standards for intimate relationships. The question becomes: What does fidelity mean, and how do we maintain a high standard of ethically vibrant and faithful unions?

If an ethical consensus is no longer securely in place about defining fidelity in terms of sexual exclusivity, doesn't the problem lie with those who fail to abide by the conventional rules? Or could it be that the deficiency resides in the rules regarding marriage? If the trouble is in the rules, then, as one ethicist puts the matter, isn't it necessary "to challenge the tyranny of a false but dominant consensus"?[2] However, a quite different critique and change strategy is called for if the problem is about the rampant, or even flagrant, noncompliance with respect to a good rule. How an ethical problem is framed goes a long way toward determining the appropriate response.

■ Can the meaning of fidelity shift depending on circumstances?

Reading an obituary not long ago in my local newspaper brought these concerns close to home.[3] The death notice for William Harkins describes "an exceptionally kind, thoughtful, and generous man" who was "a source of support and inspiration to everyone in his life." As a young adult in his early twenties, Bill filed as a conscientious objector to the Vietnam War, and soon after he became a high school math teacher. In 1970 he married Susan Gluck, "his eighth-grade sweetheart," with whom he parented two sons. After twenty-five years of marriage, Susan suffered two debilitating strokes and was institutionalized in a residential facility near their home. As the obituary records, Bill "visited his wife every night up until the time of his death. Reading, singing, and talking with his wife was one of the great pleasures of his life." The newspaper story then mentions how Bill in recent years had cohabitated with Ruby Wilde, also named as "his partner," with whom he "lived an active and enjoyable life at their home on the Cushing Briggs Road in South Freeport." The article closes by affirming how Bill Harkins provided "for his sons and for all, the model of a man: caring, committed, thoughtful, strong, and loving."

Because the Christian tradition has upheld the norm for marriage as a lifelong, sexually exclusive intimate partnership between a man and woman who promise to maintain their marital bond "in sickness and in health" and who pledge to "forsake all others," is it not contradictory, or at least puzzling, to praise a married man, who has lived openly with another woman, as a model of a "caring, committed, thoughtful, strong, and loving" husband and father? Bill Harkins, recognized by many as a principled person who took his ethical obligations seriously, was married his entire adult life to Susan, but he entered into an intimate relationship with a second woman, who was also publicly acknowledged as his intimate partner. From the evidence available, it seems that he broke the marital rule about monogamy, or, more accurately, because he was legally married to only one of the women, he violated the principle of marital fidelity as sexual exclusivity and did so openly. His community knew about, and seemingly affirmed, his nonmonogamous pattern of relational intimacy.

What does this say about prevailing marital rules, about rule breaking, and about the task of figuring out what is going on in the midst of changing mores? In approaching such questions, Christian ethicist Larry Rasmussen warns us to proceed with caution in light of the sobering realization that "the religiously committed are often poorly poised by their traditions to discern the new, the deviant, and the non-normative, much less to judge these with clarity, insight, and foresight."[4] This warning is especially warranted whenever Christians deal with matters of sex and sexuality. Because of the long-standing sex-negativity within this tradition, Christians are often at their worst about these matters: fearful, rigid, judgmental, and punitive. This is no accident, for as historian Mark Jordan points out, "Preaching against sex may be the most familiar Christian speech of all in our pluralistic, secular societies. People who know nothing of Christian creeds or scriptures can recite the most notorious Christian sexual prohibitions. . . . In the public imagination, Christianity can figure as nothing more than a code of sexual conduct, a code that likes especially to elaborate prohibitions."[5]

■ When is breaking a rule the right thing to do?

In ethics, rules have an important place, but the moral life is about more than following rules. In fact, ethical inquiry often gets under way as an effort to discern which moral principle may best apply among competing values and obligations, and we may end up identifying compelling reasons to break rather than keep a rule. In the midst of moral controversy, a first step is to figure out what's going on, but that's often not a quick or easy matter. How best to interpret reality and find moral meaning in a particular context can itself be highly contested. Much is at stake in how well we engage in our ethical explorations, because if we misread situations or misname the moral problem, we're not likely to come up with helpful responses.

That said, ethical inquiry cannot proceed without principles even though moral principles are only part of the effort. Moral principles direct us, among other things, to tell the truth, keep our promises, and be faithful in our connections with others. They encourage us to act in certain ways and avoid acting in other ways, and in so doing they convey the community's inherited wisdom about right living and about promoting the good of persons in relation to the common good. Rules provide a kind of moral trajectory for doing good, avoiding harm, and living right. However, rules are only rules. They offer important, at times indispensable guidance, but the ethical life involves more than knowing and following rules.

By themselves rules are good, but not good enough. They're necessary, but not sufficient. First of all, rules often provide only general guidance ("Be loving"), but not the specificity required to figure out what loving actually means in a concrete instance. Similarly, the same principle may be interpreted quite differently by different people, all of whom sincerely wish to do the loving thing, but who have conflicting notions of what that implies. Furthermore, we may encounter situations in which more than one rule applies, and we must determine, as best we can, which guidance fits the situation. For example, when faced with end-of-life care decisions, family members may all agree about doing the most loving thing for Grandmother as she lies comatose in a hospital bed, but they may disagree on whether that loving care requires them to place her on a respirator ("Protect and extend life") or to refuse the respirator ("Avoid unnecessary pain and suffering"). Therefore, rules have limits. They are not self-interpreting. Moreover, good rules allow good exceptions. Sometimes we disregard or "break" a rule, not because the particular rule does not matter, but rather because we come to the judgment that in this particular circumstance this particular rule does not hold because another moral value takes precedence for guiding our actions, and we can provide warrants or good reasons for our decision.

For these reasons, Catholic theologian Daniel Maguire suggests that the ethicist's role is like that of "a detective in search of clues," who must resist premature certainty, patiently figure out what's going on, and not short-circuit the process "of deciding which principle connects most valuably to a particular situation" before proposing any resolution to the problem at hand.[6] When confronted with messy life situations, the ethicist is charged with locating the various pieces of the puzzle, fitting them together to make sense of the whole, and thereby reaching moral insight. As Maguire observes, "We all like tidy explanations, and that is fine, but when reality is messy, our tidy talk may miss the point."[7] Again, he points out, while "the moral tabooist holds that certain actions are wrong regardless of the circumstances," in contrast, the ethicist understands that ethical discernment is a "dialogue of principle and context" and that good ethics necessarily pays significant attention to the particularities of our lives and to the ongoing project of figuring out critically "what is going on." Furthermore, it bears emphasizing that "ethics rests on the art of questioning. The unasked (or poorly framed) question is the bane of ethical inquiry."[8]

The process of ethical discernment begins with reading the circumstances, describing what is, and moves to prescribing, figuring out the moral principles that apply for making a moral assessment. Knowing the rules is therefore not the whole ethical project; it's only the beginning. As Maguire explains, "Ethics is the art of weighing and balancing. It is a pondering activity. . . . The task is to weigh and balance amid competing values and disvalues. The morally good choice is the one that is most humanly valuable."[9] This interpretive art draws on the community's moral wisdom, but in the midst of multiple perspectives and conflicting insights, we may need to critique and reshape prevailing moral perceptions and patterns of actions. Therefore, when it comes not only to the complexities of sexuality but also to the demands of ethical inquiry, we are wise to prepare ourselves for a certain amount of messiness and ambiguity. Few things in life are neat and tidy, including the outcome of ethical inquiry that rarely results in a "neat code of dos and don'ts." As Maguire puts it, "Noonday clarity is not available at dusk, and there are many dusks in matters moral."[10]

■ Why do we need to reframe our question?

To illustrate, consider a case study that first circulated among clergy counselors and hospital chaplains. Rabbi Richard Address, director of the Union for Reform Judaism's Department of Jewish Family Concerns, describes a scenario that "is not at all fiction. I have heard versions of this story over and over again, across the country." The dilemma he shares is "of a healthy spouse—let's call her Sarah—caring for her husband, who is restricted to an Alzheimer's facility. Sarah must deal with the extended institutionalization of her spouse. She cares for him with love and dignity, *but also feels that he is not really her spouse.*"[11]

The question Rabbi Address poses is this: "How does Sarah handle the reality that, while on a brief respite from the demands of care giving, she met someone with whom she became friendly and intimate? She cannot discuss this with her children, or even with her circle of friends. So Sarah asks her rabbi, 'Tell me, rabbi, am I doing something wrong? I love and care for my husband. But I am a healthy 70-year-old woman, who goes to work, enjoys life and has needs. Is it wrong? Am I supposed to just put my needs on hold?'" The title Rabbi Address offers for this dilemma is "Is it still adultery if the spouse has Alzheimer's?"[12]

Among the online responses to this situation, some answer Sarah's question by saying that, yes, she did something wrong. The wrong is committing adultery by becoming sexually involved with someone other than her husband. In doing so, she has violated her marriage vows. At the same time, the responders continue, Sarah should be met with compassion, not judgment, given the heartbreaking circumstances of her husband's dementia and subsequent institutionalization. Nevertheless, rules are rules, and by definition, having sex outside your marriage is morally wrongful. Moreover, because casting stones at Sarah, literally or figuratively, would not be an effective strategy to curb the misconduct, some admonish the community to "love the sinner but not the sin."[13]

In these responses, the adequacy of the moral code is not in question. The moral onus is placed instead on the noncompliant person who is more likely to receive, in a liberal democratic society, a compassionate rebuking than either condemnation or punitive expulsion from the community. Other bloggers who weighed in on this question agree, but with differing emphases on the sin, the sinner, and the just response. One wrote, "In short, the answer is, 'Yes.' But I am not without empathy." Another wrote, "Under any circumstances, it's adultery unless you've divorced or your spouse has died." A third commentator opined, "Yes, she has to remain celibate because she is a married woman. Marriage is not a conditional contract that you will stay with someone when they are healthy but leave when they are sick." Then with a heavier hand the blogger added, "Such a person when caught should lose all rights to the family assets. Every penny ever saved should contribute to the support of the ill spouse. The adulterer can go live off the earnings of their lover."[14]

In pondering this question, I've reached a different conclusion, in large part because I define the problem differently. I would argue that it is a mistake to categorize the ethical problem as adultery. This case is not, first and foremost, about the supposed infidelity of a caregiving spouse, but rather a sad story about partner abandonment on the part of the Alzheimer patient. Granted, this abandonment is nonvoluntary, but it is the patient-spouse who disappears, emotionally though not physically, and leaves the caregiving spouse. Subsequently, this becomes a story about the caregiving partner's moral wrestling about whether she is entitled to receive as well as give love, including the sexual love of a third party.

■ Are there good limits to love?

About the reframing of this matter, two guides have informed my perspective, but neither is responsible for the position outlined here.

The first guide is ethicist Stephen Post in *The Moral Challenge of Alzheimer Disease*.[15] Post writes: "Seldom does human experience require more courage than in living with the diagnosis and the gradual decline of irreversible progressive dementia."Alzheimer's disease, he suggests, is "like a tidal wave disrupting everything in its path. The person with dementia is eventually swept away, while caregivers look back and feel forever changed by their experiences."[16] Along with Post I want to praise caregiver spouses and "recognize the remarkable depths of affection, care, and loyalty" they express toward their life partners.[17] The real story here is not any perceived betrayal of the caregivers' relational commitments to their Alzheimer partners, but rather their exemplary fidelity. Caregiver spouses manage to stand steadfastly by their beloved partners through horrendous loss and diminishment, and their loyalty is often grounded in their prior promises to be there "in sickness and in health." As research indicates, there is a remarkably low divorce rate, lower than the national average, between caregivers and their spouses living with Alzheimer's, which underscores how seriously they take their vows.[18] As Post reports, "The family is very often uniquely caring because of a deeply personal memory of and gratitude toward the affected person, formed before the onset of illness. There is among most family caregivers a loyalty based on this gratitude, without which 'society simply could not exist.' . . . Empirical studies have pointed out that many spouses also continue to value their mates as unique persons 'despite cognitive impairment and sometimes difficult behaviors in the afflicted spouse.' . . . In other words, they continue to find fulfillment in the quality of their lives together, however complex the marital relationship becomes when someone is afflicted with AD [Alzheimer Disease], sexually and otherwise."[19]

At the same time, Post argues that "there are limits" to what a caregiver can provide, and no one should be made to feel guilty when the time comes that at-home care is no longer advisable and the better course is to place a loved one in a residential care facility. As Post states, "The caregiver counts ethically, too," and "some balance" should be found "between what is best for the person with dementia and what is best for the caregivers."[20] These considerations gain urgency in light of gender injustice, often at play in caregiving insofar as the responsibility for care falls disproportionately on women's shoulders. Post writes: "While women caregivers must be appreciated for all they do, significant numbers of women are harmed by the gender expectation that they—and not men—[must] embrace care-giving as their vocation in life," even to the extreme of sacrificing their own well-being. A needed corrective is to encourage far more equitable if not "equal sharing between the sexes of family responsibilities," what Susan Moller Okin describes as "the great revolution that has not happened."[21] Another corrective is to challenge the simplistic notion that "love bears all things," which can harm and further burden caregivers. It is unjust and damaging to encourage caregivers to attend only to the needs and interests of others—even deserving others like a spouse with Alzheimer's—or in the name of love be expected to neglect and even deny their own needs.

In contrast, a life-giving ethic will encourage caregivers and, specifically, women to honor their own dignity and value and not discount their right to a personally fulfilling life. Therefore, it is important to acknowledge that the caregiver spouse has a very demanding job, which includes attending to their own grief and loss while at the same time extending devotion and care to the person who is the source of that loss. Again, the real story here is the caregiver spouse's fidelity and vigilant generosity. Post is helpful in this regard by pointing out that "women vary as individuals, of course, and many may find care-giving roles to be profoundly meaningful and even inspiring."[22] Many will testify that no matter how arduous, caring for another was more blessing than burden.

At the same time, the fact remains that too often the caregiver is left uncared for. That problem is compounded not only by the scarcity of resources and support services, but also by the difficulties of sorting out and ranking multiple, often competing obligations. "If choices must be made," Post asks, "does one care first for one's children, then one's spouse, one's parents, and finally one's siblings?" In this mix, where does "Sarah" in our case study fit in, and how much consideration should she give to her own needs and interests? Post insists, and I agree with him, that "it is wrong for caregivers to state, 'We just want to do what is in [the other person's] best interests and we have no concern about what's good for us.' The interests of the person with dementia and of his or her caregivers," he rightly contends, "are practically and ethically interwoven and interdependent."[23] That said, it is telling that theologians and philosophers have not provided concrete proposals for ordering the multiple, sometimes conflicting responsibilities that confront caregivers on a daily basis. Such efforts to prioritize, Post recognizes, are "difficult and distasteful," so he proposes, as an alternative, that we should not "be overly rigid in this area of ethics, since a great deal of individual variety in priorities and interpersonal proximities is understandable."[24]

■ What can we learn from those with insiders' knowledge?

My second guide is Helen Davies and her colleagues at the Veterans Administration Medical Center in Palo Alto, California. Their research underscores three things about sexual intimacy between Alzheimer's patients and their spouses. First, because sexuality is part of the human experience from birth to death, it is appropriate to view both the Alzheimer's patient and his or her partner as sexual persons with sexual feelings and interests. Second, Alzheimer's disease is likely to have significant effects on sexual behavior. Third, this topic to date has received far too little attention and understanding.[25]

Like Post, Davies notes how seriously caregiver spouses take their marriage vows. In fact, their marriage commitment typically plays a vital role in their sustaining care through difficult times. However, because one component of the marriage commitment is the expectation to share sexual intimacy, and because for most married people emotional intimacy is a condition for acceptable sexual engagement, a poignant problem arises with the progression of Alzheimer's disease, precisely because emotional intimacy is lost. It is not unusual for spouse caregivers to cite numerous reasons for their loss of interest in sexual intimacy with their spouse living with Alzheimer's: their partner may no longer remember their name or know who they are, the patient's incontinence or poor personal hygiene may become off-putting, or the character of the relationship changes to the extent that the caregiver comes to feel more like a parent than a spouse.[26]

In these circumstances, at least some caregivers face a difficult choice: either to engage in sex *within* marriage, but absent the authentic mutuality and emotional intimacy that are typically desired between intimate partners, or to find emotional intimacy, including sexual intimacy, where it is possible, namely *outside* the marriage with a mutually consenting, emotionally available partner. However, because of the stigma attached to sex outside marriage and the cultural prejudice that associates sexual desire only with the young and healthy,[27] some outsiders may try to forestall this possibility, especially if the caregivers are women, by desexualizing the caregivers or by caricaturing them as morally selfish for taking seriously their desire for intimate connection, including emotional and sexual bonding. Neither reaction is warranted, nor is it helpful to misname the problem as if the moral problematic is marital infidelity. Circumstances matter in shaping the moral meaning at hand, and in this circumstance, the caregiver's dilemma has been created, albeit unintentionally, by the Alzheimer partner's nonvoluntary abandonment of the marriage. The resulting moral and spiritual challenge is how to support the caregiver spouse in living their life to the fullest extent possible while they continue to care for their loved one.

As the research documents, the vast majority of caregiver spouses do not divorce or abandon their partners living with Alzheimer's. The truth of the matter is the reverse: gradually, the Alzheimer patient leaves them, and so caregivers must deal with the ambiguity of having and, at the same time, not having a marriage partner. In these challenging situations, some caregivers will show their faithfulness through their devotion and care of their spouse and not enter into an intimate sexual relationship outside the marriage. Others will show their faithfulness through their devotion and care of their spouse, but also choose to love another person. The parties involved, as well as their communities, will need to ethically assess whether only one of these responses, or both, give evidence of a principled large-heartedness and the human capacity for expansive loving.

I wager that for some, their nonmarital loving will result in greater good than harm. Loving a person outside their marriage may well enhance their caregiving of their marital spouse by providing the support and nurture that make it possible for them to keep on loving and caring for the spouse living with this awful disease. In addition, loving a person outside the marriage may even deepen their attachment to the loved one living with Alzheimer's, which gives testimony to the mystery that love does not operate on the basis of a zero-sum calculation. Rather than negatively judging such persons, we should stop to listen and learn from them. They have much to teach about loving well under adverse conditions and about surviving broken-heartedness. For all parties concerned, including ministers and health professionals, the moral challenge of meeting both patients and caregivers where they live requires us to pay greater attention to their legitimate interest in, and need for, sexual and emotional intimacy.

■ When should we make, break, or enlarge our commitments?

Nothing here is meant to make light of partner abandonment within marriage or to encourage a casual attitude about adultery. Taking relational commitments seriously is at the heart of the moral life. "To give our word," Roman Catholic moral theologian Margaret Farley explains, is "to give to another a claim over our selves—a claim on our doing and being what we have promised."[28] Such promises make interpersonal and social relations possible because they "provide some reliability of expectation regarding the actions of free persons whose wills are shakable. Commitments give us grounds for counting on one another, even on ourselves."[29] And yet, adultery happens. A recent study reports that while there is "almost universal denunciation and disapproval of infidelity," there is, in fact, a "high incidence" of noncompliance to the marital rule of sexual exclusivity, to the extent that "55% of married women and 65% of married men report being unfaithful at some point in their marriages."[30] When adultery happens, it causes harm because it is experienced as a betrayal of one partner's commitment to another, which then ruptures the relationship, breeds mistrust, and causes pain for the partner betrayed.

While some marriages survive such harm, many do not. Marriages may end, Farley argues, because even an "extremely serious, nearly unconditional, permanent commitment may cease to bind."[31] Beyond adultery, other reasons may also release people from a marital commitment entered into with the expectation of permanence. As Farley notes, "There can indeed be situations in which too much has changed— one or both partners have changed, the relationship has changed, the original reason for the commitment seems altogether gone."[32]

Farley is right to emphasize, first, that commitments matter and, second, that the breaking of commitments, when done in unjust and harmful ways, can weaken and even undermine the connections between and among us. At the same time, she observes that "today . . . in Western culture (and others as well) nearly every traditional moral rule for sexual behavior is under some kind of challenge."[33] That includes challenges to the traditional rule that equates fidelity with sexual exclusivity between marriage partners. Along these lines, it is important to recognize that some people, including Bill Harkins and "Sarah" from our earlier case studies, have not been asking to leave their marriages or end their marital commitments, but rather are seeking to *enlarge* these commitments in order to accommodate "more than two" within the marriage itself. Accordingly, the very form of permanent, monogamous marriage built on sexual exclusivity is being reexamined. In addition, there are serious efforts to break the "marriage monopoly" by legitimating other options, including open-ended marriage, polygamous marriage, and polyamorous relationships, as ethically principled ways in which people may sustain intimate connections. The ethical task, within this context of moral flux and uncertainty, is to discern, as best we can, which rule changes should be encouraged and which ones discouraged.

■ How should we regard other models of love and marriage?

In speaking of shifting models of marriage and family, historian Stephanie Coontz observes that "people have always loved a love story. But for most of the past our ancestors did not try to live one. They understood that marriage was an economic and political institution with rigid rules." In contrast, "today most people expect to live their lives in a loving relationship, not a rigid institution."[34] Interestingly, among the diverse forms that marriage has taken, the historical practice that is "found in more places and at more times than any other" is not monogamy—one man with one wife, but rather polygyny—one man with multiple wives.[35] This practice has a long tenure even within Jewish and Christian traditions, beginning with the polygamous marriages of the ancient Hebrew patriarchs. Perhaps surprisingly, nowhere does the Bible condemn this family model. In the early fifth century theologian Augustine acknowledges in "The Good of Marriage" that the ancient patriarchs did, indeed, marry polygamously out of a "need of procreation," but he insists that a "difference in times" means, in contemporary parlance, "that was then, and this is now."[36] This theologian, so enormously influential in shaping the Western Christian tradition, recognized the need to balance ethical rules with historical context.

By the twelfth century polygamy had been prohibited in Christian Western Europe, but as Coontz explains, women rather than men were the ones more greatly penalized by this prohibition, insofar as "many men kept mistresses, and wives were expected to ignore such behavior. But mistresses had no legal rights or social standing. By the fifteenth century the children of mistresses had lost the inheritance rights they had had in the early medieval period."[37] A century later, the Protestant Reformer Martin Luther, while not endorsing polygamy, had to concede that the practice does not contradict the Scriptures and that Christianity cannot condemn it outright. "I confess, indeed," he writes, "I cannot forbid anyone who wishes to marry several wives, nor is that against Holy Scripture; however, I do not want that custom introduced among Christians among whom it is proper to pass up even things that are permissible, to avoid scandal."[38]

Feminist critiques of polygyny are grounded in the ethical value of protecting the dignity and well-being of women. *Genuine mutuality and sharing of power between intimates are marks of ethical marriages,* but these are missing in polygamous arrangements where husbands are entitled to exercise sexual control over their wives but women lack reciprocal power and authority. To the contrary, women are prized as sexual property, and their worth is dependent on their childbearing and their ability to enhance the husband's wealth. As Farley summarizes, polygamy is "an arrangement for the sake of men and harmful to women"[39] because this marriage model not only subordinates women to men, but also subordinates some women to other women in terms of the prerogatives of first wives over other wives. "Even where it continues to exist as a majority pattern for marriage," as in parts of Africa, "the critiques it receives, especially from women within it, grow louder and clearer."[40]

Where practiced in the United States, polygyny is illegal, but it is not uncommon among fundamentalist Mormons, who measure a man's righteousness by the size of his family and, in keeping with a strongly pro-natalist belief system, regard women's primary role as bearing and raising as many children as possible. The cover photograph of an issue of *National Geographic* that investigates polygamy in North America describes the reality in a straightforward way: "One Man, Five Wives, 46 Children."[41] Criticism of Mormon plural marriage practices focuses on the harm done to women, especially underage females "sealed" to older men, and, interestingly, the harm done to young men, referred to as "Lost Boys," who have either left or been forced out of their communities because of the paucity of eligible females in their peer group and the threat of competition. However, polygamy has its defenders, including women in this fundamentalist culture who "know little else" and who can scarcely imagine an alternative life. "Walking away" would mean "leaving everything behind," including their families and the material and psychological security provided them through the community and the family system that is familiar to them.[42] They would need to leave their social world behind in order to change their lives in a more mutually empowering way with other women, as well as with male partners.

Because of the nonconsensual and exploitative character of polygamous unions between (often very) young females and older males, it is not difficult to challenge polygamy as unethical, especially in a form that exaggerates gender hierarchy and reinforces male power and control over women's lives and labor, including their bodily labor. However, is there an *ethical* polygamy that deserves further scrutiny? At least one feminist Muslim theologian makes the case that polygyny is "apparently a growing phenomenon in the United States among African American Muslims" because it serves as a practical alternative to single-women, head-of-household families and because it offers a creative response to the shortage of available male partners for heterosexual women, due to the high incarceration rate of adult males in the African American community.[43] Calling for "a serious debate about standards of justice and sexual ethics," Debra Mubashshir Majeed acknowledges that while "polygyny is not for everyone," it may be a welcome option for women whose religious tradition gives explicit permission for plural marriage and who find themselves struggling with their economic displacement and their children's vulnerability in a class- and race-segmented economic system.

As Majeed explains, some women "may choose polygyny because they believe it to be the only way they authentically can practice half of their religion, since marriage and family life are believed to be integral to their religious practices."[44] At the same time, in a post-9/11 environment, because Muslims are at risk for any perceived departure from dominant cultural norms, few may be willing to draw negative attention to themselves or their community by openly discussing, much less practicing, this alternative marriage pattern, especially if that would reinforce the prejudicial view of Islam as a patriarchal religion hostile to women's dignity, safety, and well-being. As a feminist theologian, Majeed argues that if polygamy is to be recognized as ethically principled, it must not appear as a threat to women that keeps them "invisible, voiceless, and without power," but rather be perceived as a freely elected option "determined by the force of women behind it."[45]

■ What happens when we reconsider our definitions?

Another pattern for marriage may be described as open-ended marriage, the "new monogamy," or even monogamy-plus. As married couples weigh the value of their union's permanence over against the traditional obligation of sexual exclusivity, they may choose to give greater emphasis to relational permanence and embrace a more fluid marriage model that allows for secondary emotional and even sexual relationships. At the same time, the couple maintains their primary commitment and loyalty to their marital bond by avoiding any secrecy or deception about satellite relationships, by operating with a single rather than double standard for husband and wife, and by their ongoing willingness to negotiate fairly and openly about this arrangement and revise its terms as needed. As one theorist explains, "To couples engaged in the new monogamy, it isn't the outside sexual relationships themselves, but the attendant secrets, lies, denial, silences, and hidden rendezvous that makes them so destructive to the marriage. Rightly or wrongly, today, many couples consider that honesty and openness cleanse affairs, rendering them essentially harmless."[46]

Although the Christian tradition has long promulgated a negative view of sex as sinful and redeemable only for the purposes of procreation and containing lustful desires, the new monogamy, based not on sexual exclusivity but on relational loyalty and fair negotiation, does not focus on sex as problematic, but rather on the harmful consequences of the betrayal of trust. Along these lines, theologian Scott Haldeman, writing in the context of what may be learned from many gay male relationships, offers an alternative view of fidelity, which he defines as relational loyalty and mutual investment in each person's well-being and in the integrity of the relationship itself. "Queer fidelity," he contends, requires a "shift from a norm of exclusivity in the realm of touch to a new norm of self-care and truth-telling." Because the bulk of Christian history has regarded marriage as more about the regulation of sex and the suppression of erotic desire than ever about embodied love and the sharing of mutual pleasure, Haldeman cautions against placing ethical attention on the wrong question. "Could it be that defining sex as the problem makes it the problem rather than it actually being so?" If so, then Christians need to shift from a control model of sex and marriage to one of mutual empowerment that accepts "the risk of ongoing negotiation in the context of loyalty."[47]

In the 1970s James B. Nelson, in discussing marriage and fidelity in his groundbreaking *Embodiment: An Approach to Sexuality and Christian Theology*, cited four "unproven assumptions" that have reinforced a more restrictive notion of fidelity centered on sexual exclusivity: "that we cannot love more than one person . . . concurrently; that co-marital or extramarital sex always destroys a marriage; that 'good' marriages are totally self-contained and self-restrictive and sufficient; [and] that only emotionally unstable people seek and need intimate relationships outside the husband-wife bond."[48] In addition, he observes that contemporary marriages face a serious challenge in maintaining marital permanence over the course of as many as forty, fifty, sixty, or more years because of people's increased longevity and greater health, but there are other challenges as well: the narrow focus on the nuclear couple as disconnected from community, the propensity toward possessiveness and the "failure to meet the growth needs of the parties," the legacy of sexual inequality and skewed power dynamics within heterosexual coupling, and the heavy load of unrealistic expectations that one partner can fulfill all the social, emotional, and material needs of the other.[49]

In these circumstances, with the values of permanence and sexual exclusivity in tension, some couples may give priority to permanence, especially if both parties consent to, and benefit from, an open, fairly negotiated arrangement in which one or both may engage in secondary relationships of an emotionally intimate and perhaps also sexually intimate nature. Nelson proposes, therefore, that it is appropriate to draw a distinction between adultery and infidelity. Adultery is engaging in sex with someone other than one's marital spouse, which may or may not be a breach in the marital covenant or an indication of infidelity. Why not? Because infidelity, which Nelson regards as a more comprehensive notion than adultery, means a "rupture of the bonds of faithfulness, honesty, trust, and commitment between spouses."[50] By this definition, some couples may, indeed, maintain a strict sexual exclusivity, but their union may lack authentic fidelity because of dishonesty, manipulation, emotional and sexual coercion, and so forth. In contrast, fidelity requires the couple to grant primacy to their marriage over other connections and to invest in the well-being of both partners, as well as the vitality of their union. For other couples, being faithful to one another may include "certain secondary relationships of some emotional and sensual depth," which Nelson contends can be "compatible with marital fidelity and supportive of it."[51]

■ How do we sort out the arguments and counterarguments?

Counterarguments in favor of maintaining sexual exclusivity as an intrinsic requirement for marital fidelity appeal to biblical and traditional injunctions against adultery, emphasize that the two partners become "one flesh" through an irrevocable ontological bond established by the radical nature of heterosexual intercourse, invoke Christian symbols of divine faithfulness that demand an exclusive kind of loyalty, and express concerns about the harmful consequences to the couple, as well as to their children.[52] In response, advocates for a more fluid notion of relational fidelity point out that the biblical prohibitions of adultery define women as men's sexual property and therefore typically view adultery as the woman's violation of her husband's property rights.[53] A double standard has long existed that allows "him to play" and requires "her to pay." Furthermore, feminists warn against an escalated rhetoric of the "total gift" in which one person gives his or her entirety to another in marriage, which, if taken literally, "suggests a form of self-sacrifice that has never been good, especially for women."[54] Finally, the "two in one flesh" imagery is problematic if it suggests a "fusion between persons" that "risks ignoring the realities of individual persons, and rests too often on symbols of purity/defilement . . . that can no longer be sustained."[55]

In her critique of open-marriage options, Farley acknowledges that "marriage as a lifelong commitment has obviously come upon hard times," but she contends "those who made these proposals" in the 1970s for a more fluid, even relaxed notion of fidelity "abrogated them some years later on the grounds that they had proved unrealistic and unworkable." Monogamy, she argues, remains "the model of choice for most persons in our culture, and certainly for committed Christians."[56] Marie Fortune, a student of Farley and a feminist ethicist who writes extensively about domestic abuse, clergy sexual misconduct, and other forms of relational betrayal, agrees that monogamy will likely be the most common choice, but she leaves room open for a principled notion of fidelity that does not require of all married partners that they sustain a commitment to sexual exclusivity.

In her analysis of ethically principled relationships, entitled *Love Does No Harm*, Fortune proposes that relational faithfulness depends on four value-commitments: truthfulness, promise-keeping, attentiveness, and the absence of violence. The promise-keeping component allows Fortune to affirm couples who reserve their sexual activity within their pair-bond, but also to affirm those couples who "are comfortable having sex with someone outside their primary relationship." "Whatever promises are made," Fortune writes, "need to be made with the intention of being kept."[57] That said, she also acknowledges that for many and perhaps most couples, their religious values will undergird a commitment to sexual monogamy and, further, that as a general rule, "monogamy is a good idea these days" because it focuses people's emotional and sexual energy and highlights the value of safer sex requirements for maintaining sexual health. Sexual exclusivity is "also practical," she suggests, because "given limited time and energy, it is simply easier to manage intimate involvement with only one other person."[58]

Emphasizing the freedom of individuals to come together and work out their private arrangements, Fortune is right to emphasize that "whatever promises are made," they should be kept, but she is also right to move beyond liberal individualism's "anything goes" framework to invoke religious values about not only personal freedom, but also personal responsibility and the call to justice to promote the good of persons in their intimate and communal relationships. Along these lines, ethicist Eric Mount lifts up, in contrast to private contracts, the "deep symbol" of covenant. Covenant making requires an emphasis on obligation, commitment, promise, responsibility, and fidelity, but it also conveys a strong commitment to the common good, which is the "holding context" and grounding for people's personal well-being. "Contracts tend to be minimal, short term, and presumptive of little or no community bonding," Mount explains, while "covenants presuppose community, lasting commitment to the other's total well-being, and the assumption of obligations to each other and to shared values that change one's life."[59] Doing good means not only keeping our promises, but also making the kinds of promises that promote the dignity of persons and strengthen our mutual respect and care of one another. In other words, it matters not only that we keep our promises, but also what the content of these promises are. Moreover, fidelity may have different meanings and requirements, depending on different stages within a given relationship. Ethicist Mary Hobgood notes, for example, that early marriage and childbearing years are a different context for covenant making than thirty, forty, or more years later in the same marriage, and responsible adults seek to sort out how best to meet changing needs and expectations that affect each person, as well as the relationship itself.[60]

For Mount and Fortune, "covenantal moral formation should keep intimacy and commitment together,"[61] including a commitment to justice as communal right-relatedness, both within and beyond the intimate partnership. To speak about marriage in terms of justice and love pushes us to revisit the meaning of marriage. On the one hand, if marriage is a contract, then perhaps it is enough to say that persons are free to contract with a partner or perhaps even several partners whom they love and with whom they are interested in bonding. On the other hand, if marriage is a covenant, we may agree to limit intimate relationships to those connections that contribute not only to the individual's private good, but also to the common good. The community's role is significant here for at least four reasons. First, while a couple may privately regard themselves as married, it takes the community's validation to make that pronouncement real and true. Second, good marriages are good not only because they benefit the married partners, but also because their intimate love spills over and energizes those partners to nurture and care for others beyond their twosome. Third, the vitality of any marriage depends not only on the personal investment of the partners in their relationship, but also on whether prevailing social conditions provide adequate economic and other kinds of support for their lives together. Personal well-being is intertwined with and utterly dependent upon communal conditions of relative justice and a fair distribution of goods, resources, and power. Finally, because few if any persons find that a marriage alone or any other intimate relationship alone can meet all their needs for connection, support, nurture, challenge, and even companionship, we need to rely on a broader set of community ties to foster our human development and growth and provide a secure sense of belonging and purpose. In speaking of the necessity of building what he terms an "affectional community," historian John D'Emilio speaks about the broadly inclusive LBGTQ justice movement, but his claim extends beyond social identities: that creating life-enhancing social and affectionate connections "must be as much a part of our political movement as our campaign for civil rights."[62]

■ Is polyamory an ethical practice?

Beyond considering the possibilities and the limits of covenant making in relation to polygamy and the "new monogamy," another relational pattern to explore is polyamory, which may be distinguished from the other two options in several ways. First, polyamory, from the root words meaning "many" and "love," is not a variation on marriage so much as a friendship-based commitment to share emotional and sexual intimacy with various partners who intentionally do not limit their affection or bonding to romantically linked dyads. Polyamory specifically differs from polygamy in the fact that the latter is historically rooted in a patriarchal marriage model and is almost always a heterosexual arrangement. In contrast, polyamorous connections "may cross all lines of sexual orientation and expression," and participants "variously consider themselves straight, gay, bisexual, or just plain 'poly.' "[63] Furthermore, polyamory as an ethical practice depends on mutual consent, honesty, and a commitment to the safety, care, and well-being of each and all parties. "Open communication and honesty in emotions are important hallmarks of sincere, effective, functional polyamorous . . . relationships that strive for power-sharing, consensus-building, and equality for all involved parties."[64]

Advocates for this pattern of intimacy challenge those who would try to reduce polyamory to unprincipled, self-indulgent hedonism and insist, to the contrary, that loving multiple partners is an ethically demanding commitment that requires moral maturity and emotional strength. As Valerie White puts the matter, "We wish to cultivate the development of a responsible attitude toward sexuality in which humans are not exploited as sexual objects, and in which intimacy, sensitivity, respect, and honesty in interpersonal relationships are encouraged."[65] If the promise of polyamory is to move "beyond possessive binary coupling," the antidote to jealousy may be what J. N. Ferrer called "compersion," the feeling-response of "taking joy in the joy that others you love share among themselves."[66] This generosity toward the other has been modeled publicly by retired United States Supreme Court justice Sandra Day O'Connor, whose late husband lived with advanced Alzheimer's disease. Justice O'Connor regularly visited Mr. O'Connor, who had been institutionalized in a residential facility where he had entered into several romantic relationships with other Alzheimer's patients, all of whom were women. Mr. O'Connor and his women friends "[spent] time together, holding hands, even when Justice O'Connor [was] nearby," reports the *Washington Post*, and the retired Justice had given her blessing to these intimacies. After all, Alzheimer's patients continue to have emotional lives and need social interaction, even as they lose awareness of their own family members and their intimate histories with them. As one medical expert reports, "'For some [people living with Alzheimer's], their thinking and memory are largely gone, but their emotional expressiveness may be relatively intact.'" Furthermore, "'As Sandra Day O'Connor and others say, they are just thankful that there is a moment of happiness that comes into their loved one's life.'"[67]

Queer theologian Robert Goss proposes that polyamory may be viewed religiously as a practice of communal loving with warrants from the Christian monastic tradition, which provided its members an alternative form of intimate life outside the marital, monogamous family. These typically single-gender communities were also, Goss surmises, "erotic communities, whether implicitly or explicitly expressed,"[68] for which the biblical imagery of Christ as the bridegroom (Eph. 5:25-33) had deep resonance. "When the church is understood as a collective of countless men and women, married and unmarried, with a variety of sexual orientations and gender expressions, then Christ becomes the multi-partnered bridegroom to countless Christian men and women. His faithfulness and love to them may well express the growth of love, mutual devotion, and faith commitments in pair-bonded heterosexual and same-sex relationships. Yet Christ is polyamorous."[69] As Goss concludes, "Christian ethics has too long spent time in dualistic theological thought that poses a series of binary oppositions: celibacy vs. marriage, monogamous marriage vs. polyamorous relationships. . . . The differences between monogamy and polyamory recede as we understand that Christ is the sexual outlaw, the multi-partnered bridegroom whose erotic visitations and love-making render the differences slight."[70] In this theological frame, Christ's expansive love incarnates the radical grace of divine generosity and openness to all creation, without distinction. Similarly, church historian Mark Jordan observes that Christians have long been troubled by the prospect that the gospel invitation to "love one another" could become eroticized in a radically inclusive manner and thereby disrupt, if not undermine altogether, the traditional Christian emphasis on sexual regulation and control.[71]

■ How would focusing on justice-love reframe the question of relational fidelity?

In postmodern culture, we are witnessing diverse patterns of marriage and family, including monogamous unions, plural marriages, open marriages, and polyamorous connections. Because this is our context and because good people will disagree about how to balance conflicting ethical principles, we would be wise to keep the ethical focus not on the particular relational form but on the moral quality or character of the relationship. The norm for guiding intimate associations should be justice-love in all connections, meaning a strong commitment to the dignity and well-being of persons, a fair sharing of power and pleasure, concern for each person's safety and health, and a mutual pledge to foster respect and care for each other and to invest, as well, in the vitality of our wider communities. As I have written elsewhere, "neither marriage nor heterosexuality, but *justice in sexual relationships* should be morally normative." Marriage remains a valued and important place in which people live out their ethical commitments, but marriage should not be granted a special status or be privileged above other relationships that display deep intimacy and mutual love. Rather than serving as a "license for sex or establish[ing] ownership rights over another human being," egalitarian, justice-bearing marriages offer "a framework of accountability and a relatively stable, secure place in which to form durable bonds of mutual trust and devotion. Marriages should deepen friendship beyond, as well as within, the primary relation and avoid fostering patterns of dependency and control."[72]

Learning to live more gracefully in the midst of cultural diversity will no doubt challenge us all, but not necessarily in the same way. Some of us have need of greater personal security and may hesitate to expand relational options beyond the familiar; others may tolerate more fluid patterns of relational commitment because of the stability they find in their own personal and community ties. At the same time, we need to appreciate how contemporary sexual ethics, among Protestant and Catholic theologians alike, is shifting away from a restrictive marriage ethic to a more pluralist justice ethic of sexually intimate and other kinds of social relations. This shift involves making a break with marriage exclusivism, the notion that heterosexual, monogamous marriage—usually also characterized as a permanent and (preferably) procreative union—is the only right mode for living as responsible, sexually active persons. A narrowly restrictive marriage ethic would claim that all sexual activity outside marriage is morally wrong and that all sexual activity within marriage is "beyond reproach," which is certainly untrue, given the pervasive patterns of marital rape, domestic abuse, and partner abandonment and neglect within supposedly reputable marriages.

If monogamous heterosexual marriage is no longer the presumptive norm for all right loving, then it becomes necessary to make discerning judgments about a diversity of relational patterns, but on the basis of moral quality, not relational status. To paraphrase philosopher Anthony Weston, our project is not to ask which pattern is right and, thereby, judge all others as defective, but rather to ask, at least provisionally, what is each pattern right about?[73] How, and to what extent, does any relational pattern express justice-love commitments?

No doubt many people, including many Christians, will enter into and sustain sexually exclusive, monogamous marriages. James Nelson's observation seems accurate, that "for most of us the better rule is marital genital exclusivity," but this rule is presumptive, not absolute, and may admit good exceptions.[74] About marriage, as about other relational commitments, our ongoing task will be to figure out, as best we can, where to draw our lines and then be prepared to give an accounting for our artistry.

CHAPTER 4

Is Same-Sex Marriage a "Must" or a "Bust"?

Obtaining a right does not always result in justice.

PAULA ETTLEBRICK[1]

Humor can be a seriously effective way to acknowledge the difficulty—and the delight—of putting conflicting issues into perspective, which is one of the ongoing tasks of ethical inquiry. As ethicist Daniel Maguire observes, "Often the cartoon is more insightful than the editorial." Or, again, with a bit more solemnity he points out that humor is "good for ethics" because "humor has an epistemological function: it shakes the foundations of settled surety."[2]

With that insight in mind, consider a cartoon that appeared during the presidency of George W. Bush when one social crisis seemed to follow quickly upon another. The president is pictured at a press conference with a reporter asking, "Mr. President, Iraq and Afghanistan are in chaos, polar ice is melting, and the middle class is disappearing. What response do you have to all of that?" Mr. Bush replies, "Marriage is between a man and a woman."

Here the cartoonist's humor hinges on briskly "[shaking] the foundations of settled surety" after juxtaposing three claims: first, that there are matters far more momentous than making marriage available for same-sex couples; second, that politicians may try to dodge difficult questions by "waving a red flag" about such private yet deeply contentious matters as homosexuality and family values; and third, that the conventional wisdom about marriage as an arrangement exclusively "between a man and a woman" is settled in a way that matters of war and peace ("Iraq and Afghanistan are in chaos"), ecological degradation ("polar ice is melting"), and economic disruption ("the middle class is disappearing") may never be. Perhaps so. But doesn't this cartoon's punch line work because it suggests a more jarring reality? Even supposedly fixed verities about marriage and family are no longer quite so private, fixed, and unassailable. In fact, marriage, a personal relationship as well as a political institution, is both politically significant and culturally contested. Moreover, the outcome of the current marriage debate is far from certain. Therefore, ethical inquiry is needed not only about peacemaking, ecology, and economic policy, but also about the future of marriage and the eligibility of same-sex couples to participate in that civil and religious activity. What does it mean, then, to put same-sex marriage in proper perspective?

■ A sampling of discordant perspectives about same-sex marriage

Even a quick sampling indicates that multiple voices are in contention about this marriage question. One voice is that of marriage traditionalists. When Tony Perkins of the Family Research Council was asked during the 2008 presidential election campaign about California's ballot measure to restrict civil marriage to heterosexual couples only, he remarked, "[Proposition 8] is the most important thing nationally on the ballot. We have survived bad presidents. But many, many are convinced we will not survive [a] redefinition of marriage."[3] Glenn Stanton at Focus on the Family has argued similarly: "[So-called] same-sex 'marriage,'" he asserts, "is being forced upon us by a small, but elite, group of individuals dressed in black robes — judges — who say that thousands of years of human history have simply been wrong. That is a very arrogant notion that will bring great harm to our culture." "God bestowed [marriage] upon mankind [*sic*], and we tamper with it at our own peril." "Redefining marriage in this way [is] the first step toward abolishing marriage and the family altogether."[4] Why so? Because marriage equality, Stanton argues, erases gender differences. If men can marry other men and women other women, "gender would become nothing," he conjectures, "[even though] real, deep, and necessary differences exist between the sexes. [Same-sex marriage] rests on a 'Mister Potato Head Theory' of gender difference (same core, just interchangeable body parts). [However,] if real differences exist, then men would need women, and women would need men" in order for each person to find his or her "other half" and thereby be completed.[5] For marriage traditionalists, same-sex marriage is a "bust."

A second voice is that of marriage advocates. The United Church of Christ in 2005 became the first mainline Christian denomination to support same-sex marriage by affirming "equal marriage rights for couples regardless of gender." Marriage exclusion, this liberal denomination has noted, is a form of discrimination that violates the principle of equal protection under the law. However, this church's stance in favor of marriage equality is rooted more fundamentally in theological and biblical affirmations. "The message of the Gospel," the UCC resolution reads, "is the lens through which the whole of scripture is to be interpreted," and it is a message that "always bends toward inclusion."[6]

Social critic Andrew Sullivan, another marriage advocate, has written, "This debate is ultimately about more than marriage and more than homosexuality. As an argument it is a crucible for the future shape of democratic liberalism."[7] "Including homosexuals within marriage, after all, would be a means of conferring the highest form of social approval imaginable."[8] Again, Sullivan writes, "Gay marriage is not a radical step; it is a profoundly humanizing, traditionalizing step. It is the first step in any resolution of the homosexual question—more important than any other institution, since it is the most central institution to the nature of the problem. . . . If nothing else were done at all, and gay marriage were legalized, ninety percent of the political work necessary to achieve gay and lesbian equality would have been achieved. It is ultimately the only reform that truly matters."[9] For marriage advocates, same-sex marriage is a "must."

A third voice is that of marriage critics. Historian John D'Emilio argues in an article titled "The Marriage Fight Is Setting Us Back" that "the campaign for same-sex marriage has been an unmitigated disaster. The battle to win marriage equality through the courts," he writes, "has done something that no other campaign or issue in our movement has done: it has created a vast body of *new* antigay law. Alas for us, as the anthropologist Gayle Rubin has so cogently observed, 'Sex laws are notoriously easy to pass. . . . Once they are on the books, they are extremely difficult to dislodge.'" Moreover, D'Emilio argues, "as a movement" haven't we been "pushing to further de-center and de-institutionalize marriage? Once upon a time we did."[10]

Jewish feminist theologian Judith Plaskow and her partner Martha Ackelsberg agree. "We love each other," they write in the *Journal of Feminist Studies in Religion*, "and we've been in a committed relationship for nearly twenty years. We are residents of Massachusetts. But we're not getting married." Why not? Because, they explain, "focusing on the right to marry perpetuates the idea that [social and economic] rights ought to be linked to marriage. Were we to marry, we would be contributing to the perpetuation of a norm of coupledness in our society. The norm marginalizes those who are single, single parents, widowed, divorced, or otherwise living in non-traditional constellations." They question the wisdom of reinforcing "the centrality of marriage to the social order."[11] For them and other marriage critics, the problem is not, as Focus on the Family insists, the cultural devaluation of marriage, but rather its *overvaluation* as a privileged marker of social status and as the exclusive conduit for allocating a range of social and economic benefits from health care to inheritance rights. Similarly, Catholic feminist theologian Mary Hunt argues, "I remain of mixed mind, not to mention mixed emotion, on the question. I seek relational justice for all rather than legal remedy for a few. . . . Although I support enthusiastically the right of same-sex couples to marry, I am not persuaded that it will inevitably lead to greater relational justice, a feminist goal."[12] Ironically, for marriage critics as for marriage traditionalists, same-sex marriage is a "bust."

Despite their differences, where both marriage advocates and marriage critics agree is that if different-sex couples have the freedom to marry, then same-sex couples should be afforded that same freedom as a simple matter of justice. Because marriage advocates and marriage critics within the LBGTQ movement also agree that homosexual love and heterosexual love are no different in moral substance ("love is love"), they insist that justice as fairness requires "treating like cases alike." However, justice is rarely simple or easily accomplished. Therefore, a two-pronged approach to marriage is called for. First of all, it is necessary to mount a compelling and principled defense of the freedom to marry for same-sex couples, but it is also then necessary to clarify how limiting justice to the acquisition of equal rights is terribly problematic insofar as other compelling requirements of justice are downplayed or ignored, including the reordering of social power and the debunking of the reigning cultural ideology, including religious claims, that legitimates sexual and other social hierarchies.

■ Why constructing a Christian defense of marriage equality must begin with repentance

At the outset of constructing a Christian defense of marriage equality, it is wise to remember that historically many Christians have been on the wrong side of previous marriage controversies. At various moments in United States history, a Christian majority has refused to allow slaves to marry, affirmed women's status as property of their husbands, questioned the need for laws against marital rape, and as recently as the late 1960s opposed legalizing interracial marriage. Additionally, for centuries Christian theologians promoted marriage as a patriarchal ownership arrangement and touted this model as ethical, even sacramental. Therefore, it would be wise to begin not by making grand theological pronouncements, but by listening to those with fresh insights about these matters, especially gay, lesbian, bisexual, and transgender persons who have gained moral wisdom about intimate matters by managing against the odds to love well, sustain partnerships and families, and build community within often hostile social and religious environments.

In considering whether the civil right and religious freedom to marry should be extended to same-sex couples, I start with several assumptions. First, marriage is a changing, ever-evolving institution with a history, some of which has been oppressive. Second, not only is marriage changing, but it should change in order to be in better alignment with the best of civic and religious values. Because social change aims at reordering distorted social relations and strengthening community, such transformation is often precipitated by a shift in moral perception and deepening recognition of the humanity of those marginalized as Other. Coming to respect the personhood of the "culturally despised" requires honoring and protecting their human rights, including their freedom to enter into intimate association and marry. Third, how we answer the question of whether to support or oppose the freedom to marry for same-sex couples depends on the interpretive framework utilized for moral and theological discernment.

My constructive proposal is to use a justice lens in order to gain perspective about these matters and then to pursue a twofold agenda: first, to correct injustice, in this instance the oppression—the stigmatizing and devaluing—of gay, lesbian, bisexual, and transgender persons, including the denial of their full civil and human rights and, second, to promote the conditions so that all people, gay and nongay alike, can flourish not only in terms of meeting basic needs, but also in terms of exercising basic human capacities, including entering into and sustaining intimate affiliation with a significant other as a life partner and next of kin.

In contrast to definitions of marriage that emphasize both gender difference ("marriage is between one man and one woman") and gender hierarchy ("marriage requires male headship"), I define marriage as the covenanted or vowed union of two persons as committed life partners. In a similar way, Catholic theologian Daniel Maguire speaks of marriage as "the highest form of interpersonal commitment and friendship achievable between sexually attracted persons."[13] Two men or two women fit this definition, as do a man and a woman. Moreover, the goods of marriage as traditionally defined are companionship, mutual trust and fidelity, economic sharing, and the nurturing of children, and these values are central concerns not only for different-sex couples, but also for same-sex couples, many of whom are currently parenting children and caring for elderly and other dependent family members. For these reasons, philosopher Richard Mohr suggests that we focus on marriage as a "lived moral reality," defined as "intimacy given substance in the medium of everyday life, the day-to-day." Because gay and lesbian couples are already "doing the work of marriage" and, in fact, are living together and acting *as if* married, it is only a rather small step to grant these committed partnerships legal standing and protection that would benefit them as well as society.[14]

Beyond the re-imaging of marriage as an intimate partnership between co-equals, the other cultural shift that makes same-sex marriage imaginable is the deep rethinking of sexuality and sexual ethics now under way within Christianity and other religious traditions. Sexuality, the capacity for physical, emotional, and spiritual connection and communion with one another, is a defining characteristic of human beings. Because the human need to love and care for one another in intimate relationship is constitutive of personhood, the freedom of intimate association between adult peers merits moral respect, as well as the community's protection. As legal scholar Carlos Ball argues, "Lesbians and gay men, like everyone else, pursue and express their humanity, in part, through their intimate relationships, including sexual ones. . . . If we morally strip lesbians and gay men of their same-gender sexuality, and thus deny that they have needs and capabilities for meaningful physical and emotional intimacy along with everyone else, we fail to recognize them as human beings."[15] The *morally relevant* point here is the shared human need and capacity for physical and emotional intimacy, which for many is most fully expressed in a sexually intimate relationship. The *morally irrelevant* point about intimate relations, marriage included, is the gender of the partners. As Ball concludes, those in the cultural majority who increasingly support gay rights do so "because they are seeing enough of themselves reflected in the homosexual 'other'—not, of course, in the more superficial sense of being attracted to someone of one's own gender, but in the deeper sense that the attraction (whatever its object) is driven by common needs, capabilities, and vulnerabilities that we share . . . as human beings."[16] Being gay is not only one way of being human; it is also a good, complete, and fully normal way of living and loving humanly.

Rethinking marriage and sexual ethics also requires challenging heterosexual exclusivism, the pernicious notion that the only acceptable sexual expression is heterosexual, marital, and procreative. In contrast, a revised ethical paradigm recognizes a diversity of human sexualities, that sexual orientation is morally neutral, and that the ethical focus belongs not on identity but on conduct and the character of the persons-in-relation. The truth of the matter is that same-sex love and intimate relationships are morally comparable to heterosexual love and intimate relationships with all their strengths, flaws, struggles, and hopes. That is something many clergy, myself included, have witnessed in performing covenant ceremonies for same-sex couples. Granted, two men or two women exchanging vows may look different from a heterosexual couple getting married, but they are engaged in the identical practice of making promises, seeking the support of their community, and receiving a blessing.

■ Legal recognition affirms the dignity of same-sex couples and their full humanity

In its November 2003 *Goodridge v. Department of Public Health* decision, the Massachusetts Supreme Judicial Court ruled to end that state's marriage exclusion and grant same-sex couples the freedom to marry civilly. The law should affirm the dignity and equality of all persons, the Court said, and forbids the creation of second-class citizens. This ruling reflects the understanding that marriage is both a mark of first-class citizenship and a basic human right, so precious that even incarcerated inmates on death row have a constitutionally protected right to marry. Moreover, the Massachusetts court argued that a marriage ban "works a deep and scarring hardship" on same-sex couples "for no rational reason." Therefore, for the purposes of law, the court defined marriage as "the voluntary union of two persons as spouses, to the exclusion of all others."

The Goodridge decision marks a change in the history of marriage, but as the court observed, marriage equality for same-sex couples "does not disturb the fundamental value of marriage in our society." In this regard, the recognition of same-sex marriages as legally valid is a conservative move, part of the ongoing effort to guarantee basic rights and freedoms for all citizens in a pluralistic society in which some families are formed by same-sex couples. Broadening access to marriage rights, benefits, and responsibilities is, above all, a means to acknowledge the humanity of gay persons. When the Vermont Supreme Court in late 1999 declared that the state's ban against same-sex marriage was unconstitutional, it went out of its way to make a remarkable public confession: "The past provides many instances where the law refused to see a human being when it should have." In recognizing that gay people also love, form families, and would benefit from the protections and entitlements that civil marriage provides, the court concluded, "When all is said and done, [this is] a recognition of our common humanity."[17]

October 1, 2008, marked the sixtieth anniversary of the *Perez v. Sharp* decision, another landmark legal case in which the California Supreme Court in a 4 to 3 decision became the first court in the United States to strike down race restrictions on marriage. That courageous Court affirmed that the freedom to marry is a precious freedom that belongs not only to white people, but also to persons of color and, specifically, to interracial couples with the audacity to cross the color line for the sake of love. "The essence of the right to marry," the Court said in 1948, "is the right to join in marriage with the person of one's choice." Sixty years later the California Court cited *Perez* in its own courageous ruling that cleared the way for gay men and lesbian women to "join in marriage with the person of [their] own choosing."[18]

Some Christians, and here Robert Knight at the Family Research Council comes to mind, insist that there is no real discrimination in the United States preventing gay men and lesbians from marrying—as long as gay men marry women and lesbian women marry men! However, as the California Court recognized sixty years ago, any person seeking a state license to marry the "wrong" kind of person—whether interracial couples then or same-sex couples today—would soon find "himself [*sic*] barred by law from marrying the person of his choice and [yet] that person may be to him irreplaceable. Human beings are bereft of worth and dignity by a doctrine that would make them as interchangeable as trains." As legal scholar Evan Wolfson points out, "The courageous California Supreme Court decision in *Perez* marked the beginning of the end of race discrimination in marriage, much as the November 2003 decision of the Massachusetts high court [has marked] the beginning of the end of sex discrimination in marriage."[19]

For religionists, this affirmation of the full humanity of LBGTQ persons and advocacy for securing their human rights, including the freedom to marry, establishes a noticeable dividing line. On one side stand those who would divide the human community according to sexual orientation and grant heterosexuality special status and privilege. On the other side are those who recognize that "the desire for a significant other with whom we are uniquely conjoined is not a heterosexual but a basic human desire."[20] This does not mean that either marriage or sex is necessary for human fulfillment, but it does mean that it is wrong, arbitrary, and cruel to exclude an entire class of persons from these routes to intimacy, shared pleasure, and mutual commitment.

■ A biblical mandate for marriage equality

I support the freedom to marry for same-sex couples because I take the Bible seriously. More to the point, I take the God of the Bible seriously, whose divine passion is for justice and an end to oppression. However, the truth of the matter is that not everything in the Good Book is good. For that reason, the Bible must be read prayerfully and with critical discernment. As William Sloan Coffin has queried, "Why can't Christians just admit that there is such a thing as biblical deadwood, not to say biblical folly?" Some of that deadwood is about women, some about slavery, and still other is about homosexuality, which the Bible says little about and what it does say is either misinformed, plain wrong, or irrelevant to contemporary discussion about intimacy and covenantal love between two coequal partners. As Coffin sums it up, "It's time we grew up." Moreover, "The problem is not how to reconcile homosexuality with scriptural passages that condemn it, but rather how to reconcile the rejection and punishment of homosexuals with the love of Christ."[21]

For those who decline to treat the Bible as a rulebook or "seamless garment" about sex and marriage, the challenge is to listen to the diverse, often conflicting voices within scripture and yet identify the compelling motifs and insights that still command attention and loyalty. Comedian Lynn Lavner's observation may be helpful in trying to keep matters of biblical directives in perspective: "The Bible contains six admonishments to homosexuals and 362 admonishments to heterosexuals. That doesn't mean that God doesn't love heterosexuals. It's just that they need more supervision."[22]

A constructive and entirely welcome move would be to reclaim the centrality of the biblical mandate for justice and compassion and keep front and center the Jesus story, including his own nontraditional stance with respect to family and his challenge to tradition insofar as tradition was invoked to legitimate divisions within the human community. However, the authority for welcoming same-sex couples into the pool of those eligible for marriage is, when all is said and done, not the Bible and not tradition, but rather the movement of God's Spirit at work doing a new thing, troubling the waters, and empowering self-respecting gay people to claim their rightful place alongside others. Others are called, then, to respond in a manner consistent with such a gracious, inclusive God.

■ Why marriage equality is a mixed blessing

While it is necessary to make a compelling religious case for marriage equality,[23] it is also important to recognize that extending marriage to same-sex couples would be, at best, a mixed blessing. On the positive side, marriage equality would affirm gay and lesbian intimate partnerships as morally principled, loving relationships. On the negative side, it would mean reinforcing compulsory coupling, a dynamic that Protestant Christianity has encouraged by expecting all (or at least able-bodied, nominally heterosexual) adults to marry. As ethicist Beverly W. Harrison observes, "The Reformers, none more passionately than Calvin, embraced marriage almost as a duty." In fact, marriage had to be compelled within a patriarchal religious system because "if men must marry women, whom they view as deficient in humanity, the external role of 'duty' necessarily must be invoked."[24] Furthermore, by focusing exclusively on the duty of marriage, Protestant Christianity has consistently failed to celebrate other ways in which people make families and engage in meaningful intimate association.

This point cannot be overemphasized: although the exclusion of same-sex couples from marriage is an injustice that needs correction, the trouble with marriage does not lie primarily in this exclusion. The problem lies in marriage itself or, more precisely, in the institutionalizing of compulsory heterosexuality. Therefore, the larger problematic is how a religious tradition has fostered fear of sexuality, legitimated male control of women's lives, and promulgated compulsory (patriarchal) marriage in response, thereby causing great damage, first, by reinforcing gender oppression and placing women tightly under male authority and control; second, by making alternatives to sexist and heterosexist relationships seem unimaginable; and, third, by demonizing sexual nonconformists as moral deviants and "enemies of God" whose bodies and lives could then be excoriated with impunity.[25]

In contrast, a liberating Christianity, in promoting sexual justice as an indispensable component of a more comprehensive social justice, must advance a larger change agenda than extending the freedom to marry to gay men and lesbians or even restructuring marriage on egalitarian terms, as necessary and important as these changes most certainly are. Relational justice, if it is to take firm root in this religious tradition, requires more: a positive revaluation of sexuality, including appreciation for the goodness of gay (and nongay) sex; the dismantling of the prevailing sex/gender paradigm that privileges heterosexuality; and conscientious efforts to provide the social, economic, and cultural conditions so that all persons, whether partnered or not and whether heterosexual or not, may flourish and be honored within their communities, including their faith communities.

Feminist and LBGTQ marriage critics agree that the ethical agenda should be the promotion of relational justice *for* all families and relational justice *within* all families. In a pluralistic society, people of faith and goodwill should be concerned about more than the vitality of the (heterosexual) marital family. At the opening of the twenty-first century, we must draw a larger picture of love, commitment, and family with ample room for same-sex partnerships, one-parent households, extended families, blended families, and other relational configurations, including plural relationships. Because the strength of family as a crosscultural institution is its adaptability, we should be focusing not on family or relational form, but rather on things that truly matter: protecting the dignity and well-being of all persons; insisting on the qualities of mutual respect, nonviolence, and care in every relationship; sharing power and goods fairly; and making sure that every family, regardless of form, receives the support and resources necessary for its members to thrive. Not marriage, but relational justice as a component of a more comprehensive social and economic justice should be our moral vision.

While it is true that winning (or beginning to win) the freedom to marry for those unjustly denied this right is a good and worthwhile pursuit, it is also true that gaining equal marriage rights is not unambiguously good. The inclusion of gay men and lesbians within the ranks of married couples may be beneficial for those who can elect this newly available option, but it may also further entrench the hegemony of state-sanctioned marriage and strengthen the "special rights" accorded to the marital family to the detriment of other relational patterns. If so, then same-sex marriage would not have a broadly transformative effect, especially if it continues to privilege the married, devalue the unmarried, and reinforce current patterns of social and economic inequities. Expanding marriage rights by itself will not accomplish what truly needs doing: to promote a more complex, more demanding, and ultimately more liberating justice agenda that aims, in Mary Hunt's words, at "relational justice for all rather than legal remedy for a few."[26]

Stated differently, a comprehensive justice requires more than adding queer families to the mix and stirring. Inclusion is good; transformation is better. Expanding the circle is a necessary but insufficient change strategy. More challenging is to dig deeper and transform the cultural assumptions and power dynamics that place so many at disadvantage while granting others unearned privileges. Marriage equality matters, but only within a comprehensive justice framework that confronts not only sexual and gender oppression, but also white racism, economic exploitation, and cultural elitism. Moving in the direction of greater relational justice will mean *queering* our communities, such that all persons, whether partnered or not, and all families, whether state licensed, church blessed, or not, are guaranteed the resources necessary for flourishing.

A social justice framework for thinking about marriage and the common good is urgently needed to highlight the fact that the quality of our marriages, partnerships, and other social relations rises and falls in relation to prevailing social, economic, and cultural conditions and their relative fairness. The personal is not only personal; it is at the same time political, economic, and cultural. The church, because it has an explicit mandate to pursue compassion and justice in all things personal and political, may make a significant contribution in education and advocacy for relational justice, but only if it can deal constructively with three hotly contested matters: the sex question, the assimilation question, and the question of how best to frame the cultural crisis in marriage and family.

■ Addressing the sex question: What makes sex holy and good?

Marriage is about many things, including economics and property, reproduction and childrearing, caregiving and community responsibilities. It is also about the regulation of sex. Sex is an occasion for great cultural anxiety, given how sexual mores have been so thoroughly influenced by Christian sex-negativity. This sex-negativity is reinforced by sexual fundamentalism, the notion that the only morally acceptable sex is heterosexual, marital, and procreative. Those abiding by this standard believe that they have a moral duty to police others and keep them under control. Respectable people are those who marry, restrain their sexuality, and "settle down," thereby establishing their credentials as responsible adults. In contrast, gay men and lesbians are, by definition, "out of control" because they reside outside the marriage zone. Queerness has become cultural code for a generalized immorality and sexual immaturity, again because gay sex is not marital and, therefore, not properly constrained.

Advocates of same-sex marriage have by and large dodged the sex question and not dealt forthrightly with the sexual ethics question, including what makes sex holy and good. Instead, they have tried to make their case for equal marriage rights by downplaying sex. Often they seek to normalize gay men and lesbians by desexualizing homosexuality. Their constant message is that gayness is a nonthreatening difference similar to left-handedness and eye color. Moreover, they insist that same-sex couples are not really interested in altering the institution of marriage, but only in joining the ranks of the "happily conjoined," thereby reinforcing rather than upsetting the status quo.

Playing down sexual difference and sanitizing gay sex are efforts to reduce the threat that gay identity and queer culture pose to dominant norms. According to this strategy, safety and access to basic rights, including the right to marry, require making queerness invisible. In the process, the prevailing norms and structures of compulsory heterosexuality go unchallenged. The moral problem becomes mystified, once again, as the "problem" of homosexuality and whether a minoritized group of outsiders can ever properly qualify to gain access to majority-insiders' privileges by becoming "like them." Defined this way, the solution to injustice is for gay men and lesbians to conform, as best they can, to heterosexist norms or at least not flaunt being too happily deviant.

Take, for example, William Eskridge, a gay legal scholar, who defends the legal right to marry for same-sex couples, but in buttressing his case relies on sex-negative and homophobic arguments. His book, subtitled *From Sexual Liberty to Civilized Commitment*, suggests that even in the midst of an HIV/AIDS pandemic, gay men have been "more sexually venturesome" than others and are, therefore, "more in need of civilizing." His argument in favor of marriage rights is that "same-sex marriage could be a particularly useful commitment device for gay and bisexual men."[27] If marriage becomes the normative expectation among gay men, he argues, gay male cruising and experimentation with multiple anonymous sex partners will give way "to a more lesbian-like interest in commitment. Since 1981 and probably earlier, gays were civilizing themselves," he continues. "Part of our self-civilization has been an insistence on the right to marry."[28]

To argue that marriage is a necessary social control mechanism to tame men's sexuality only reinforces the sex-negativity already so much in evidence among social conservatives. To argue, as Eskridge does, that "same-sex marriage civilizes gay men by making them more like lesbians" presumes, first of all, that women are not really interested in sex or sexual pleasure, but instead concerned only with intimacy and making relational commitments.[29] Moreover, marriage's primary purpose becomes sexual control, this time of gay men. In the process, sexual fundamentalism is never critiqued, much less debunked.

If some marriage advocates have adopted a strategy of desexualizing homosexuality or safely containing homoeroticism within marriage, an alternative, riskier, but in the long term more productive change strategy is to launch an enthusiastic, nonapologetic defense of gay and lesbian sex (and, more generally, of healthy eroticism), spell out a principled critique of heterosexist norms, and reformulate a sexual ethic no longer based on heterosexual marriage as normative. On this score, a *non-reconstructed* Christian tradition will hardly be helpful. The conventional Christian approach does not offer a positive ethic of sex. Rather, it promulgates a highly restrictive moral code aimed at controlling and containing sex within strictly defined marital boundaries.

The prevailing Christian code—celibacy for singles, sex only in marriage—is no longer adequate, if it ever was, for anyone, gay and nongay alike, for at least three reasons. First, this code is fear-based, punitive, disrespectful of human personhood, and aimed at control rather than empowerment of persons. Second, the Christian marriage ethic is not sufficiently discerning of the varieties of responsible sexuality, including among singles and same-gender loving people. Third, it is not sufficiently discriminating in naming ethical violations even within marriage and has been far too silent about sexual coercion and domestic abuse. A reframing of Christian ethics is needed to realistically address the diversity of human sexualities and place the focus not on the "sin of sex," but on the use and misuse of power, the dignity of persons, and the moral quality of their interactions.

The renewal of Christian sexual ethics depends on making justice-love rather than procreative heterosexual marriage the normative expectation for intimacy and erotic exchange. This single relational standard calls for mutual respect and care, a fair sharing of power and pleasure, the maintenance of health, and, in those cases where it applies, the avoidance of unintended pregnancy. This normative shift signals further changes as well.

First, the decentering of marriage. While marriage may be one place in which people live responsibly as sexual persons, it is not the only place. Therefore, it is appropriate not to privilege marriage as the exclusive site for human intimacy. In fact, it would be far better to reclaim the notion of marriage as a vocation to which only some are called or actually well suited. At the same time, we should insist on egalitarian partnerships whether these are marital or not. Friendship, as many feminist and queer theorists suggest, is the most enduring basis on which to construct relationships of mutual respect, care, and abiding affection.[30]

Second, the decentering of heterosexuality. What would it mean to recognize a plurality of sexualities, including bisexuality, intersexuality, transsexuality, asexuality, homosexuality, and heterosexuality, and show respect for the amazing diversity of ways in which people live and love? What matters here is not the sex or gender expression of the partners or their marital status, but the moral quality of relationships and the ongoing commitment of the partners to live in responsible accountability to each other and the community. This framework also defends the freedom of sexually active adults not to marry, without penalty or prejudice.

Third, mutual pleasure as a morally worthy pursuit within intimate relationships. The guiding interest should not be to discourage sex or promote marriage, but rather to equip people with skills and insight for assessing the quality of their intimate (and other) relationships and for negotiating how their needs and the needs of others will be fairly met. A justice-centered ethical framework can, in fact, give pride of place to mutually shared pleasure, as well as responsible freedom, as moral resources and guides.

■ Asking the assimilation question: Are gays only mimicking nongays?

Some queer-identified marriage critics worry that the current push to acquire marriage rights reflects how (at least some) gay men and lesbians are seeking status and safety by mimicking heterosexuals. Of course, that may well be happening here and there, but it can be fairly argued that something far more interesting and potentially transformative is also under way.

Considerable evidence supports the claim that the majority heterosexual culture is coming increasingly to resemble gay culture with its gender flexibility, experimentation with family forms, and celebration of the pleasures of nonprocreative sex. "Contrary to popular belief, and even some gay rights rhetoric," Michael Bronski observes, "gay people have not been patterning their lives on the structures of heterosexuality; rather, the opposite has occurred. Heterosexuals who have increasingly been rejecting traditional structures of sexuality and gender have been reorganizing in ways pioneered by gay men and lesbians." This process may be thought of as *reverse assimilation.* The lesson, Bronski suggests, may be that "only when those in the dominant culture realize that *they* are better off acting like gay people will the world change and be a better, safer, and more pleasurable place for everyone."[31]

The Religious Right with its notorious "straight and narrow agenda" is hardly enthusiastic about queering the church or world. LBGTQ people, singles, and cohabitating heterosexual couples are all morally suspect as "displaced persons" outside the marital system, but it is precisely their marginality that grants them a measure of freedom to invent alternative ways of creating intimate partnership and family. "Banished from the privileges of marriage," Alison Solomon writes, "we have been spared its imperatives,"[32] including its gender rigidity, its preoccupation with the couple in isolation from the community, and procreative duty. Perhaps the more pressing question is not whether same-sex couples should marry, but whether *any* couple should seek a state license for their intimate relationship.

The Religious Right, fearful that this precious freedom *from* marriage and its mandates may catch on, has launched a "traditional family values" campaign in order to depict queerness—that is, life outside patriarchal, procreative marriage—as dangerous, difficult, tragic, and pitiable. By targeting LGBTQ people for condemnation, this campaign is aimed at keeping same-sex couples out of the marital "inner circle," but their primary target audience is the heterosexual cultural majority. Focus on the Family and other organizations certainly want to keep gay and lesbian couples from marrying, but their overriding agenda is *to keep heterosexual couples pinned into a hierarchical sex/gender system* that also naturalizes race and class inequities as divinely sanctioned. Gay bashing sends a signal, to gays and nongays alike, that any deviance from patriarchal norms will be subject to ridicule, violence, and even death. Such threats are highly effective in dissuading people from giving credence to, much less acting on, the intoxicating notions of sexual freedom, gender flexibility, and bodily self-determination.

One way to break the marriage debate "logjam" would be for heterosexual couples to begin living and acting more like their LBGTQ counterparts. Acting in solidarity to rebuild community might well require heterosexually married couples to renounce their marital privilege. After all, why shouldn't *heterosexual* couples be satisfied with having only the more limited legal options of domestic partnerships and civil unions? Why should anyone, gay or nongay, seek the state's licensing or authorization for their intimate relations? Moreover, should it not be enough for different-sex couples to receive a blessing of their relationships from their religious tradition, but not seek "special rights" above and beyond this communal affirmation?

Along these lines, I've been impressed by the change initiated by a United Church of Christ congregation in northern New England. This church has been involved for more than a dozen years in the Open and Affirming movement, advocating the full and equal participation of gay, lesbian, bisexual, and transgender persons in the life and leadership of the church. A few years ago, when reviewing their policies regarding the use of the church building for weddings and other public functions, this congregation decided to discontinue authorizing marriage ceremonies altogether. Instead, in the church they permit only covenant or union ceremonies for same-sex and different-sex couples alike. If two people wish to marry civilly and have that option, they are encouraged to enter into that legal contract at the city hall, but for the purposes of what happens at church, only a witnessing to and blessing of their covenant making is offered with no double standards according to the gender of the covenanting partners. This approach does not rule out state licensing of intimate partnerships, nor does it demarcate the word *marriage* as "state only" or "religion only," but it offers a creative strategy for gaining greater clarity about the purpose and role of church in people's lives.

■ Reframing the crisis in marriage and family: late capitalism's erosion of community and the collapse of liberal democracy

The feminist and queer justice movements struggle to make explicit the connections between people's personal pain and turmoil in their daily lives and how sexism, racism, poverty, and ecological degradation undermine personal well-being and community coherence, especially for those without social power. What is undermining family life for the vast majority in the United States and elsewhere is not same-sex love or same-sex partnerships, not even marriage equality, but rather advanced capitalism's erosion of social and economic security and the destruction of communities, as well as the earth, for the purpose of maximizing wealth for a few.

Under conditions of capitalist modernity, a cultural sea change has taken place that has loosened social obligations to neighbors and strangers and eroded communal ties of affiliation and connection. In the process, people increasingly turn to private relationships, primarily marriage and family, for identity, emotional support and fulfillment, and economic survival. Here a large caveat is in order: intimate, romantic relationships, even enduring ones, are no substitute for the security of a richly textured community life. As historian Stephanie Coontz points out, "It has only been in the last century that Americans have put all their emotional eggs in the basket of coupled love. Because of this change, many of us have found joys in marriage that our great-great-grandparents never did. But we have also neglected our other relationships, placing too many burdens on a fragile institution and making social life poorer in the process." The consequence, Coontz continues, is that "as Americans lose the wider face-to-face ties that build social trust, they become more dependent on romantic relationships for intimacy and deep communication, *and* more vulnerable to isolation if a relationship breaks down."[33] The private good is simply no substitute for, nor adequate compensation for, a genuinely robust public common good.

So what is the solution? Again, Coontz is helpful: "We should raise our expectations for, and commitment to, other relationships [in addition to marriage and family], especially since so many people now live so much of their lives outside marriage. Paradoxically, we can strengthen our marriages the most," Coontz argues, "by not expecting them to be our sole refuge from the pressures of the modern work force. Instead we need to restructure both work *and* social life so that we can reach out and build ties with others, including people who are single or divorced."[34] In other words, we must refuse to reinforce privatized marriage as "you and me against the world," but rather help each other connect more strongly to our communities and empower each other to participate in, and contribute to, the broader social world. This connection to community is especially important at this historical moment in which marriage is no longer the major social organization organizing most people's lives, and even those who marry often spend half or more of their adult years outside marriage itself.

In the midst of this cultural crisis, the challenge to people of faith is to hold on to a much larger gift than families, valuable as these may be. Our calling is to embrace and revitalize *community* and celebrate how our lives are utterly social and deeply, deeply intertwined. Our mutual dependence is a gift from God, or as theologian Carter Heyward expresses the matter, " 'We are the boat. We are the sea. I sail in you. You sail in me.' This is the truth of our lives, and it is the essence of our goodness."[35]

In terms of both caregiving and prophetic social witness, we must also pay close attention to the stresses mounting on almost every household. During the past thirty years, beginning with the Reagan revolution and its dismantling of the liberal welfare state, corporate capitalism has demanded that taxes on the rich be drastically cut and social spending radically curtailed. With the morally callous demands for privatization and deregulation, which result in little if any public accountability or responsibility, neoliberal economic policies have undermined—destroyed is not too strong a word—the common good and steadily pushed economic and social responsibility away from employers and government and onto private households. The mounting personal and communal strains have pushed millions beyond the breaking point, especially the growing numbers of economically vulnerable and racially marginalized.

Neoliberalism's ideology of radical individualism and market fundamentalism has cultivated a gross cultural lie in many hearts and minds: that whether a person or a community sinks or swims, it is entirely up to that person or community alone. Success belongs to the individual alone. If you fail, no one will come to your aid, especially if you're poor, nonwhite, and non-English speaking. (Think New Orleans and Hurricane Katrina, think Darfur, and think Cleveland, Ohio.) As one example of the erosion of social solidarity, consider how care for the most vulnerable among us—children, the frail elderly, and people living with cognitive, emotional, and physical disabilities—is no longer defined as the community's responsibility, but rather as a private family burden that has shifted steadily onto the shoulders of women, mostly unpaid women at home or privately employed, often poorly paid immigrant women of color. As sociologists Lisa Duggan and Richard Kim observe, "In this context, household stability [and household security have] become a life-and-death issue."[36]

At the same time, an interstructured gender, race, and class analysis helps to decipher why marriage equality evokes such fear and negativity, perhaps especially among men. In a globalizing capitalist market economy with ever-widening economic inequalities and severe disruptions of work and family life, increasing numbers of heterosexual men are experiencing a crisis in masculinity as they confront unemployment, underemployment, and the necessity of depending increasingly on their wage-earning wives and female partners to subsidize the family's income. The Christian Right encourages men to compensate for their heightened economic and social dependency by reasserting their male and heterosexual privilege. The entire "traditional family values" campaign emphasizes how "normality" for men requires their being head of—and therefore in charge of—a heterosexual marital family. Heterosexuality, and especially male heterosexuality, has come to represent not only compliance to conventional patterns of male-female exchange, but also loyalty to an entire cultural paradigm of work, family, and community life. For beleaguered men, their heterosexual identity has become a hard-won but mostly token badge of personal virtue, even superiority. Even though a man may not be as successful an economic provider for his family as he might wish in an eroding economy, he can still claim his manliness and hold on to his self-worth by reassuring himself, and perhaps others, that he has at least not shirked his family responsibilities by "turning queer." Without a critical religious perspective to help him connect his suffering with the multiple forms of injustice that afflict countless others, he may be easily manipulated into believing that queer people, "uppity women," and the other "usual suspects" are to blame for his woes rather than a callous economic system that exploits even white males as readily as it does others.

To stem the tide against further erosion of male power and to block additional gender changes in and beyond marriage, traditionalists seek to draw a line to prevent queers, those most publicly identifiable as sex/gender nonconformists, from gaining state sanctioning or religious blessing for their partnerships and families. While denying civil and religious marriage to gay people is their immediate objective, the Christian Right's major preoccupation is to monitor and police the *heterosexual* cultural majority, significant numbers of whom are already in noncompliance—or at risk of noncompliance—with respect to conventional sex and gender norms. What the Christian Right fears most is the dreaded prospect of mass ethical and spiritual defection as "straights turn queer." However, to my mind this cultural upheaval is not a problem to fix, but rather an opportunity to seize for cultivating emerging "wild spaces" of freedom from which to mount social resistance to sexual and other forms of injustice.

In the midst of this cultural crisis, the Right has cruelly played the race card and the sex/gender card, again and again, to scapegoat vulnerable groups and divert attention from the real source of our cultural woes, runaway capitalism and the collapse of democracy. The Christian Right, in particular, has latched onto a conservative sexual agenda to distract people from their economic woes and from understanding the economic structural crisis in late capitalism that is at the root of the deteriorating quality of their lives.[37] If faith communities have hope to offer, it will only be by encouraging us to name and resist this social and economic madness. To put it bluntly, our credibility, ethically and spiritually speaking, now depends on our willingness to resist capitalist plutocracy and our conscientious efforts to dismantle Christian patriarchalism while we seek to embody a truly liberating spirituality of justice.

■ How a queer turn toward radical equality lies at the heart of social and spiritual renewal

If the twin problems with respect to Christian marriage reside, first, in positing gender difference (in actuality, gender hierarchy) as the core structure of marriage and, second, in defining the twin purposes of marriage as containment of erotic desire and male control of women, then re-visioning marriage as right-related mutuality between sexually attracted coequals would be no threat to marriage, but rather a real threat to *patriarchal* marriage and, by extension, other social hierarchies. In point of fact, *affirming same-sex partnerships could serve as an impetus for the ethical and spiritual revitalization of marriage* and other relations by insisting that the doing of justice should lie at the heart of *all* social relating, beginning with the most intimate. If mutual respect, caring, and equitable sharing of power and resources were the expectation for marriage and other social relationships, then extending the freedom to marry to same-sex couples might prod faith communities to acknowledge that what matters is not the gender configuration or how body parts fit together, but rather the moral quality of people's connections and their commitment to change the world for the better.

As Southern author Flannery O'Connor is reputed to have quipped, "You will know the truth, and the truth will make you odd." Celebrating our common humanity requires making an odd, decisively *queer* turn toward radical equality and plunging in together to rebuild a vibrant, just, and wildly inclusive social order. Rather than embrace a more modest marriage equality agenda, I encourage us to embrace a larger, more disruptive queer agenda. The queer agenda has never been only about sex or even sexual justice, but rather remains a persistent, unwavering demand for a comprehensive renewal of life-in-community. The change we desire, deep down, is *not mere inclusion* but rather spiritual, moral, political, economic, and cultural transformation from the grassroots upward and from our bedrooms to far beyond.

This progressive justice agenda reflects an unquenchable spiritual desire for right relation not only in our families, but on our streets and throughout our social, political, and economic institutions. But I would go even further. Turning queer is also a spiritual pathway for remaining loyal to God, who, as these things go, is also rather odd: passionate about justice, no respecter of social rank or status, and forever graciously at work "making all things new."

CHAPTER 5

Why Don't Batterers Just Leave and Rapists Just Cease and Desist?

*The primary task of Christian faith communities is "truth work,"
that is, embodying the ways of Jesus and speaking truth
against death-dealing realities.*

LAURA STIVERS[1]

*When a man hits a woman, he has not lost control;
he achieves and maintains control.*

CAROL ADAMS[2]

A Christian ethic seeking to promote sexual justice dare not gloss over the fact that people often live and love in social and relational contexts of power inequities, violence, and injustice. As ethicist Karen Lebacqz rightly suggests, "To be adequate, Christian moral reflection must begin with real experience, not with romantic fantasies about love, marriage, and the family."[3] Accordingly, in sorting out our ethical roles and responsibilities, what if we begin by paying attention to the pervasive patterns of sexualized violence and coercion that occur between intimates in this culture? What do we make of the fact that interpersonal violence most frequently takes place as men's violence against women, children, and less powerful men? Furthermore, what is the impact of this violence not only on the victims, but on the perpetrators themselves? While it is safe to assume that fomenting intimate violence may well deform the moral character of those who instigate the violence, what about the effects on communities, including faith communities, that ignore, minimize, or even tacitly accept such violence as life, as in "That's life"?

■ Both women and men fear men's violence

Certainly one consequence of intimate violence, for persons and their communities, is the loss of safety and a diminished sense of security. The Yogyakarta Principles, developed in 2006 by international jurists and human rights activists as guidelines for protecting the human dignity of women and sexual minorities, affirm as a universal good the "right to the security of the person." Basic human freedom includes protection "against violence or bodily harm, whether inflicted by government officials or by any individual or group."[4] However, this ethical principle stands in stark contrast to the reality on the ground, which for countless numbers of people does not mean living in safety and security, but rather living in chronic fear and experiencing profound suffering of body, mind, and spirit. Precisely because of such trauma, many individuals and their communities spend considerable time and energy, day in and day out, on strategizing about keeping safe or, in the aftermath of violence, about how to keep going, make healing possible, and prevent further violence.

While it is true that men as well as women fear men's violence, there are significant differences to sort out with respect to men's and women's experiences of violence and violation. First, as Carol Adams and Marie Fortune explain in their edited volume *Violence against Women and Children*, "For men, personal violence is episodic. It occurs occasionally to individuals. It occurs more frequently to men who, by virtue of their occupation, are at great risk, e.g., in the military, professional sports, or police work. Their occupations may require them to be in harm's way." For women, however, "violence is the *context* of [their] lives rather than separate, individual episodes in [their] lives." As they explain, "As women, we live in harm's way: everyday, everywhere. There is no respite. . . . Physical and sexual violence is the context of [women's and children's] lives."[5]

Second, men's violence is more common, more destructive, and results in more frequent hospitalizations for those harmed, while women's violence, especially when directed at men, is typically reactive and undertaken in self-defense.[6] As pastoral counselor and theologian James Poling points out, "One in every three women will experience at least one physical assault by an intimate partner during adulthood." In addition, men's violence is usually deadlier insofar as "women are more frequently injured or killed by male partners than men" are killed by their female partners. In fact, Poling cites statistics that show that "'over half (52 percent) of murdered women are killed by their male partners, compared to only 12 percent of murdered men who are killed by their female partners.'"[7]

Third, male violence against women, including battering of women by their male partners, is viewed by many as customary, ordinary, and even normative behavior, while women's violence, especially directed at men, is regarded as exceptional, extraordinary, and deviant. "This is why women are so harshly punished for using violence in self-defense," Carol Adams argues. Citing criminal justice statistics, she observes that "the average sentence for a woman who kills her spouse or companion is fifteen to twenty years compared to an average sentence of two to six years for a man."[8] While men's violence is regarded as normal and unexceptional, women's violence is viewed as abnormal and blatantly transgressive of social norms and expectations.

For those affected by intimate violence, helpful responses include publicly naming the violence as wrongful and undeserved, offering support and resources to victims/survivors so that they may reclaim safety and bodily integrity, and holding abusers accountable by requiring them to stop their violence and make restitution to those harmed. The community's tasks include critiquing the cultural norms that justify or excuse the violence, joining with others in a coordinated community response to protect the safety and well-being of all persons, and consistently maintaining the norms of nonviolence and of mutual care and respect within all interactions. However, none of this is likely to take place until there is truth telling, the necessary first step in the process of both healing and justice making.

■ Truth telling is the first step

Telling the truth about these matters requires acknowledging that while intimate violence affects individuals, it is a societal problem. The root of the problem is social injustice and the ideologies of race, gender, class, and sexual supremacy that sustain it. In a white racist, class-stratified, and patriarchal social order, some groups have historically claimed entitlement to exercise power as control over other groups while those with less power are obligated, by force if necessary, to show deference and serve the interests of those "above them." Violence and threats of violence maintain an unjust and complexly multilayered power structure by means of enforcing compliance and punishing dissent. In a hierarchical social system that grants prerogatives to white over black and other persons of color, male over female, rich over poor, able-bodied over the disabled, and Christian over non-Christian, violence is used as a mode of social control. Intimate violence is social oppression writ small within interpersonal relationships.

Whatever we have come to understand about the dynamics of coercion, abuse, and sexualized violence between intimates, about the personal and social costs incurred, and about appropriate interventions and prevention strategies, we have come to understand because of the moral wisdom and collective savvy of the survivors of such violence. While facing enormous pressure to "keep the secret," not "break up the family," and avoid "bringing shame and dishonor" to their communities,[9] survivors of rape, domestic abuse, and other forms of intimate violence have courageously come forward, shared their stories of victimization and resilience, developed a wide range of practical resources to aid other victims and their families, and created a grassroots social change movement in the hope of helping others avoid the pain and suffering they have been forced to endure. What do we learn by taking their witness seriously?

First, we learn that intimate violence is commonplace. The National Coalition Against Domestic Violence provides some sobering statistics: in terms of adults, one in four women experiences domestic abuse during her lifetime; 85 percent of victims of intimate violence are adult women; and one in six women and one in thirty-three men have experienced rape, either attempted or completed. Moreover, forced sex or sexual assault occurs in approximately 45 percent of battering relationships.[10] In terms of children and youth, the Maine Coalition Against Sexual Assault reports that in the United States, more than half (54 percent) of females who have been raped experienced this assault before the age of eighteen. One of every seven victims of sexual assault is under the age of six; one in four victims under the age of twelve is a boy. Among college women, about one in seven have been forced to have sex in a dating relationship. Moreover, the United States has the highest rate of rape among countries that maintain such statistics, thirteen times higher than Great Britain and twenty times higher than Japan.[11] In a survey of college men, 51 percent reported that they "would rape if they could get away with it."[12]

Second, in addition to the fact that rape and abuse are commonplace, it is also a matter of great consequence that so much of this violence takes place in a particular context: within intimate relationships. Contrary to popular thinking, most women and children are "considerably less safe in the home than anywhere else."[13] The United States Bureau of Justice confirms the fact that "historically, females have been most often victimized by someone they knew."[14] Typically, the source of endangerment for women and children is someone they live with rather than the presumed stranger who attacks randomly. Accordingly, is it any wonder that "the single most common occasion for female homicide is not robbery, gangs, or drugs, but an argument with a man?"[15] Furthermore, in commenting on women's experiences of rape, Karen Lebacqz observes that "while roughly one woman in ten had been attacked by a stranger, more than one woman in three had been attacked by someone she knew." An even more disturbing finding is that "nearly two-fifths of rape crimes are perpetrated within the presumed intimacy of heterosexual marriage. Thus," she concludes, "it is not only in *public* spaces that women must fear for our safety: the nuclear, heterosexual family is not a 'safe space' for many women. . . . The net result is that sexuality and violence are linked in the experience, memory, and anticipation of many women."[16]

As discussed in chapter 2, the Christian tradition has long sanctioned marriage as a patriarchal arrangement based on gendered roles of domination and submission. Therefore, when heterosexual erotic coupling has been permitted, it has been permitted only within patriarchal marriage, an unjust relational structure based on a gendered power imbalance. The gendered hierarchy of "two becoming one flesh" has brought together a husband-provider with a dependent wife in order to form a next-of-kin unit. Although each party in marriage has presumably had exclusive rights to his or her spouse's body, the two have been united in such a way that the husband has remained in charge and the wife has been subsumed under his authority. "Marriage then is too easily a loss," observes British theologian Adrian Thatcher. "The new one flesh created by marriage has too often been his. Without a mutual contribution to the married relationship, an entire 'gender-sex system' is encouraged in which wives exist through their husbands and subordinate their interests to those of men. Such relationships are clearly unjust."[17]

One of the casualties of this hierarchical gender order, feminists have long insisted, has been the marital relationship itself. Patriarchal power structures do not foster intimacy. As Catholic moral theologian Christine Gudorf explains, "When one person has power over another—and the greater the power, the more profound the effect—trust becomes difficult. The powerless party is unlikely to fully trust the powerful party, and therefore avoids complete vulnerability."[18] However, without mutual respect, reciprocal vulnerability, and power shared consistently and fairly between intimates, intimacy is compromised. "To merge with someone of superior power is dangerous," Gudorf continues, "for we can disappear completely, be swallowed up by the other—which has been women's experience of the legal, political and economic consequence of marriage historically understood as 'two in one flesh.' "[19]

Only late in the twentieth century, with the dismantling of marital rape exemption laws, has one of the last vestiges of the patriarchal doctrine of coverture or "two-in-one flesh" marital unity been discarded. Women's right to bodily integrity and self-determination, including a married woman's self-possession and freedom from coerced sex by her husband, has at long last been affirmed as a legal principle throughout the United States and Canada. Even so, the marital family has not necessarily become a safe zone of freedom for women, especially when the vestiges of Christianized patriarchy have not been critiqued and discarded. As a consequence, Lebacqz observes, "because violence and sexuality are linked in the experiences of women, the search for loving heterosexual intimacy is for many women an exercise in irony: women must seek intimacy precisely in an arena that is culturally and experientially unsafe, fraught with sexual violence and power struggles."[20]

■ Domestic abuse is oppression within intimate relationships

Battering destroys safety for many women. Domestic abuse takes place when one person, usually a man, believes that he is entitled to control his intimate partner and uses a variety of tactics to gain and maintain that control, including threats, isolation, degradation, enforcement of trivial demands, and occasional indulgences, which are offered as positive motivation for further compliance. These tactics are the same ones used against prisoners of war by their captors who deploy a variety of psychological and emotionally manipulative measures to "bind" their prisoners. As Ginny NiCarthy explains, "Most people who brainwash their intimate partners use methods similar to those prison guards, who recognize that physical control is never easily accomplished without the cooperation of the prisoner. The most effective way to gain that cooperation," she argues, "is through subversive manipulation of the mind and feelings of the victim, who then becomes a psychological, as well as a physical, prisoner."[21] Therefore, it is important to recognize that while all domestic abuse includes emotional and psychological abuse, not all abuse is necessarily physical. In fact, if we focus too narrowly on physical violence alone, we may mistakenly assume that some abuse is not "serious" or "bad enough." However, if an abuser can gain what he wants and maintain control by other means, he may never become physically violent, what some experts refer to as exercising "hands-off" rather than "hands-on" battering. Therefore, outsiders will do well to focus not so much on what a particular abuser *does* (in terms of specific tactics of control), but rather on what the abuser *gains* by what he has chosen to do. An abuser abuses in order to gain something he desires: control over another, compliance to the abuser's "rules," and enforced loyalty.

While not all men are batterers and not all women are victims, the ethical problem goes beyond the personal or individual level to the sociocultural. Even when a husband or male partner is *personally* loving and not abusive, the fact that he has membership in the dominant social group has great import. Because men as a group hold a near monopoly on the means of aggression, have a historical track record of employing violence as social control, and receive cultural permission to exercise dominative power, all of this sends a strong signal that *politically* he represents to her, whether intentionally or not, the possibility of danger and harm. As Lebacqz summarizes the matter, "What we need is an approach to sexual ethics that can take seriously the power that attaches to a man in this culture simply because he is a man (no matter how powerless he may feel), the power that he has as representative of other men, and the power that he has for women as representative of the politics of dominance and submission and as representative of the threat of violence in women's lives. . . . In other words," she emphasizes, "we need to keep the political dimensions before us, rather than retreating to a private language of mutuality, relationality, and sharing."[22] The persons we are in relation to others are more than our personal or private identities; we also convey the history, meaning, and cultural baggage associated with the social roles we inhabit and the groups to which we belong. "A role-based morality," Lebacqz concludes, "never ignores the fact that the other by whom I am confronted is historically conditioned by a specific culture and will represent and carry the scars of that culture, just as I do."[23] For better or worse, men as a group represent "the socialization of heterosexuality into patterns of domination and submission," and therefore it is wise to remember that while sexuality may well be God's wondrous gift, that gift is always culturally mediated and in this culture remains "a social construction fraught with the problems of human power relations."[24]

Survivors bear witness to the painful reality that intimate violence is not necessarily recognized as wrong. To begin with, in a violent society male violence is tolerated as the way things are, at least until it really gets out of hand. Moreover, male abusers typically evade responsibility for relying on violence, minimize the harm done, and attempt to "exteriorize the problem" by blaming the victim for somehow causing her own difficulties. It is also common for people to construct an explanatory schema or "tell a story" in order to make sense of what is going on. Often the story told reflects the interests of the powerful to minimize any abuse of power on their part and to suggest that the real trouble lies in the defective character or life situation of the other, the one conveniently designated as the "appropriate victim."[25] "The problem with story telling," Carol Adams contends, "is that it is most frequently a story about the woman (I did something wrong, God is punishing me, I provoked the beating [or the rape]). With story telling the explanations that form the narrative change, but they always deflect the focus from the behavior of the man who batters [or rapes]."[26] In addition, as we will soon explore, a whole set of unexamined cultural assumptions about power, gender roles, and "normal" sexual patterns provides an assortment of justifications and excuses that make male violence appear legitimate or at least inevitable.

■ The cultural construction of men's violence: the insiders' view

In order to explore the motivations and dynamics of sexually violent men, sociologist Diana Scully went directly to the source by interviewing 114 convicted rapists, along with a contrast group of 75 other incarcerated felons, with whom she and a research colleague conducted face-to-face interviews in seven maximum- and medium-security prisons. Although other research about battering and rape has focused on the experiences of victimized women, Scully argues that that victim-as-central approach has avoided dealing with a larger, more troubling truth, namely, that "women are not the clue to men's sexual violence. In fact," she argues, "focusing on women can lead to blaming the victim and to perceiving rape as women's, rather than men's problem."[27] To counter that misperception, Scully makes two points, one about women and the other about men.

About women she notes that while they have been the primary recipients of men's sexual violence, women have never been simply passive victims. To the contrary, women have organized, protested, changed laws, built shelters, developed theory and practical strategies of defense and social change—"everything," she notes, "but commit[ted] acts of violence. Yet," she surmises, "no fundamental change will occur until men are forced to admit that sexual violence is *their* problem."[28] About men she contends that it is necessary to listen to and learn from convicted rapists in order to discover, from firsthand sources, why and how men rape, what incentives and rewards men find in such behavior, and what keeps them (and the society at large) from seeing rape as their problem. The purpose of her project, she writes, is "to understand sexual violence from the perspective of men who rape—to provide outsiders with a view inside."[29]

This insiders' view is disturbing. One rapist told Scully, "Rape was a feeling of total dominance. . . . I would degrade women so that I could feel that there was a person of less worth than me."[30] Another man reported, "Rape gave me the power to do what I wanted to do without feeling I had to please a partner or respond to a partner. I felt in control, dominant. . . ."[31] Many men, linking sexuality and violence, associate violent acts with sexual pleasure, but they also insist that their victims "enjoyed themselves." One man decided to rape because his older brother had repeatedly told him that "forced sex is great, I wouldn't get caught, and, besides, women love it."[32]

In critiquing the psychiatric model that suggests that men who rape are "sick" and suffering from an idiosyncratic pathology, Scully underscores how little incarcerated rapists differ from the general population of prison inmates. She also debunks the myth that rape results from men's uncontrollable sexual impulses or from sexual frustration or deprivation. Her findings show that "men who rape . . . are not frustrated by a lack of consensual sexual opportunity. They are," in fact, "as likely as other men to have significant relationships with women although . . . more likely to have abused these women, and they father children."[33] The medical model of rape-as-pathology also does not adequately explain why all men with similar personality traits are not rapists, nor does it account for the frequency or ordinariness of sexual assault. How could responsibility for such a common occurrence rest solely with a purported "lunatic fringe" of pathological men? By falsely assuming that aggressive male sexual behavior is unusual, even strange in this culture, the psychopathology theories portray men who rape as if they are outsiders, thereby missing the point that *men are regularly socialized to be dominant in their interactions especially with women* and, therefore, primed to act out as potential offenders just as girls and women are socialized to be socially submissive and "legitimate" victims.

As a feminist theorist, Scully locates the problem of men's sexual violence not in men's psyches or "essential nature," but rather in gender socialization that encourages conformity to prevailing cultural patterns of gender imbalance and power inequities. The origins of sexual violence lie in the social subordination of women and the maintenance of a gendered system of male privilege and control that also explicitly eroticizes men's power over women as sexy and "naturally arousing." Rape is not only a singularly male form of sexual coercion. It is also an extension of, not a deviation from, normative male behavior insofar as men shape their lives and interactions to conform to patriarchal values and prerogatives.

If rape is to be understood as learned behavior that is culturally constructed, it is also behavior that is purposeful. Men abuse in order to gain something they desire. As Scully's informants disclosed, they regard rape as a "low-risk, high-reward crime," which from their perspectives serves several positive purposes. Rape is used for revenge and punishment of women who "step out of line." It is a "bonus" that occurs during the commission of another crime. It happens for adventure and recreation. For some, rape is a readily available source of impersonal sex and power. Nearly all the men reported that "it is an act that makes them 'feel good.' "[34]

Even more telling, the incarcerated rapists by their own testimony emphasized their belief that "their behavior is within the normative boundaries of the culture."[35] What distinguishes rapists from other patriarchalized men is that they are only more extreme in their beliefs about male power and women's subordination and in their willingness to act on those beliefs. As Scully documents, the most consistent predictors of male sexual aggression are callous attitudes toward women and acceptance of cultural myths about rape, such as the belief that women find sexual aggression stimulating and pleasurable. Men who rape are thereby showing their allegiance to the norms of patriarchal male culture with its rigid double standard, its "pedestal" values regarding women as more virtuous and in need of male protection (read control), the hostility toward women as defective and subversive of male authority, and the presumption of a male right to discipline and punish women. It is also quite significant that Scully's research substantiates that men who rape are not social deviants, but rather social *conformists* who overidentify with a traditional model of masculinity.

Moving beyond examining men's motivations, Scully analyzes how men who rape construct their social reality and draw on cultural values and beliefs to justify and excuse their behavior. She remarks that "from the perspective of these men, almost no act is rape, and no man is a rapist."[36] As the men Scully interviewed disclosed, learning how to rape involved acquiring a vocabulary along with a set of excuses or justifications that could be called upon to explain sexual violence against women in more socially acceptable terms. "As men who have mastered this vocabulary," Scully argues, "convicted rapists have much to tell us about how sexual violence is made possible in our rape-prone society."[37]

Classifying the men as either "admitters" or "deniers," Scully notes that admitters express the conviction that rape is morally reprehensible and also acknowledge women's fear of sexual violence, but they explain away their own actions by appealing to forces beyond their control. They cite emotional problems or alcohol and drug use to "excuse" themselves and insist that engaging in rape was not a reflection of their "true selves." While not altering the facts of the rape, they typically try to minimize the amount of violence used or insinuate that they have been grossly misunderstood. Yes, they've been convicted of a crime, but they're not "really" victimizers. In contrast, deniers justify rather than excuse their acts. They accept the fact that they were responsible for "an act," but they claim that the act was not wrong or inappropriate. For example, they portray their victims as willing, even enthusiastic participants in seduction and "wild, abandoned" sex in which their "dreams came true." Or, again, deniers portray their victims as the type of woman who "got what she deserved." Since *she* is not a "nice girl," *they* (the men) are not rapists. Deniers operate out of a value system that provides no compelling reasons not to rape. Developing their justifications from cultural stereotypes about men as sexually masterful and women as coy but seductive, deniers ultimately deny the existence of victims. If no man is a rapist, then no woman can rightfully claim to have been harmed.

Despite their differences, both admitters and deniers share in common an absence of feelings and a remarkable (and remarkably disturbing) capacity to ignore or misinterpret how they appear to their victims. The majority of men interviewed did not experience guilt or shame for their violence against women, nor did they report feeling any emotions for their victims during or after the rape. As Scully notes, "Instead of experiencing feelings that might constrain their sexually violent behavior, these men indicate that rape causes them to feel nothing or to feel good."[38] The conclusion she draws from her research is that men are able to rape precisely "because their victims have no real or symbolic meaning or value outside the role rapists force them to perform."[39] Women are not regarded as real persons, that is, as human subjects with rights and feelings, but rather as objects, jokes, sexual commodities, and targets of abuse. One prisoner succinctly summarized the rules of male sexual terrorism: "Rape is a man's right. If a woman doesn't want to give it, a man should take it. Women have no right to say no. Women are made to have sex. It's all they are good for."[40]

Is Scully's analysis nothing more than a sociological exercise in male bashing? We might have reason to believe so if Scully has assumed that "rapist" is a fixed, essentialized identity and, therefore, a descriptively accurate term for literally Everyman, but this is not the conclusion she draws. Even though male sexual aggression is commonplace, Scully argues that men learn to rape and use sexual coercion against women (and against children and other men, as in prison same-sex rape) in a cultural climate that tolerates violence generally and, more particularly, promotes hostility toward women. Misogyny has distorted and inhibited these men's moral awareness and responsiveness by encouraging them to ignore the impact of their violence on other people's lives, especially when those other people are women.

Because men who rape have been desensitized by the pervasive cultural devaluing of women, their moral frame of reference not only excludes women, but also allows them to consistently misinterpret how they appear to the women they rape. Deficient in the moral imagination to "take the role of the other," especially when the other is female, men who rape can neither see themselves as their victims see them, nor imagine how their victims feel. The men Scully interviewed were able to say things like, "She felt proud after sex with me," "Once we got into it, she was okay," and "I shouldn't have all this time [i.e., a prison sentence] for going to bed with a broad."[41] What we need to appreciate is how masculinization, the process of "hardening up" by losing touch with feeling-connections to and about one's self and others, deprives men who rape ready access to the full range of human emotions that would ordinarily regulate sexually violent acts. This includes not only feelings of shame, guilt, and embarrassment, but also the capacity for empathy.

■ The problem is political as well as personal

Instead of "telling a story" that either blames women for provoking their attackers or excuses men who use violence by pathologizing them and thereby making them not "really" responsible, we should tell the truth that in this culture, sexual and domestic violence is something, as Susan Schechter proposes, that is "individually willed, yet socially constructed."[42] Men who harm others are personally responsible for the choices they make, but the problem of men's violence against women will not be corrected solely by stopping individual men from acting in destructive ways. The problem is political as well as personal. It is lodged in the social construction of sexuality that sets up erotic exchange as a power dynamic between unequal parties in which one is expected to exercise control or mastery, the other is expected to submit willingly, and this conquest-and-surrender pattern is supposedly pleasurable for both.

Because patriarchal patterns of heterosexual intimacy are based on dominance and submission as erotically stimulating and "normal," the result, as Lebacqz explains, is far from surprising: "Men are expected to disregard women's protests and overcome their resistance." In this cultural climate, sexuality and violence have become fused for many. The rapist is not alone in viewing sex as the violation of the less powerful by the more powerful, but also in his expectation that he can act with impunity because sex-as-domination is a male prerogative. Moreover, he believes, often correctly, that he will not suffer negative consequences for his abusive conduct. Accordingly, in this cultural context, given the particular social construction of sexuality in terms of dominance and submission and given the confusion between sexual violence and sexual activity, the answer to the following question will likely remain ambiguous: "When a man 'overpowers' a woman, is he raping her, or is he simply being a man in both his eyes and hers?"[43]

The moral challenge to consider is whether men alongside women will create a countercultural perspective that consistently challenges the legitimacy of intimate violence, advocates "the right to the security of the person" for all adults and children, affirms bodily integrity as a foundational human right, and holds abusers accountable, or whether people will continue to "tell a story" that minimizes the abuse, blames the victim as the "identifiable" problem, and excuses the victimizer. As Carol Adams acknowledges, it is hard to hold on to the truth that "abusive men know what they are doing, to whom they are doing it, and what it is they are doing."[44] Many prefer to see battering, for example, as a "misunderstanding" caused by stress, abuse of alcohol, or anger that "gets out of hand." The problem then becomes localized within the individual, and the corrective is some kind of therapeutic response. However, this privatized, individualistic framework ignores the centrality of power in all social and intimate interactions, as well as the patriarchal construction of heterosexuality as a dynamic of male dominance and female submission.

A contrasting interpretive framework understands that intimate relations are political as well as personal. Abuse is a problem of injustice. As psychologist Ellyn Kaschak explains, in a male-supremacist culture "[boys] will be taught that a certain amount of threat to women is an acceptable expression of masculinity. . . . She is supposed to be fearful and vulnerable. He frightens as well as protects her. Her vulnerability and his power to frighten and to protect supposedly enhance his masculinity and sexuality, as well as her femininity and sexual interest."[45] Therefore, in order to make sense of why some men batter their intimate partners, the explanation is not to be found, for the most part, in mental illness or individual pathology. Moreover, there is no psychological profile that is able to identify batterers or distinguish them from "ordinary men" because of certain idiosyncratic characteristics. To the contrary, what abusers have in common is their belief system. They are persuaded that intimate relations require someone to be in charge, that the man is entitled to control "his" woman, that violence or threatening violence is permissible and will be effective in achieving the desired outcome (compliance and loyalty), and that the abuser will not suffer negative consequences for his abusive behavior.[46] In other words, battering is a pattern of coercive tactics that a person employs in order to dominate another person; it is willful, purposeful, and intentional behavior that is chosen in order to accomplish a goal.

In her study of battering in intimate relationships, Carol Adams describes the abuse dynamic this way: "Battering is learned behavior. With it the perpetrator gains his way. Because it works, battering is repeated."[47] Again, "perpetrators believe that they are entitled to have their own way at the expense of others. Their tendency is to deny (I didn't do it), minimize (it didn't cause any harm), or externalize (she caused it) their behavior."[48] Similarly, as a pastoral counselor working with abusive men, James Poling observes, "Denial and minimization are common defenses by perpetrators, which makes the truth nearly impossible to discern. All perpetrators lie to avoid the consequences of their crimes."[49]

The question to ask ourselves is whether we are prepared to challenge the abuser's misinterpretation of what is going on and, in solidarity with those victimized, stand on the side of those seeking safety. Because it is beyond her power to hold him accountable, stop his violence, or make him change, it is the community's responsibility to intercede by diminishing the rewards that abusers seek and increasing the penalties for abusive behavior. As Adams writes, "Individual pastoral care [or counseling] is not the solution to ending battering behavior. A coordinated community response is. Consistently applied community sanctions for the men who choose violence [are] absolutely essential. The survivors need a community that offers safety and an opportunity to reflect in safety on the traumatic experiences of being victimized by battering. In holding the abuser accountable, society begins the work of ensuring justice for the victim and offers the possibility of repentance and healing for the abuser."[50]

■ Ending violence requires taking a countercultural stance

Understanding sexism as the root of battering means that working for change is countercultural work. It includes the personal commitment to show respect for women and support women's safety and well-being, but it also involves social and cultural change, including transforming the sexist norms that devalue women and altering the institutional power structures that grant privileges to men as men. However, sexism is not the "cause" of battering as much as it is the environmental wellspring out of which men's power to control and dominate others arises. As long as men as a social group retain disproportionate power and as long as prevailing institutional arrangements reinforce male privilege and status, then the problem of male violence against women, children, and less powerful men will not disappear. Far from it. Sexist cultural norms and values support notions of male superiority and the right to rule over and discipline others, a prerogative that some men play out violently. While sexism does not directly cause any man to choose violence toward another, it provides the cultural impetus and legitimation from which such choices are made.

The community's justice making will be further complicated because sexism does not stand alone apart from other dynamics of oppression, including racism and heterosexism. With its historical roots in slavocracy, white racial supremacy has legitimated the ownership and control of black bodies by dominant whites, who have used and abused those under their power for generations and done so with impunity. As Traci West explains, "For slaves, all whites represented an ominous, supremely controlling presence. Displeasing whites could lead to the arbitrary loss of one's children or home, to bodily brutality, even to loss of one's life, with few if any consequences for the white person."[51] Slave women were routinely raped by their slave masters, and "as forced breeders they were made to submit to sexual relations with black slave men who were chosen by the master for breeding purposes." However, as West perceptively argues, "intimate violence perpetrated by slave masters and by fellow slaves was not morally synonymous" insofar as black men were also acting under duress and forced to obey the demands placed upon them by their slave owners.[52] Accordingly, whenever black men have abused black women, black women have had to negotiate a perilous cultural situation in which calling men to account for their misconduct means taking "the risk of stoking white supremacist assumptions about black humanity" and legitimating increased white hostility toward an already disempowered and marginalized community.[53] When victimized, black women have also had the burden of their own community's expectations that they will "be strong," take care of their men, and sacrifice their own well-being for the "sake of the community," which is already under duress from white racialized assaults.

Because of this oppressive legacy, West insists that violence against black women must be contextualized in such a way that "violence against women within black communities must never be separated from an understanding of violence against the community."[54] White racialized animosity toward black women and men is accompanied, as well, by a pervasive white suspicion about black sexuality, which is routinely regarded as animalistic and prone to violence and excess. Black men are caricatured as "wild bucks" and "natural" rapists, and black women are stereotyped as "dirty temptresses" and untrustworthy Jezebels who seduce "good men."[55]

These cultural stereotypes set up barriers for black women because whenever they are victimized, they become fearful, for good reason, that they will not be believed and that white authorities will not act in their defense. As West observes, "Reporting perpetrators to white authorities can invite racial stereotyping and exploitative judgments by whites. To expose oneself to that kind of treatment is humiliating."[56]

Racist and sexist assumptions operate subtly and not so subtly to discredit a woman's truth telling, and the consequence is that the attention shifts from the fact that violence has been done to a woman to the "problem" of the victim-survivor herself. As West explains, "A black woman's testimony about rape, when filtered through the invalidating cultural lens that her status invokes, can mean to police officers that either the rape didn't happen at all, or if it did happen, it was not a big deal for a black woman (i.e., it's not really a crime)."[57] Building a social justice movement to end violence against women must therefore infuse the community "with an alternative moral consciousness" and transform "the false assumptions about women which justify the violence against them" or at least render it invisible and inconsequential.[58] This alternative consciousness must attend to the complex reality of black women's lives insofar as they must simultaneously navigate the race structure, the sex-gender structure, and often the class structure as well, which means that their experience of rape and sexualized violence is even more humiliating and stressful than what is experienced by many white women.

■ Telling another truth: same-sex domestic abuse

Not all violence in intimate relations is gender violence, and ending male violence against women, a deeply desirable goal, will not by itself end partner abuse. Another truth must be told, this time about domestic abuse in same-sex couples. Research indicates that abuse occurs at the same rate in gay and lesbian relationships as it does in heterosexual unions and, further, that same-sex victims suffer the same types of abuse as heterosexual women endure at the hands of their batterers, including physical, emotional, psychological, and sexual violence. So, too, over time the abuse typically escalates in duration and severity. In addition, victims of same-sex violence often stay for the same reasons that battered heterosexual women stay: not because they like or accept the abuse, but because they love their partner and are invested in making their relationship work, they believe in their ability to change the batterer, they blame themselves for the abuse, and they fear reprisals should they leave. Moreover, many victims are further trapped because they lack economic resources and other supports that would make it possible for them to live independently, especially if they have dependent children or family members with special needs. Others stay because it may be safer to remain with a batterer than leave and thereby risk the danger of stalking and other forms of escalating violence.

Although same-sex abuse reflects many of the characteristics of heterosexual domestic violence, a primary difference is how a heterosexist social environment and the social stigma attached to same-sex erotic relationships complicate matters. Free-floating homophobia provides a control mechanism not available to heterosexual batterers. For example, a lesbian batterer may exercise her power to "out" (or threaten to out) her partner and thereby extend her control by relying on homophobic prejudice to isolate her partner further from her family, her employer, and even their landlord. A gay-negative cultural environment not only isolates victims; it also masks abusive behavior as a serious problem and gives it no challenge because the cultural presumption is that same-sex love is intrinsically pathological or, religiously speaking, sinful and "disordered." Therefore, homophobia works similarly to racism in shaming the sexual activity from the beginning, so that ethically principled, mutually caring and respectful conduct between partners is not expected from the very start. In such a social context, without access to reliable family support, social services, or a friendly criminal justice system, battered gays and lesbians are not likely to seek assistance from the outside. If they do, they are not likely to be helped.

One ongoing task in justice making is making the connections between people's personal pain and larger social ills. In this case, the change agenda must include not only assisting victims and holding batterers accountable, but also changing the wider cultural context that sustains anti-gay oppression. Another task, equally important, is to provide a clear naming of same-sex battering as wrongful, unethical conduct. However, certain obstacles make such naming difficult. Donna Cecere, a survivor of domestic abuse, offers testimony that illuminates the problem:

> We were together for two years. The abuse began early on, though I didn't know enough then to make such a connection. Though a lesbian feminist activist for years at that point, I still thought of battering as, first, a male-against-female act, and second, as being a physically violent act. *I had no concept* of what emotional, psychological, and spiritual abuse was about.[59]

Lacking a larger cultural interpretive framework that helps people recognize healthy psycho-social relations, names the violence as unacceptable, and assigns responsibility to the batterer, people often end up telling a story, as we have already noted, usually about the person being abused and what *they* did wrong to cause their own grief. However, as long as victims are blamed or their reality is discounted, as frequently happens when the abuse is between same-sex partners, no liberating action is possible. This communal inaction is compounded when people hold on to their settled belief that abuse can happen only when the recipient of violence ("the victim") has less social power and status than the abuser. Survivors of same-sex abuse tell a different story: that abuse can and does occur even when the parties have roughly equal social power and status. It can happen whenever one person is willing to abuse their power and role, has the opportunity to abuse, and chooses to abuse—and when the community fails to stop the violence.

For victims of same-sex battering, naming the abuse, being heard, and being taken seriously are made more difficult by the tendency to interpret domestic violence exclusively through a heterosexual lens. If battering is defined exclusively as male battering of female partners, and if all intimate violence is presumed to be sexist in origin, then these presumptions mitigate against recognizing women who are abusive or men who are victimized. Again, as Donna Cecere acknowledges, she "had no concept" of heterosexual women's violence or of lesbian battering. Without the experience of healthy psycho-social relations that are mutually respectful, and lacking the power to name the abuse *as abuse*, she "didn't know enough," as she put it, "to make a connection." An analytical framework that relies exclusively on gender/ sexism to assign the roles of perpetrator and victim will not readily clarify for gay men or lesbians (or for that matter, heterosexual men) their own experience as victims or as victimizers. Nor will it help keep the focus where it rightly belongs, on the abusive behavior as the moral problem, along with a sociocultural context that promotes the acceptability of power as unilateral control in the major social relations that construct our lives. Similarly, in both church and society, because homosexuality itself has long been identified as sinful or alternatively pathological, many people mistakenly identify the problem as homosexual identity rather than as partner abuse. Held captive by such cultural obfuscations, people may look and look, but they will not see.

Making sense of battering, including same-sex battering, requires developing a theoretical framework that appreciates how violence as a social control mechanism is generally tolerated in this society, how it can be used by and against anyone, and how grasping what is going on requires keeping the focus on the behavior of the abusing partner rather than on the victim's gender or sexual identity. At the same time, the interpretive framework must take into account the larger social environment, in this case the "holding context" of heterosexist values and power dynamics, which greatly expands the opportunity for the abuse to go unchecked. Heterosexism provides a convenient cultural pretext for not seeing same-sex abuse as wrongful or significant enough to warrant the majority community's time and attention.

Another obstacle to naming same-sex battering is the LGBTQ community's own inclination toward self-protection in a hostile cultural context. Like the experience of those who suffer on the underside of the race structure, the truth about same-sex battering remains hidden in part because of the shame experienced by those directly affected by the abuse and in part because of the reluctance of an oppressed community to go public with its problems and thereby give ammunition for further vilification of gay culture. Drawing attention to intimate violence *within* the community seems unnecessarily provocative and self-incriminating, just as we noted earlier a similar reluctance in communities of color. However, a lack of responsiveness to battering in same-sex or mixed-gender relationships only perpetuates the problem, by not holding abusers accountable and neglecting the needs of victims for safety and support.

As a social problem, same-sex battering requires a *social* response. Not only the gay and lesbian communities, but also the heterosexual community at large must intervene in order to ensure the safety of victims and hold batterers accountable. Together, we bear responsibility to convey the message that coercive control, whether in same-sex or other relations, is unacceptable and will not be tolerated. It is necessary to name intimate violence as both personal and structural and, further, to admit publicly that some of the families being destroyed by such violence are gay, lesbian, and transgender families. Moreover, our moral credibility on this matter depends on matching our rhetoric with policies and programs that offer effective strategies aimed at prevention, as well as crisis response.

■ Justice making as spiritual renewal

In *The Soul of Politics* Jim Wallis offers a guiding principle for restoring community and the moral integrity of its members: "Those who benefit from [an injustice] are responsible for dismantling it."[60] Similarly, in her study *Justice in an Unjust World,* ethicist Karen Lebacqz argues that justice making requires something different from the powerless than from the powerful. On the one hand, she contends that God's response to injustice encourages the oppressed to cry out, protest, and resist their abuse. On the other hand, "for the oppressor, God's response to injustice takes the form of rebuke and requisition. Both require redress—the setting right of things gone wrong."[61] As members of the dominant sex-gender class, men (and especially heterosexual white men who are likewise dominant in the race and class structures) are called, first and foremost, to repent and make amends. Men's work is not to take charge of the feminist movement or even to "help the ladies," but rather to do our own justice making with other men by transforming the norms and established patterns of dominant male culture. Throughout, we need to keep our feet off women's necks (and entire bodies!) and, instead, collaborate with them to alter the social practices and ideological underpinnings of gender, racial, class, and sexual dominance and particularly male violence in the multiple forms of battering, rape, sexual harassment, and clergy abuse of power, including sexual abuse. A progressive justice agenda for men will therefore ask at least the following of men: telling the truth, making confession, exposing dominative power and seeking a credible alternative path, becoming newly responsible, and entering into solidarity with women and with gay men, all the while facing and working through our fears of what this may cost us.

Telling the truth. Justice making begins with men's candid acknowledgment that male gender supremacy is a pervasive and personally corrupting form of social oppression. Often men dominate "in good conscience" by means of a religious ideology that downplays or erases women's reality. The moral challenge to be present with and responsive to women (as well as to less powerful men) is demanding for privileged white and affluent men, especially when it comes to lower-income women, lesbians, and women of color. When men feel little or no obligation to listen to real women as peers and companions, then it becomes more likely that they will take their own social constructions of reality for granted as really real. Male moral myopia, as we have already discussed, may be illustrated most dramatically by rapists who believe that women welcome coerced sex and that predatory sex is a "cool" male benefit.

Men have an obligation to start telling the truth about male power and its consequences, about male gender and white racial supremacy, and about how their lives have been constructed not on the basis of reciprocity and mutual respect with others, but on the basis of hierarchy, competition, control, and fear. "As men," John Stoltenberg writes, "we know more than we've ever really disclosed about how men keep women down, how men use race hate and sex hate to feel superior, how men despise 'faggots' in order to feel masculine."[62] (We should also add to this list class hate insofar as lower-income women, like women of color, are often perceived as "ready for sale" and without moral worth.) Sharing this knowledge may, and probably will, cause men discomfort, embarrassment, even shame, but men should not shy away too soon from these feelings. Shame and feelings of remorse are body-mediated moral resources that communicate to us that our actions have been wrong, disrespectful, harmful, and in need of correction. It is likely, however, that the first step in reconstructing our lives is to have our settled ways of knowing disrupted. Then, while holding on to our worth as persons, whether we are poor, gay, and of color or whether we are not, we may also confront how we have caused pain in the world and in our intimate relations.

Making confession. Justice making requires, too, that we acknowledge and sort out the mechanisms by which we have participated in, and benefited from, the gender system of injustice, as well as from white racial supremacy, heterosexism, and class elitism. Here the specific challenge is to reframe the moral problem as one that involves all men, not simply a particular segment of men.

Because men as a group benefit from unequal social power over women, men are the ones primarily responsible for restructuring social relations as well as religious traditions toward greater justice for women and for other, less powerful men. Becoming responsible as men requires giving up our innocence about male power and its effects on others. We must become *politicized*—publicly aware and accountable—as to how even good-hearted, compassionate men of faith participate in, and benefit from, systems that dehumanize, degrade, and inflict suffering on women and marginalized men.

Some men are stepping up to the plate, and Paul Kivel, an educator who works with men on ending male violence against women, speaks of this shift of understanding this way: "When confronted with the impact of male violence on women's lives, I originally wanted to say, 'It wasn't me,' 'I respect women,' 'I wouldn't hurt anyone.'. . . Yet as I learned more about male violence it became all too clear that I participated in perpetuating the system of violence that engulfs and imprisons us. Sometimes it was through my actions; other times it was through my denial or complacency. I could no longer claim innocence or feign ignorance."[63] We do ourselves a disservice by presuming that an absolute dichotomy exists between batterers (and rapists) and all other men. This dichotomizing among men discourages us from examining how as members of the dominant gender (and often reinforced by race and class structures), we participate in and, to varying degrees, contribute to a social and religious environment that promotes inequality. Candid self-reflection about male gender, white racial, and class privilege is a necessary component of our work as men of ethical integrity.

While it is true that all men are not batterers or rapists and, therefore, not all men are morally culpable of doing women direct harm, that point should not be overemphasized to allow us to evade recognizing that all men share responsibility, as members of the male gender class, for the social and cultural norms that legitimate men's violence toward and control of women. Men of faith bear particular responsibility for transforming androcentric religion into more fully humanizing and egalitarian faith traditions.

Exposing dominative power and seeking an alternative. Although men are powerful as a social group, most individual men do not consider themselves powerful. The power given men is hierarchical power that defends and upholds the system of male, as well as class and race, privilege. An alternative kind of power, one that enables critique and transformation, comes from another source entirely, namely, from the willingness to join with others to seek another way constructed on the basis of mutual respect and care. Specifically, this alternative involves transforming the model of manliness into the capacity to embrace others as equals, including the gendered, raced, and classed Other.

Any system of injustice is maintained not by external controls alone, but by becoming internalized into people's character structures. Masculinity is the culturally constructed ideal promoted for men, which invests men's lives in gaining superiority over and distance from others. However, the justice-bearing, largely marginalized traditions within Christianity carry subversive knowledge of a possible character transformation through which people gain new lives. New life in the Spirit is possible, as early Christians gave witness, by renouncing and revoking old patterns and entering into intentional community as coequals and interdependents with others, including the outcast and dispossessed. A revitalized religious tradition is needed to empower men to engage in radical experimentation with alternative, culturally subversive models of masculinity that regard battering, rape, and other forms of abuse as morally objectionable and the *least manly* things to do, ever. The masculinity needed is not based on conquest or on distancing ourselves from others, but on combining power with compassion and strength with fairness and respect for others.

Becoming newly responsible. Instead of feeling guilty, ashamed, or defensive about ourselves as men, we need to gain a critical understanding of our place in the male supremacist order and become newly responsible for using our relative privilege and social power to promote justice rather than masculinist interests. Social change arises out of two sources: shared outrage over injustice and a shared vision of possibility. At its best, Christianity sparks the heart's desire for a new thing, for genuine mutuality of respect and care between men and women, men and men, and women and women even if, and no matter if, they occupy different places in the class and race structures that must also be transformed.

Provocative theologies of desire are needed to stimulate in us a deeply felt longing for justice. However, such desire will only take place as Christians embrace the body and bodily existence as sacred. The dominant Christian tradition has focused almost exclusively on duty as a moral guide and approached pleasure with strong suspicion, but a liberating Christian spirituality must reclaim a morally principled pleasure that energizes men and women alike to claim mutual delight and enjoyment as coequals.

Entering into solidarity with women and facing our fears. Men owe women solidarity, based not on charity but rather on a respectful identification with women and on a willingness to take personal risks to advance the cause of promoting a women-friendly, gay-friendly culture, including women-friendly and gay-friendly faith traditions. To become women-identified men means running the risk that we too may become targets of male violence and be repudiated as no longer "one of the boys." Such rejection is often a man's greatest fear. Therefore, this justice work will be difficult as well as exhilarating because it will require men to face our fear that we will be perceived as being "like women" and as "no better than women," that is, as unmanly. Homophobia, including men's fear of being feminized and losing male status, is a major impediment to forming a progressive men's justice movement because it prevents men from confronting how heterosexism keeps men in fear and competition with other men. Heterosexism, the institutionalization of gay oppression, is the linchpin that keeps sexism in place by punishing gender nonconformity—that is, "stepping out of line"—as sinful, criminal, and perverted. Patriarchy and its religious cohort patriarchal Christianity make intimacy between and among men taboo, and yet without men's principled self-love and audacious love for other men (and for women) as coequals, a pro-feminist, gay-friendly men's movement is, to say the least, unlikely. If men are in the movement only for women's sake and not for our own, we are likely to bail out when the going gets tough. Because of the close affinity of sexism and heterosexism, it is doubtful that men will be able to repair their alienation from women unless and until they also repair their alienation from themselves and from other men. No oppression stands alone, and none falls alone.

At the same time, we must recognize that many men find it difficult to admit that they lack power because it is not manly to admit powerlessness or dependence on others. Therefore, it is often harder for men than women to critique the status quo and assess how they as men have been harmed by present social and cultural arrangements. Yet it is precisely this damage—for most men, the lack of individual power in a culture that demands them to exert dominative power—that lies at the root of their desire to abuse and control women, children, and less powerful men. A liberating Christian faith must provide an alternative ethical framework so that men can recognize that their own prospects for safety, well-being, and integrity are intimately bound up with the safety, well-being, and integrity of others, especially women.

The faith wager of a liberating Christian spirituality is that men can live more principled lives when we reject the belief, and the social practice, that men are more important than women, that white-skinned people are superior to people of color, and so forth. Our lives become better, more fulfilling when we refuse to take advantage of others. We become more worthy of respect when we speak up and protest sexism and other oppression. Our spiritual vitality as men of faith increases when we no longer grasp for control but enthusiastically embrace our own embodied selves first in love and compassion so that we can embrace others as our coequals. Therein lies powerful, world-altering good news.

CHAPTER 6

Is "Pro-Choice" What We Mean to Say?

Abortion debates are unacknowledged debates
about women and women's sexuality.

GLORIA H. ALBRECHT[1]

Women have as much right as men to embrace
their own well-being as a positive moral good and to be taken seriously
in their process of decision-making.

BEVERLY WILDUNG HARRISON[2]

Pregnancy happens. So does abortion. Worldwide, some 210 million women become pregnant each year. About six out of ten (63 percent) of these pregnancies result in live births, while more than two out of ten (22 percent) end in abortion and the remaining 15 percent in miscarriage. In the United States, about six million pregnancies occur annually, and half of these are unplanned. Of the total, nearly two-thirds result in live births, about one-fourth end in abortion, and the remainder end in miscarriage.[3]

Other statistics provide additional insight into contemporary patterns of pregnancy, childbirth, and pregnancy termination. Of the 64 million abortions that take place worldwide in a given year, at least one-third are illegal, usually clandestine, and often dangerous to women. Upwards of 20 percent of all maternal deaths occur as the result of unsafe abortion, and in some areas of the world, the toll is as many as half of all maternal deaths.[4] By way of contrast, for most United States women with access to reproductive health care, their risk of health complications from abortion is minimal, especially when the procedure is performed by a trained professional in an appropriately hygienic setting. Less than 1 percent of United States women experience health complications due to an abortion. In fact, the risk of death to women having abortions is less than one-tenth of the risk associated with childbirth.[5]

In terms of frequency, one in three United States women by age forty-five will have terminated a pregnancy, which means that abortion is commonplace in this society.[6] By some estimates abortion ranks as the most common gynecological procedure that women elect. On the one hand, the fact that women, now as in the past, have sought to manage their fertility and relied on a variety of means, including abortion, to limit births is nothing new. On the other hand, as ethicist Beverly Harrison points out, the "public acknowledgment of the frequency with which women resort to abortion" is a "new social reality" that has "astonished and frightened many people."[7] It may also come as a surprise that nearly 80 percent of United States women who have an abortion report that they are religiously affiliated: 43 percent identify as Protestant, 27 percent as Catholic, and 8 percent as belonging to other faith traditions. Finally, contrary to anti-abortion polemics that caricature women who terminate their pregnancies as selfish and disinterested in children, six out of ten women having abortions are already mothers.[8] More than half of these women say that they intend to become pregnant again and expect to have one or more children in the future.[9] Therefore, there are not two distinct groups of women: women who have abortions and women who value children and choose to parent. Instead, large numbers of women in the United States (and worldwide) belong to both groups.[10]

■ "Birth by choice" as a historical watershed

What statistics fail to capture is the lived reality of what a planned or unplanned pregnancy means to women and their partners. Pregnancy is always a life-altering experience. Historically speaking, women in every culture have sought to limit the number of births. The most common form of controlling family size has no doubt been infanticide, closely followed by child abandonment and the sale of children by desperately impoverished parents.[11] What marks a historical watershed, with great potential to transform the quality of women's lives, is the availability of medically safe and legal reproductive health services, including pregnancy terminations, along with the global movement for the social and economic empowerment of women. These two factors make it possible, though not inevitable, for women to direct their sexual and reproductive lives so that they may live without fear of frequent and unplanned pregnancy. The authors of *Our Bodies, Ourselves*, the Boston-based women's health collective, express the stakes this way: "Unless women can decide whether and when to have children, it is difficult for us to control our lives or to participate fully in society."[12] Therefore, making the conditions for procreative freedom or "birth by choice" widely available is a moral requisite for any good society that values women's well-being and supports their freedom to participate fully in societal as well as family life.[13]

When economic resources are adequate, when the community is supportive, and when there is physical, emotional, and spiritual readiness on the part of expectant parents to welcome new life into the world, then anticipatory parenthood can be something positive and joyful. However, when pregnancy is not desired or when a fetal abnormality renders a pregnancy problematic, then, as Catholic feminist theorist Francis Kissling observes, there is "no fully satisfactory outcome." "The choice to have a child one is not prepared to parent or cannot afford, give a child up for adoption, or have an abortion is a grim one," she writes, but "women are strong and they cope well with these lousy choices."[14] Precisely because their choices are, indeed, often lousy, women who make these moral choices require strength and courage and deserve the community's commendation, not its opprobrium, especially because the decision about how to resolve a pregnancy is often a morally ambiguous one.

While the power to create new life is an awesome power, women's procreative power, as with other forms of human power, can be used wisely or unwisely. Even when a fully considered decision about a pregnancy may be ethically principled and carefully crafted to respond to the realities of the particular woman's circumstances as well as the larger social and cultural context, she may experience lingering moral uncertainty in the aftermath of her decision. That uncertainty may persist whether she elects to continue or end her pregnancy. Women's advocacy groups[15] that counsel with women before, during, and after pregnancy decisions, including decisions to abort, report that it is not uncommon for women to experience a sense of loss because, after realistically assessing her situation and anticipating all that will be required to nurture a child over several decades, a woman has had to weigh the relative importance of multiple value claims. Because not all values may be actualized, she must decide which among many values to emphasize. Tellingly, women terminate their pregnancies for the very same reason that under other circumstances they continue their pregnancies, give birth, and rear a child: in order to demonstrate respect for the sanctity of life, including the value of emerging human life. In light of the high value they accord to the preciousness of life and out of realism about the demands that new life places on them and their community, women approach these matters with concern not to reproduce willy-nilly, especially now that human power—or, more accurately, women's power—has expanded to make it possible to continue as well as end a pregnancy safely and legally.

■ Protecting fetal life as one among other feminist values

In the decision-making process about human reproduction, a plurality of values deserves respectful attention, including most certainly the value of developing fetal life and the good of giving birth and rearing a child. Protecting fetal life is a feminist value. "We are pro-life to the extent that we do not want to abuse or harm living things if we can avoid it," Kissling argues. "That at least is our ideal—which we then regularly violate with war, torture, the death penalty, and the callous way in which we deny those in need [of] healthcare, food, shelter, and education."[16] Even though there is a moral presumption to care for and preserve human life, including developing fetal life, only a strict moral absolutist would insist that this one moral value necessarily trumps all other value claims. In potential conflict with the "protect life" principle are other values, each also expressing a serious pledge to respect life and a way to honor that moral commitment.

As a woman explores her particular life situation, she may discover that one or more of these other values become compelling as she confronts the meaning of her pregnancy, sorts out the pros and cons of the options before her, and sometimes decides that the value of preserving (developing) life must yield to a more pressing value commitment. Such positive value commitments may include giving precedence to her own well-being, her duty to protect her own health and life, her right and need to pursue her own life plan, and her need to pay attention to current obligations that she feels bound to fulfill, including responsibilities to children already born. It is not unusual, then, for women to cite more than one factor that informed their decision about abortion. Three-fourths of women who have opted for abortion say that having a child at this time would interfere significantly with work, school, or other responsibilities, including the rearing of children already born. About two-thirds report that they cannot afford to raise a child, and half share that they are reluctant to be a single parent or that they are having problems with their husband or partner.[17]

Although moralist absolutists may insist that developing fetal life is singularly the one and only value that warrants consideration, those who support women's procreative freedom to decide whether and when to give birth realize that giving birth, while a positive and communally important value, may not be the only value at stake or even necessarily the most important value. Because competing claims require their attention, women are obligated to exercise their freedom as moral agents and make conscientious choices about whether to continue a pregnancy or not. Procreation is, therefore, properly situated within a zone of moral freedom, discernment, and deliberation. No longer is biology women's destiny or the singular determining factor about these matters. With medically safe and legal contraception and abortion available as backup, women no longer need to experience pregnancy as compulsory or a biological necessity, but rather as a choice that may be elected or not, according to their best judgment. As Harrison points out, this marks "a fundamental change in human history. The expectation that women's lives may, and even should, assume procreative choice is radically new. Nothing in our lives will remain unaffected by this movement toward procreative choice."[18]

The fact that moral ambiguity accompanies these momentous decisions about childbirth and childrearing is not a sign that women and their trusted companions are failing in moral seriousness. Rather, it is the nature of the moral life. As Kissling notes, "There is nothing unusual about moral complexity. Women—and men—live with it every day. It is what it means to be a human person."[19] When it comes to pregnancy, childbirth, and childrearing, women understand that being humanly responsible requires them to exercise their procreative power conscientiously by sorting out whether they are prepared to assume the responsibilities of parenting. In doing so, they must assess not only their strengths and limits for supporting new life, but also the strengths and limits of their community. As one feminist ethicist summarizes the situation, "The power of procreation is an unqualified blessing under some circumstances, but a dreaded curse under others. Those who are realistically sensitive appreciate this fact, which accounts for many women's support of legal abortion even when they doubt that they themselves could ever choose to have one."[20] Similarly, Mary Gordon puts the moral challenge this way: "In real life we act knowing that the birth of a child is not always a good thing. . . . But this is a difficult truth to tell, [and] we don't like to say it."[21]

■ Truth telling in a pro-natalist and patriarchal culture

Telling the truth means acknowledging that giving birth is not always an unequivocal good and that sometimes *not* giving birth is the more responsible decision. Such truth telling becomes difficult, however, in a culture that has a pro-natalist as well as patriarchal bias about women's lives, sexuality, and procreative obligations. For this reason, the controversy that rages about abortion is about more than securing the legal and moral right to terminate pregnancy. At the heart of the cultural conflict is the global grassroots effort to critique and transform the long-standing patriarchal social paradigm that has placed women's lives, including their reproductive labor, under the supervision, control, and authorization of men. In recognition that women's oppression is further compounded by class and race inequities, the feminist project seeks to promote the economic, political, and cultural conditions that will enhance all women's health and well-being and also solidify their authority to exercise moral agency in the family and throughout the social order.

This justice struggle places the debate about abortion within the larger context of a global campaign to secure procreative freedom as a moral good and as a human right across cultures. The fundamental question is this: When it comes to birthing children, should nature determine the outcome, or should bearing children be intentionally subject to moral decision making and, therefore, be open to rational deliberation and choice? In other words, once pregnant, is a woman obligated to carry that pregnancy to term, regardless of the circumstances and her wishes and values? Or should she have the power and moral authority to decide how to proceed, including figuring out with whom she wants to consult along the way?

Research conducted by the Public Religion Research Institute verifies that a solid majority of religiously affiliated adults in the United States, with the exception of white evangelical Protestants, agree that abortion should be legal in all or almost all cases. However, while a majority (56 percent) says that abortion should remain a legal option, almost as many (52 percent) are conflicted about the morality of abortions and say that abortion is morally wrong or ambiguous. As the researchers put the matter, "The binary 'pro-choice'/'pro-life' labels do not reflect the complexity of Americans' views on abortion. Seven-in-ten Americans say the term 'pro-choice' describes them somewhat or very well, and nearly two-thirds simultaneously say the term 'pro-life' describes them somewhat or very well." Moreover, they document how "this overlapping identity is present in virtually every demographic group."[22]

Several factors may be at work in these responses. First, many recognize that criminalizing abortion will not end the practice, but likely only send it underground and thereby place women's health and safety at even greater risk. It is better, then, that women have access to medically safe and legal services than to return to the days of back alley abortions.[23] The question then becomes how to reduce the need for abortion while refusing to coerce women or restrict their legal and moral options.

Second, because of the high value placed on human life, including nascent human life developing in the womb, ambivalence about ending life makes good sense. I take such ambivalence as a welcome sign that these matters are approached with care and deliberation and weigh on women and their trusted companions as matters of ethical consequence. After all, there is a prevailing moral presumption that life should be protected and sustained even though it is not the only value at stake or the singular value to be honored absolutely without qualification. Sometimes values other than the protect-life value may take precedence, and navigating the moral life requires working through such morally complex and often ambiguous tradeoffs. Moreover, many people are rightfully cautious about any policy or practice that might decrease respect for persons and, in particular, engender a moral callousness toward new life. At the same time there is wide recognition that sometimes saying no to new life is the more appropriate response. Even though the ending of life may be morally justified and the best option available in difficult circumstances, many people experience this as tragic but not necessarily as immoral. For these reasons, to make the claim, as I do, that it is morally good to have the freedom not to continue a pregnancy is far different from saying that abortion itself is a moral good.

Third, when some pro-choice advocates argue that abortion is necessary so that "every child will be a wanted child," many people register discomfort with the very notion of wantedness. As Frances Kissling explains, "Our continuous talk of *wanted* children does not inspire confidence but fear. We live in a world where our value is increasingly equated with wealth, brilliance, or success. Many rightly perceive," she points out, "that they are powerless and unwanted. For the powerless, the fetus is a ready symbol of their own vulnerability."[24] Added to the symbolic weight projected onto the fetus as defenseless "innocent life" is the cultural idealization of motherhood, which makes it difficult for some to accept the fact that under some circumstances, the "all-nurturing," "all-giving" mother may decide to terminate rather than continue a pregnancy. A tolerance for moral complexity is necessary in order to grasp how ending life may be a decision also made in the name of valuing and caring for life.

■ Accounting for the intensity of the abortion debate

Given these complexities, the abortion debate remains emotionally intense in part because of human anxiety about enlarging human freedom, this time at the awesome, fragile beginnings of new life with respect to family planning and birthing. However, there is an additional reason for the intensity of this debate: not men and not even men and women together, but rather women are the ones properly authorized to make these decisions over life and death. After all, women's bodies carry the burden, risk, and even the joy of bringing new life into the world. Moreover, until feminism's "longest revolution" takes hold in every society, women will most likely remain the ones who carry the primary, if not exclusive responsibility for the care and protection of the young and other dependent, often vulnerable family members. Because women are the ones most deeply affected by this issue, they should hold the decisive power to decide how to proceed and for what reasons.

Although some moralists argue that the decisive question is "When does life begin?" that framing of the matter effectively establishes a taboo by encouraging people to believe that moral virtue lies exclusively in "letting nature take its course." Such thinking, when held consistently, also prevents human intervention in the reproductive process by prohibiting contraception as well as abortion as its backup. This life-begins-at-conception approach is reductionistic, taking into account only the biology of reproduction, but not giving weight to a broad range of relevant factors, including whether the woman has freely chosen to be sexually active as well as to become a mother, whether she has adequate economic and emotional resources, whether the developing fetus is healthy, and so on.

A rigidly prohibitive stance tries to keep the moral focus on the mere biological fact of whether a pregnancy has taken place or not. For those who embrace a more multidimensional and, therefore, complex ethic of procreative freedom, the value of emerging fetal life is surely significant, but there are other values to consider, including the health and well-being of the woman, her circumstances, and the presence or absence of community resources. While the fetus matters, so does—and so should— the pregnant woman. Stated more strongly, because of the appalling lack of justice for women in so many areas of their lives, should we not be moved by a sense of historical urgency to focus our ethical attention on transforming prevailing social, economic, and cultural conditions so that women in every community can flourish? "For many of us," Beverly Harrison observes, "this principle [justice for women] has greater moral urgency than the extension of the principle of respect for human life to include early fetal life, even though respect for fetal life is also a positive moral good."[25] Moreover, expecting girls and women to fall into line and readily comply with the patriarchal mandate to sacrifice themselves, including postponing or even denying their own needs and well-being, in order to protect and preserve [early] fetal life "at all costs" is neither reasonable nor fair. Nor is it right to place someone other than the woman in control of her reproductive (and other kinds of) decision making, no matter if that someone is her husband, father, doctor, pastor, or a judge. Whenever a woman's moral agency is downplayed and her own well-being discounted "for the sake of others," there is every reason to suspect that misogyny, the culturally debilitating mistrust of women, has raised its ugly head.

That said, it is also true that elective birth is not a simple or easy ethic. It requires moral maturity on the part of women and their trusted companions. Each pregnant woman has the moral responsibility to judge her situation and make a considered decision about whether to intervene in the pregnancy. Even if the decision is to carry the pregnancy to term and raise the child (or place the child with others to raise), she should never be made to feel guilty for the fact that she examined all her options, including the option to abort. Rather, she has exhibited moral courage about matters that are rarely if ever straightforward or neat and tidy. The bottom line is that in a world of expanded powers, in which women's procreative powers are being dramatically reshaped by modern health care and global feminism, the challenge is to sort out how best to exercise this expanded moral freedom. With enlarged freedom comes increased responsibility. Therefore, approaching these momentous matters by adopting a passive "let nature take its course" response is no longer good enough. Not nature, but historically situated, all-too-human moral agents—to the best of their ability and with their community's support—must be encouraged to engage in fully conscious, ethically principled self-direction about their sexual and reproductive lives.

■ Placing reproductive justice within its personal and sociocultural contexts

These decisions should not be approached in a context-free or context-neutral manner. Some moralists proceed as if abortion is an act that can be ethically evaluated abstractly, apart from the "mere externalities" of a woman's health, economic vulnerability, or struggle to care for already existing children. Abortion is then typically treated as an intrinsically wrong act, regardless of the circumstances. In contrast, an ethic of procreative freedom appreciates that any decision about reproduction must be contextualized insofar as an act acquires moral significance only within its meaning-giving context as people grapple with the particularities and challenges of their lives. The fact of the matter is that the "question" of abortion arises not in the abstract or as a matter of theoretical interest alone, but rather more typically as an existential moment of reckoning only after the discovery of an unintended or problem pregnancy, which then presses women and those they trust to sort out the most responsible way forward.

In the case of a pregnancy that starts well but becomes problematic, women and their partners are likely to have intentionally welcomed pregnancy and anticipated parenthood joyfully, but during the course of the pregnancy they find out, sadly, that the developing fetus has a genetic or some other significant problem that alters the meaning of their situation. They may choose to continue the pregnancy, but regardless of their decision, they now have a responsibility to take this additional information into account as they consider the wisest course available to them.[26] In terms of unintended pregnancies, again Beverly Harrison is helpful to point out that "in the best of all worlds," there would be safe and consistently reliable contraception, men and women would share responsibility for procreative decisions as well as parenting responsibilities, and there would be no sexual violence or domestic abuse. Under such ideal circumstances, it would then "probably be possible to adhere to an ethic which affirmed that abortions should be resorted to only *in extremis*, to save a mother's life." However, Harrison rightly concludes, "we do not live in the best of all possible worlds." Therefore, the widespread availability of affordable, effective, and safe contraceptive methods, as well as safe and legal abortion as a backup, "is often a genuine blessing, despite a degree of moral ambiguity that needs to be acknowledged."[27] Similarly, Catholic theologian Daniel Maguire notes that "more often than we male theologians have dreamed, abortion is the best a woman can do in a world of diversified extremities,"[28] not the least of which are threats to her own life as well as poverty, sexualized violence, and little or no access to effective contraception.

Contextualizing these concerns helps clarify how the term *pro-choice* itself does not mean "in favor of abortion," nor does it celebrate choice-making "merely" for the sake of choosing. Rather, this ethical stance, while affirming women's moral agency to exercise procreative freedom in deciding whether and when to have children, also focuses on the constraints located in the larger sociocultural context that frustrate and impede such agency. As African American theorist Jael Silliman explains, the problem with placing too great an emphasis on individual choice is that it may well "obscure the social context in which individuals make choices." For women of color, "economic and institutional constraints often restrict their 'choices,'" she writes, noting further that "a woman who decides to have an abortion out of economic necessity does not experience her decision as a 'choice.'"[29] A world characterized by social injustices, including widespread poverty and racial hierarchy, deeply constrains reproductive choices. Creating greater justice for women is necessary so that they have access to the life-conditions that would make it possible for them to actualize their decision-making power and grant them genuine choices about reproduction. Therefore, it is important to connect the struggle for procreative choice with a more comprehensive social justice agenda that includes economic and political empowerment for women of all classes, colors, and cultures.

An expanded moral vision is required that places women's lives, their limits and possibilities, within a wider social-economic framework. Again, as Silliman argues, "for women of color, reproductive and sexual health problems are not isolated from the socioeconomic inequalities of their lives."[30] Although securing access to legal abortion is essential, an ethic of procreative choice must also address the problems of forced sterilizations and medical experimentation which have plagued especially poor and nonwhite women, as well as the lack of economic resources, political empowerment, and cultural visibility that renders "choice" unlikely for so many. A genuine commitment to reproductive *justice* rather than "choice" will press the community to expand its focus and work to provide the social conditions that will, in fact, encourage women's well-being and the well-being of their children and families, including adequate economic resources and social services, freedom from violence, and safe and vibrant communities.

■ Challenging Christian sex-negativity and patriarchalism

A Christian ethic seeking to contribute to this movement for sexual and reproductive justice will need to correct two biases within the tradition that have made it difficult to embrace procreative choice as morally good: its long-standing sex-negativity that has condoned only procreative sex and its patriarchalism that has reinforced father-right and male control of women's bodies and their labor, including their reproductive labor.

Christian procreationism reinforces the notion that good sex is exclusively heterosexual, that "real" sex is penis-in-vagina intercourse, and that the only legitimate end of sexual activity is baby making. However, among contemporary Christians a shift of sentiments has occurred. Now the normative sexual practice, even among married heterosexual couples, is contracepted, not procreative sex. As the Alan Guttmacher Institute points out in its research about sexuality and family planning, United States women typically want and have two children and then spend roughly three decades trying to avoid becoming pregnant. (Even with the best medical technology available, women experience their fertile decades as extremely stressful, and many women welcome the freedom, including sexual freedom, that comes with menopause or after tubal ligations or hysterectomies.) That pattern is now a global expectation. "In general," the research indicates, "women worldwide are sexually active but do not want to have a child throughout most of their childbearing years."[31]

In addition to the normativity of non-procreative (heterosexual) sex, there is a rising expectation among many, including conservative Christians,[32] that sexual exchange should be pleasurable for women as well as men. However, a procreative mandate reinforces the problematic notion that the "best sex" is male-dominant, female-submissive in the missionary position. As Catholic ethicist Christine Gudorf explains, that may be the official "theory," but it is no longer the practice among most couples, married and unmarried. "We have a growing body of research that demonstrates that penile-vaginal intercourse is not the only avenue to sexual satisfaction," Gudorf writes, "and [it] may not even be the most effective avenue to sexual satisfaction, especially in women. Women report that masturbation produces stronger orgasms than penile-vaginal intercourse, and lesbian women report higher rates of orgasm than heterosexual women." In addition, Gudorf points out that "some men report that their most frequent sexual fantasy is not of penile-vaginal intercourse, but of fellatio."[33] Therefore, a contemporary Christian ethic of intimate touch, while refusing to privilege any particular mode of erotic exchange, must also insist that all sexual touching should be consensual and responsibly principled. In other words, erotically powerful and ethically principled relationships are those in which the parties are intentionally good stewards of their erotic power and plan carefully to maintain their health, avoid unintended pregnancy, and do what they can to compensate for power differentials in their relationship while keeping their interaction playful and mutually pleasurable.[34]

A procreationist bias is also at work whenever children are identified as the inevitable "cost" of being sexual. A double standard has traditionally operated to allow men to claim exemption from the consequences of "irresponsible" sex, but women are constantly warned that if they "play," then they must "pay." This is particularly true, Mary Gordon observes, "if a woman is consciously and volitionally sexual" and violates cultural norms for "good" women (that is, those who are chaste, compliant, and virginal and also white, middle class, and Christian). This posture of sexual control reflects not only ambivalence about sex, but also patriarchal discomfort with female sexuality, sexual pleasure, and, most certainly, sexual autonomy on the part of women. In contrast, a commitment to procreative freedom as well as sexual and reproductive justice are indispensable requirements if women are to have self-directed and fulfilling lives, including self-directed and fulfilling sexual lives. "It is possible for a woman to have a sexual life unriddled by fear," Gordon writes, "only if she can be confident that she need not pay for the failure of technology or judgment (and who among us has never once been swept away in the heat of the sexual moment?) by taking upon herself the crushing burden of unchosen motherhood."[35]

Finally, there is not a clear and consistent view about abortion within the Christian tradition despite claims that the church has "always and everywhere" protected fetal life as an absolute value. Although abortion has almost always been condemned as sinful, some of the most influential and revered theologians, including Augustine and Aquinas, refused to equate destruction of the fetus with homicide until later in a pregnancy after ensoulment had taken place, usually marked by "quickening" or noticeable fetal movement. Contrary to the presumption that there is a long-standing Christian tradition of protecting fetal life from the earliest moments, the primary motivation for prohibiting abortion has not been defense of the fetus, but rather worry that abortion would cover up illicit sexual activity, especially nonmarital sex. Christian sex-negativity, not protection of "innocent" fetal life, has been a primary cause for associating abortion with sin. Moreover, as Kissling wagers, the punitive, anti-sex, and woman-devaluing legacy of the Christian tradition makes it reasonable to conjecture that "for those opposed to abortion, it is not saving fetuses that matters but preserving a social construct in which women breed" and do not "get away with" sexual autonomy.[36]

In patriarchal societies, especially under the influence of Christian sex-negativity, there is palpable anxiety about women's empowerment as self-determining subjects of their own lives. This anxiety is most acute when it comes to women's sexual and reproductive lives. Historically, the principle of father-right has placed women under the social control of men, and women's lack of social power has only further reinforced their subordination within the family. Today it requires an exercise in moral imagination, especially on the part of women with some measure of economic and race privilege, "to grasp how very little choice women had, in every arena of their lives, prior to [the] organized social movement for women's right. Patriarchy or the rule of the fathers," Sylvia Thorson-Smith writes, "was codified into all social and legal institutions. Wives were subject to their husbands, and their sexuality was truly not their own in any of the ways we assume today."[37] Not only did women lack decision-making power; they were valued primarily for their instrumental use as objects of men's sexual pleasure and for their role in producing male offspring. Furthermore, patriarchal Christianity idealized the "good woman" whose virtue resided in her docility and compliance to male authority and in her willingness to serve men's needs, even to the point of sacrificing herself.

With the rise of global feminism has come a push to shift from father-right to human rights and to recognize women as persons morally entitled to exercise a range of human rights and responsibilities, including the moral freedom to enjoy bodily integrity or bodily self-determination. In a statement in support of procreative choice entitled "African American Women for Reproductive Freedom," feminists of color acknowledge that freedom means not only the absence of coercion and bodily control by another, but also the capacity to make decisions according to one's own values and beliefs, especially about such highly personal and life-altering matters as reproduction. Their statement reads, "This freedom—to choose and to exercise our choices—is what we've fought and died for. Brought here in chains, worked like mules, bred like beasts, whipped one day, sold the next—244 years we were held in bondage." The slavocracy principle held that a slave's body and, accordingly, a slave's body-self was property owned by a master, and only the master had the power and moral authority to decide what happened to slaves and their procreative capacity. Those historically subjected to such dehumanization know the reality of moral evil from the inside even as attempts were made to "prettify" it and render it less blatantly offensive. But as these women of color underscore, the fact remains that "somebody said that we were less than human and not fit for freedom. Somebody said we were like children and could not be trusted to think for ourselves. Somebody owned our flesh and decided if and when and with whom our bodies were to be used."[38]

In contrast, a liberating social ethic of embodiment insists on transforming alienating, oppressive, and unjust property relations into just, compassionate, and life-affirming *moral* relations in which women are honored in their personhood, not "merely" for their motherhood or their service to others. In particular, women are encouraged to make their own well-being and life-plans central to their decisions when contemplating childbirth and childrearing. Again, the fundamental question is whether women should have the freedom to exercise procreative choice and not only have access to abortion. As these women of color explain, "As black women we have never been able to say clearly that we support abortion. But being able to control our reproduction directly affects the quality of our lives and, in some cases, whether we even have lives." Under the constraints of racist patriarchal Christianity, they also recognize that "it is very hard for women to say that when the deal goes down, we choose ourselves."[39] However, when women choose themselves, they are not being selfish, uncaring, or indifferent to the value of developing fetal life, but rather giving themselves their appropriate due as persons who matter and whose lives have value, even exceeding the value of emergent human life.

■ The harm of denying women procreative self-determination

When women are denied the freedom to direct their own lives and control what happens to their bodies, they are at risk of becoming infantilized, disempowered, and unable to develop the necessary capacity for self-initiating moral agency. Denying women procreative self-determination is harmful and disrespectful. The message delivered is that their bodies and their labor, including their reproductive labor, are not their own, but belong to someone else. As Beverly Harrison sums matters up, "What women have discovered, signaled in the phrase 'we are our bodies, ourselves,' is that in the absence of freedom to understand, control, and direct our own sexuality, our power as self-regulating moral agents does not develop."[40] Given the fact that our humanity is validated through social recognition that we as persons are self-directing moral agents and that abuse occurs whenever there is theft of bodily self-determination, any violation of the principle of noncoercion in child-birthing is fraught with great risk as women's moral freedom is curtailed and their dignity becomes reduced to their reproductive role. Feminist scholar Emily Culpepper, speaking of women's ongoing contributions as culture-creators, notes that women's insistence about "our right to choose" is fundamentally a claim about women's empowerment as ethical agents. In asserting her procreative freedom, a woman is asserting that "even more fundamentally than being 'she who can bear children,' a woman is 'she who can create values.' This act is," Culpepper proposes, "an even deeper threat to male superiority."[41]

Women's collective assertion of procreative choice is precipitating a cultural power shift that makes many people nervous. While the Christian tradition has long celebrated human freedom to reshape life conditions, including intervening in natural processes so that human well-being is enhanced, there has been a noticeable reluctance to celebrate *women's* power to shape the procreative process and especially to exercise the power to terminate pregnancy. Catholic ethicist Christine Gudorf notes that her tradition has given men wide latitude, for example, with respect to the ethics of war, but it has not been as generous with women when it comes to life-and-death decisions about pregnancy and childbirth. Church leaders and theologians have recognized a legitimate diversity of moral opinions about state violence and warfare, all of which have been placed under the rubric of a respectable, morally principled debate. Rather than coerce, the church has attempted to persuade people regarding war making while acknowledging that these decisions about using killing violence are morally complex and should be approached through dialogue, moral education, and ongoing discernment. Critical of the church's absolutism when it comes to reproductive ethics and its rigidity when women's lives are at stake, Gudorf asks, "Is it so clear that the abortion decision is never complex?" Again, when it comes to abortion, isn't a gendered double standard at work? After all, "women are threatened with dire sanctions; men in the military are treated to an exercise in persuasion."[42]

Gudorf and other feminists share Harrison's suspicion "that the near hysteria that prevails about the immorality of women's right to choose abortion derives its force from the ancient power of misogyny rather than from any passion for the sacredness of human life."[43] When men are no longer in control, then women are perceived to be untrustworthy and even recklessly, subversively out of control. The heat surrounding the abortion debate rises not only because the question deals with the fragile beginnings of life, but even more so because of the patriarchal bias that continues to rage about women's lives, their sexuality, and their moral agency, especially when not under male supervision.

■ What about men in relation to procreative freedom and responsibility?

Because of historical patterns of male sexual exploitation and social control of women's lives and bodies, including their procreative power,[44] men who wish to stand in solidarity with women owe women a radically different response to pregnancy, childbirth, and childrearing. A constructive response will ask of men that they take their fair share of responsibility for family planning, reproductive health (including protection from disease), and the care of children. Men will also need to advocate publicly for women's sexual health and well-being, as well as honor women's primary decision-making authority. Solidarity with women is therefore best grounded in two moral principles: the principle of maximizing respect for women as moral authorities who have also historically carried the greater weight in bearing and caring for children, and the principle of minimizing coercion, such that no woman should be made to act against her own will or pressured to sacrifice herself in order to demonstrate her virtue as a "good woman."

Defending women's moral authority and legal right to make informed decisions about pregnancy and childbirth threatens racist patriarchy at its core, the presumed right of the socially powerful and privileged to exercise control, even ownership, of others and use them as they wish. It is no surprise, then, that severe conflict about these matters has been stirred up by the Christian Right in an effort to reassert male control of women's lives and to return women to their traditional place of social and domestic subordination (or, more euphemistically, gender complementarity).

A Christian pro-feminist stance must encourage men, and especially sexually active heterosexual men, to take responsibility for their behavior, to take steps to avoid unintended pregnancy, and to speak out in support of women's empowerment and reproductive freedom.

At its best the Christian tradition has celebrated the fact that new times bring forth new questions and often new duties. In an age in which the global feminist movement has raised critical awareness of women's full humanity and their decision-making authority, religionists are no longer in a credible position to question whether women have the right or the competence to make these decisions. Misogyny is at work, in law and tradition including religious tradition, whenever women's capacity to make responsible decisions is denied and whenever others are turned to as the experts better qualified to decide about pregnancy and childbirth. Furthermore, we are living in a time when, because of advances in scientific knowledge, we have finally gained the power to create human life purposefully. Therefore, for the first time in history, we possess the means to guarantee that every child is able to be welcomed and cared for. Because of these two historical developments, the world has changed, and we no longer have the right to create life unintentionally, against a woman's will, or in defiance of her best judgment about whether it is timely and right to give birth.

While the question of abortion will not likely arise in most pregnancies, when it does it should be recognized as a courageous and principled effort to exercise pro-creative responsibility and make a decision based on the woman's freely formed conscience and her religious and ethical convictions. Given the ubiquity of unjust social, political, and economic relations that impinge on women's lives, their decision making most often occurs within a context they do not and cannot fully shape, much less control. We should applaud, not condemn or second-guess, the moral courage of women as they proceed, often in less than optimal circumstances, to consider the best course of action. Moreover, when a pregnancy is terminated, the appropriate moral response, as discussed earlier, should not be guilt or shame, but perhaps regret (that it was not possible to birth a child at this time), relief (that pregnancy did not obligate the woman to bear a child), and affirmation (that she has exercised her moral freedom with courage and dispatch).

The question now before Christian and other faith communities is how they can support women, recognize and honor their moral courage, and help them integrate the decision to have an abortion with a view of themselves as responsible and faithful persons. In the past, the church has either condemned or silenced women about these matters. Today we must accept the leadership challenge to create the conditions for safety, respect, and forbearance that will allow more candid and constructive conversations to take place within churches and other houses of worship, so that women can speak the truth about their experiences and "hear one another into speech" as Nelle Morton invited us to do.[45] Then we may come to appreciate with greater realism and honesty, the joys and the burdens of pursuing reproductive justice as a moral good in our communities. We men are long overdue in acknowledging that women have struggled, against incredible odds, to exercise their procreative powers wisely. Often they have had to take great risks, including risks to their lives and health, to avoid unwanted or problematic pregnancies. Too often, in the midst of these struggles, we have allowed them to stand alone without support, guidance, or our abiding respect and gratitude.

It has been the Christian tradition's moral failure not to recognize and support women's reproductive freedom. Women, including our grandmothers, mothers, aunts, sisters, wives, and daughters, have not been the sinners, but the sinned against. To repair this moral damage, the church and its majority male leadership must now declare their resolve to defend women's moral and legal right to birth by choice and also fearlessly advocate for public policy that reflects this commitment. Given the reality of an unjust world and the significant constraints most women encounter in their sexual and reproductive lives, the ethical principle that should guide us in these matters is a shared commitment to promote reproductive justice for all women, especially those marginalized by race and class disparities, rather than "mere" advocacy for the far more elusive freedom, at least for most women and men, to exercise something called unfettered choice. In the best sense of the word, being "pro-choice" should mean taking a robust stand on the side of justice for women and investing one's life energy to help create a world of far greater equality and respect for women's well-being and bodily integrity, a world which we do not yet inhabit, but the vision of which sparks our religious and moral imaginations as a good worth living and struggling for, together.

CHAPTER 7

What Do We Have to Learn From, as Well as Teach, Young People about Sex?

I agree that the church needs to help kids know how to handle sex, but I don't see that as a complicated thing. Having sexual intercourse before you're married is a sin. We need to teach that. Teens need to know that they should say NO.

ADULT YOUTH GROUP ADVISOR, CHURCH OF GOD[1]

My priest, the church, my parents would consider me a slut if they knew what I did. . . . I don't think I'm that different than any other teenager. . . . Like I take my religion seriously, but I can't agree with NO birth control, NO premarital sex, NO abortion under any circumstances.

FEMALE TEENAGER, ROMAN CATHOLIC CHURCH[2]

Just as faith communities have a mandate to promote justice and compassion in all things and strengthen our interpersonal and communal ties as sexual-spiritual persons, so too do they have a responsibility to equip people for the challenges and joys of becoming passionate and principled lovers in the bedroom and beyond. Sexuality encompasses genital sex but refers more expansively to our divinely given desire for physical, emotional, and spiritual embrace and to this amazing capacity we humans enjoy for sustaining intimate relationship. Finding pleasure in an ethical eroticism is a spiritual blessing insofar as it sparks in us a sensuous, embodied desire for right relation with ourselves, other earth creatures, and the earth itself. Throughout our lifetime, then, we find ourselves in an ongoing process of shaping and reshaping our connections so that they may exhibit genuine respect, consistent care, and true delight.

In keeping with this more comprehensive and sex-positive perspective, ethicist James B. Nelson encourages us to appreciate *eros* as a moral power, nothing less than "our hunger for pleasurable and fulfilling connections." While he acknowledges that erotic power can become sinfully distorted and that we are capable of doing great harm, especially as patterns of dominance and submission become eroticized, he proposes a grace-filled remedy. "Our hope lies," he affirms, "in eroticizing patterns of sexual justice and mutuality." Furthermore, "it is the design of God that truly fulfilling pleasure comes only in such [just and mutually loving] relationships."[3] The good news here is the prospect of life-enhancing relationships that are both pleasurable and ethically principled.

■ "What we're teaching is terrible"

The bad news is that few faith communities do a decent job of educating youth and others about erotic power, sexual intimacy, and the demands as well as the blessings of the moral life. For the most part, the focus in Christian circles has been on conveying an exclusivist (heterosexual only), restrictive (sex only in marriage), and often punitive message in order to prevent, or at least discourage, sexual activity among adolescents, unmarried adults, and those who are nonheterosexual. At the same time, many church members have discovered that their friends, neighbors, family members, and perhaps they themselves no longer abide by the conventional rules, including restrictions on sex outside marriage, divorce and remarriage, contraception and abortion, and same-sex affiliations. Increasingly Christians find themselves questioning whether the prevailing prohibitions make sense and whether conducting "ethics by taboo" is sufficient. As historian Mark Jordan observes, in much Christian discourse "human sex is usually not about reciprocal love; it is about selfish gratification."[4] Furthermore because of the frequent link Christian theologians have drawn between sex and sin, even married heterosexuals, the "normatively normal," find that the church fails to provide adequate guidance about intimate matters, much less helps them address the social, as well as personal, implications of a robust justice-love ethic. While the married are often convinced that silence is best ("just say nothing"), the unmarried receive a minimalist and mostly negative message ("just say no"). For Christians, sex continues to be approached as shameful, dangerous, and fearful, and the moral watchwords remain avoidance, control, and containment.

In assessing the church's role in promulgating this kind of fear-based and restrictive sexual morality, ethicist Beverly Wildung Harrison sums up matters this way: "What we're teaching is terrible. We're not helping people. In the local church, people are starving for a more mature conversation about how to live in self-affirming, other-affirming, non-hurtful ways. Putting forth a wider framework [about human sexuality and values] and identifying what else we need to learn is part of the work."[5]

By and large, however, faith-based sexuality education is either not being done or not being done in a sex-positive and justice-centered manner.

Church of the Brethren minister and researcher Steve Clapp, after surveying young people about these matters from forty faith traditions (and from every state of the Union except New Hampshire and Utah), confirms that even religiously active youth complain that their faith communities are not teaching them how to integrate sexuality and spirituality. Across the theological spectrum, Clapp writes, congregations are failing "to help [their youth] understand themselves as sexual beings and to prepare them for the sexual relationships which will be part of their lives." Moreover, "many youth feel they have received little information about sexuality from their faith-based institutions *except prohibitions* and that too much sexuality education has been primarily fear-based."[6]

Adding yet another perspective, theological educator Marie Fortune, whose ministry has focused on the church's role in justice making and healing in response to sexual and other forms of abuse, argues that the development of sexually healthy persons and of sexually healthy communities requires a sustained commitment to education and ongoing advocacy for personal and social change, but her assessment of current efforts is equally sobering. "As a society," she observes, "we have all but abandoned the responsibility to equip people with the skills to make serious ethical choices. . . . Many of our religious and community leaders, lacking courage and imagination, have remained virtually speechless in the face of critical ethical questions about sexuality and relationships."[7]

■ Sexual ethics over coffee

These critical assessments do not nullify the religious mandate to assist persons of all ages in learning how to live and love responsibly, but they indicate the urgency of finding a better way to promote effective sexuality education within congregations and the wider community. The Religious Institute on Sexual Morality, Justice, and Healing expresses the moral obligation this way: "Religious leaders today have a special responsibility to help adolescents [and others] achieve moral, spiritual, and sexual health. . . . We call for faith communities to move beyond silence about sexuality or a fear and shame-based ethic that is based only on rules and prohibited acts. Young people [especially] pay too high a price when those in religious communities ignore their responsibilities to help them understand, affirm, and embrace their sexuality."[8]

Similarly, in a publication titled *A Time to Speak: Faith Communities and Sexuality Education*, the Religious Institute's Debra Haffner and Kate Ott point out that faith communities not only have a responsibility to educate for sexual health, but also have a unique opportunity to do so. Citing statistics showing that two-thirds of Americans belong to churches or synagogues, they observe that faith communities have access to significant numbers of young people as well as adults. "After schools," they point out, "religious institutions serve more teens and young adults than any

,mmunity agency," and, furthermore, faith communities "are the only ones which. are specifically empowered to do so from a moral perspective."[9]

In conjunction with a mandate and the opportunity to provide sexuality education, faith communities also face a compelling need insofar as sexuality for many people, including youth, is a source of pain, suffering, confusion, and struggle. Statistics tell the story in one way: 8 percent of high-school-aged youth report that they have experienced or caused a pregnancy; annually, about 8 million young people ages 15 to 24 contract a sexually transmitted disease; of the 400 million Americans currently living with HIV/AIDS, a large proportion became infected as teens; and each year at least 500,000 children experience sexual abuse at the hands of an adult they know and quite likely trusted, typically a parent or other family member, teacher, neighbor, or religious leader.[10]

Another way the story about the need for faith-based sexuality education can be told is through face-to-face encounters. Anglican priest Sarah Park describes an exchange that she has experienced multiple times in her ministry with adolescents and young adults in her Auckland, New Zealand, parish. "The conversation about sexuality and spirituality almost always begins with a seemingly unrelated question," Park explains, usually along the lines of the young adult inquiring whether the clergyperson is available for coffee. "For half an hour, or perhaps an hour, the young person talks generally about life, school, work, and things which seem inconsequential. Then . . . they find the courage to ask the question I've been expecting," Park reports. "It's to do with their intimate relationship and their life of faith. . . . The young person wants me to tell them what level of sexual relating I think is appropriate." As Park recognizes, she is being sought out because she represents the faith tradition, because she's assumed to have authority as well as insight, and, importantly, because "I am not of their generation, yet I am not as distant as their parents. So the question unfolds in parts: 'This is my relationship. This is how I feel. What's appropriate?' "[11] In other words, where is the line drawn, and how much sexual engagement is allowable before crossing that line, compromising Christian values, and getting into trouble?

■ How do youth regard sexuality and spirituality?

As the Religious Institute's "Open Letter to Religious Leaders on Adolescent Sexuality" acknowledges, while sexuality is an aspect of our humanity from birth to death, "forming a sexual identity is a key developmental task for all adolescents." Among other things, this means that "as young people mature biologically and emotionally into adults, they experience their first erotic feelings and romantic relationships, and confirm their gender identity and sexual orientation."[12] Current research also verifies that, generally speaking, youth and young adults are a sexually active cohort group. Although advocates of educational programs that promote "abstinence only until marriage" insist that reserving sex exclusively to marriage is a core religious (and

American) value, the reality on the ground is far different from the rhetoric that espouses "celibacy in singleness, sex only in marriage."

A 2007 study documents that the median age of sexual initiation in the United States is 17 while the typical age for (heterosexual) marriage is 26 for women and 27 for men, almost a ten-year gap. Moreover, 95 percent of adults ages 18 through 44, when surveyed about their sexual histories, acknowledge that they engaged in sex before marriage while "even among those who abstained from sex until age 20 or older, 81 percent reported having had premarital sex."[13] In addition, the United States continues to have the highest teen pregnancy rate among industrialized nations with almost 750,000 teenage women experiencing pregnancy during a given year. In fact, "nearly three in 10 U.S. teenage women experience pregnancy."[14] Finally, the most reputable social scientific research confirms that abstinence-only sexuality educational programs are not effective either in delaying the initiation of sexual activity or in reducing teen pregnancy. A federally funded evaluation of these programs reports that "the youth enrolled in [these abstinence-only] programs were *no more likely* than those not in the programs to delay sexual initiation, to have fewer sex partners, or to abstain entirely from sex."[15]

Researcher Steve Clapp's findings in *Faith Matters: Teenagers, Religion, and Sexuality* are based on surveys and interviews conducted in 635 congregations with nearly 6,000 high school students actively involved in their faith communities, representing over 40 different faith traditions. About the demographics reflected in this study, two-thirds of the teens belonged to Protestant denominations and included mainline, evangelical, and fundamentalist Christians. A sizable group of Roman Catholics, as well as Reform and Conservative Jews, were involved in the study along with some Muslim youth and a smaller number of Hindus and Buddhists. As Clapp notes, two-thirds of the teens were white and one-third African American, Latino, Native American, or Asian American. "Over 80% of teens in this study attended religious services at least two or three times a month," Clapp writes, and "over 90% participate in a youth group, class, choir, or other congregational program at least two or three times a month."[16]

A telling finding from Clapp's research is that religiously active youth report lower rates of sexual intercourse than their secular peers. Thirty-one percent of seventeen-year-olds involved in congregational life report that they have had sexual intercourse compared to more than 60 percent of all teens in the United States who admit being sexually active. Although Clapp had initially speculated that evangelical and fundamentalist youth would be the ones most likely to report the lowest rate of premarital sex, he found instead that "no particular religious traditions showed markedly lower rates of sexual intercourse than other religious traditions except for Jewish and Muslim youth, who were less likely to have had intercourse than Christian youth."[17] Moreover, while one in five of the teens had signed a pledge to abstain from sex until marriage, "that subgroup was not any more or less likely than others in our sample to have had sexual intercourse or to have experienced pregnancy or caused a pregnancy."[18] At the same time, while only about half of these religiously affiliated youth share the conviction that premarital sex is wrong, the vast majority of them—more than 90 percent—said that sexual intercourse should only happen between persons who have a commitment to each other.[19] As Clapp summarizes the situation among religiously affiliated youth, "Many of the teens are not ready to say that sexual intercourse is only all right in marriage, but there is nothing casual about the view of most of these teens toward intercourse."[20]

Several other findings are also noteworthy. First, while youth who are regularly involved in faith communities are more likely than the general youth population to delay sexual intercourse, and while these youth cite the importance of their faith values for discerning their readiness for a mature relationship, these young people report that they are far from sexually inactive. From his survey of these 6,000 high school students in faith traditions representing the entire theological spectrum from liberal to conservative, Clapp discovered that "religiously involved teens have high levels of sexual involvement besides intercourse: 29 percent of males and 26 percent of females engage in oral sex; 70 percent in fondling; 50 percent in nudity with the opposite [sic] sex; 89 percent of males and 71 percent of females masturbate; and kissing is universal."[21]

In terms of engaging in oral sex, religiously affiliated teens are no different than their secular peers, about one-third of whom also report having had oral sex with at least one partner. The teens in Clapp's survey also insisted that oral sex is safe insofar as it runs no risk of pregnancy, but they incorrectly assumed that oral sex carries no danger of infection with sexually transmitted diseases (STDs). At the same time, these youth drew a carefully delineated line between intercourse and oral sex in terms of what they believe is permitted by their liberal-to-conservative faith traditions. "While they see premarital intercourse being prohibited by the teachings of their tradition, many of the teens feel that the Scriptures and tradition are silent on the matter of oral sex."[22] Accordingly, while nearly 93 percent agree that their faith community regards premarital sex as immoral, less than 30 percent believe that oral sex, including oral sex before marriage, is wrong.[23]

Second, a large number of youth (one in five males and four in ten females) reported unwanted sexual experiences, sometimes the result of physical force but often due to emotional pressure from their peers and their own desire for social acceptance.[24] An additional factor is the lack of clear communication before, during, and after an intimate encounter. As Clapp writes, "Most teens have not talked together about what they do and do not want to do sexually." Moreover, "the desire to be accepted and loved is a major factor in some teens going further than they really want sexually." Significantly, a gendered double standard plays out among youth in which "boys are 'supposed to' try to go further, and girls are 'supposed to' stop them," and all these dynamics are further complicated when alcohol and drugs are introduced.[25] Some unwanted sexual activity takes place not with other teenagers, but with adults, and the most commonly reported sexual abuse involves teen girls and their stepfathers. If these youth tell anyone connected with their faith community about these experiences, they are most likely to share the confidence with a youth minister or another trusted adult in a faith-based youth program.[26] As Marie Fortune rightly points out, "An adult who has clear boundaries, is willing to listen and impart solid information and discuss ethical dilemmas, and will take the time to be with young people without sexualizing the interaction [can be] a vital resource in their sexual development" and an advocate for their safety.[27]

Third, almost all the young people know someone who is gay, lesbian, or bisexual within their own age group, and as Clapp notes, their awareness of diverse sexual identities and gender expression is "a part of life for teenagers today."[28] However, what surprised Clapp and his research colleagues is how many of these religiously affiliated youth self-identify as gay, lesbian, bisexual, or questioning about their sexual identity. About one in seven males and one in ten females describe themselves as nonheterosexual, figures that run counter to Clapp's initial assumption "that teens of homosexual or bisexual orientation would be somewhat less likely to be involved in a faith-based institution, given the number of traditions with a negative view of homosexuality."[29] Moreover, why would people even suspect that there might be LBGTQ youth in their congregation, given how nearly half of the youth surveyed have not talked openly with their parents and nine out of ten are not out to their pastor, priest, or rabbi? By and large, they are living "secret lives," Clapp observes. Furthermore, "non-heterosexual teens in our study were almost twice as likely as heterosexual teens to have seriously considered suicide. This should be a matter of significant concern for those of us in faith-based institutions," especially those in leadership roles.[30]

In those faith traditions in which there are strongly negative views about homosexuality, almost no youth had spoken openly about their identity or their struggles. Among these traditions, Clapp discovered that pastors in predominantly black congregations were among those who identified themselves as most disapproving of gay sex. This is not surprising, as African American theologian Kelly Brown Douglas has argued, because many black Christians, in reacting to Christian sex-negativity as well as white cultural suspicion about black sexuality as animalistic and promiscuous, have adopted what she terms a Christianized "hyper-proper" sexual morality as a survival strategy. A strict code of hetero-normativity condemns nonmarital sex along with any nonconformity to heterosexual expectations. This rigid code is deployed as a socially constructed defense against white racialized judgments about the so-called deficiencies of black (sexual) personhood. As Douglas writes, within many black church traditions "not only is [nonmarital] heterosexual intimacy unacceptable, but homoerotic . . . love becomes unforgivably intolerable. It is that about which one 'never dares to speak' and in which one never dares to participate."[31] In such religious contexts, in which it is difficult to talk not just about homosexuality but about any sexual topic, sexually active youth are likely to be both stigmatized and silenced, especially if their erotic attractions are toward members of the same gender.

■ A discrepancy between adult and teen perceptions of the faith community's leadership

Finally, there is a noticeable discrepancy between adult and teen perceptions regarding the adequacy of their faith community's spiritual leadership when it comes to matters of sexuality and moral formation. There is an encouraging acknowledgment among almost two-thirds of the clergy and adult leaders surveyed that faith communities should offer comprehensive sexuality education, including but not limited to information about abstinence. In interviews clergy shared these kinds of comments: "We don't do a good job of teaching abstinence or teaching something more comprehensive. Anything we would do would be an improvement." "I support sexuality education in the schools, but we're fooling ourselves in the religious community if we think that does the job. [Our youth] need a moral and ethical framework for sexual decisions. That has to come from the religious community and from parents." "We need to give them tools for living as sexual persons even though we hope they'll wait until they are married or at least older before having intercourse."[32] However, when asked to grade their performance in terms of actually providing sexual information as well as tools for developing relationships, including dating, marriage, and parenting, clergy and youth ministers rated their performance as "good" or "fair to good" in all categories, but the youth gave them a "poor" grade across the boards.

The youth struggle in particular with the negativity of their faith communities about sex and sexuality. Although three-fourths of the clergy and youth advisors agreed with the statement "My congregation portrays sex in a healthy and positive way," only 44 percent of the youth agreed with that perception. A male teen in a Southern Baptist congregation said, "Our pastor and our teachers make me feel like sex is an ugly, dangerous thing. But if that's what it is, why would anyone want to do it?" A female teen who belongs to the Presbyterian Church (U.S.A.) spoke appreciatively of the good intentions of adult leaders, but offered this critique: "I know that the adults who work with us care about our well-being. They don't want us getting pregnant or getting AIDS. But the way they talk about sex is always emphasizing the negative. They say it's 'God's good gift,' but the way they talk about it doesn't make it sound good."[33]

Again and again, youth relay the message that they need—and desire—more from their faith communities: more information about intimate relationships, more support as they develop into young adults, more practical guidance about ethical decision making and how to exercise refusal skills, and, above all, a more positive, less anxious approach to sex and sexuality that underscores how it is possible to claim one's sexuality and one's spirituality in a holistic, self-respecting, and other-respecting manner. As Clapp argues, the focus of many faith-based resources "is so much on discouraging youth from early sexual intercourse that an overall healthy, positive view of sexuality isn't always conveyed."[34] However, when congregations do provide more comprehensive and positively framed sexuality education that includes, for example, contraceptive information, the research underscores that the result is not that teens are more likely to engage in sexual intercourse, but rather that they become less likely to experience unintended pregnancy or sexually transmitted diseases.[35] Furthermore, as Clapp points out, while the teens surveyed viewed sexual intercourse as "a serious step" about which careful spiritual and ethical discernment is called for, the majority "were not committed to waiting until marriage." Providing quality sexuality education that is scientifically accurate and values-based will, therefore, "help protect the well-being of those who do not wait until marriage" and also likely "result in better sexual experiences for those who do wait until marriage."[36]

■ Updating the assumptions that undergird our sexual ethic

Many faith leaders recognize that they should be doing more to prepare youth for sexually healthy lives and responsible loving. At the same time, they also report being most comfortable communicating an abstinence message. Dutch scholar Claire Gresle-Favier, in her study of how fundamentalist Christians in the United States have pushed abstinence-only education as part of a political agenda to reshape society in a more conservative direction, notes that there is a strong cultural consensus among adults "that abstinence for teenagers is the best option" even though, she underscores, "in practice few youths remain abstinent throughout their teenage years and . . . even fewer remain abstinent until marriage."[37]

This call for sexual abstinence is apparent, for example, in a pastoral letter entitled "Learning to Love in the Lord," issued to Catholic young people by Bishop Joseph Gerry of Portland, Maine, my hometown. The bishop, clearly concerned that many teens feel strong cultural pressure to become sexually active prematurely, called for a dialogue with younger people about ethical values and human sexuality. At the same time, he left no uncertainty about his own stance: only sex within heterosexual, procreative marriage is acceptable. For the unmarried, abstaining from sex is the goal. Accordingly, to aid the young in "keeping chaste," he proposed a six-step guide for avoiding sex until a marriage commitment can be solemnized. As he elaborated in his pastoral letter, faith and prayer can aid in "avoiding temptation."

While I share the bishop's interest in furthering dialogue about sexuality and ethical responsibility, I want to suggest another framework for moral education about these humanly important matters, but first it is important to acknowledge where the bishop has been helpful. First of all, I agree wholeheartedly that young people along with adults need ongoing dialogue about human sexuality and its meaning and place in their lives. Productive dialogue requires access to scientifically sound information as well as an ethical framework, what the bishop speaks of as a "moral compass." Equipping young people for decision making includes addressing how to integrate sexuality into their whole lives as responsible, self-respecting persons and also exploring the intimate connections between sexuality and spirituality. In the dedication to her book on positive approaches to adolescent sexuality, Peggy

Brick, a sexuality educator, acknowledges how young people are often ill served in this regard: "To the young people of this nation who must find their way to sexual health in a world of contradictions—where media scream, 'Always say yes,' where many adults admonish, 'Just say no,' but the majority just say . . . nothing."[38] The bishop has it right: ongoing, candid dialogue is needed that will break the silences, avoid negativities of shame and guilt, and honor the questions, struggles, and insights of younger people.

Second, I agree that it is incumbent upon faith communities to offer age-appropriate sexuality education not only to younger people, but also to adults. Most parents want to teach values to their children and be the main source of information about sex and ethical responsibility, but they often need help in this process of moral formation. The bishop is right that congregations are ideal places to offer value-based sexuality education and that faith-based programs can easily complement what parents do at home. To be worthwhile, a sexual ethic must attend to the pleasures as well as the dangers of sexuality in this culture and manage to keep both in perspective. When a young person or anyone else is made ignorant about sexuality, they are placed at greater risk of being harmed and possibly of doing harm. Such risks run especially high in this culture because it is saturated with sexualized imagery and because bodies, especially female bodies, are so flagrantly commodified and objectified. Ironically, even though sex talk is seemingly everywhere, a majority of people remain woefully ignorant and sadly misinformed about their own bodies and about sexual matters generally. A few years ago, the Kinsey Institute and Roper Organization tested for basic knowledge about human sexuality in a random sampling of United States adults. What did they discover? Of the nearly 2,000 people who took the 18-question exam, only 5 percent received an A grade while 82 percent received a D or F. *Ours is a sexually illiterate society, and dangerously so.* The bishop has it right: youth and adults need help, and faith communities have an obligation to promote the kind of education that fosters personal well-being while serving the common good.

While I agree that dialogue is in order and that faith communities have an important leadership role to exercise, I part company with the bishop when it comes to the moral compass that he proposes as effective guidance about these matters. To begin with, I am persuaded that the credibility of religious people on matters of sexuality depends, to a great extent, on our public candor about the Christian tradition's long-standing ambivalence, if not outright negativity, about the body, sexual difference, and pleasure, as well as its devaluing of women and complicity in giving theological legitimacy to male gender supremacy. A patriarchal religious tradition has reinforced the fear, shame, and guilt that many people experience about passion and bodily pleasure, including masturbation. Speaking as a Protestant, I witness a widening gap between the church's traditional teachings about procreative hetero-normativity—lifting up as exclusively normative only sex that is heterosexual, marital, and procreative—and how many people, including many people of faith, actually live their lives. While the human capacity for sin and irresponsibility is always a factor in the moral life, the truth of the matter is that the conventional Christian sex ethic is no longer adequate and increasingly not compelling for many.

One of the ways religious tradition fails young people (and adults) is to allow outmoded assumptions to go unquestioned. It is not true, if it ever was, that everyone is heterosexual, that marriage is the only place in which people can live sexually responsible lives, and that sex is exclusively (or even primarily) for the purpose of making babies. Yes, we need a moral compass, but we also need to revisit and, when necessary, update the assumptions that undergird our ethic if we are to speak truthfully and if our intention is to empower rather than merely assert disciplinary control over people.

A contemporary sexual ethic must begin by affirming that sexuality is a broader notion than (genital) sex. Traditional Christian morality has been narrowly preoccupied with prohibiting certain acts and with preserving male-dominant marriage as the exclusive site for morally legitimate sexual activity. As Marie Fortune notes, "The traditional *rule* which said categorically that sexual activity before [or outside] marriage was wrong implied that sexual activity in marriage was right; no other criteria need be applied. The primary consideration was *when* sexual activity took place. It gave little consideration to the substance or quality of the sexual interaction after marriage."[39] In addition, a rule-based, act-focused, and legalistic "thou shalt not" approach has focused people's energies on not making mistakes rather than on discovering what is genuinely loving and pleasurable for themselves and their intimate partner. Although often fearful of sex, Christians have become nearly fixated on these matters, especially the sex lives of others. People have readily come forward to police the sexual lives of single persons, but denied how frequently battering and rape happen within marriages. Through it all, faith communities have failed to attend to the things that truly matter, namely, the quality of relationships, the use and misuse of power, and how people might more fully integrate their sexuality with their commitments to justice and other core religious values.

At the same time, Christians entrapped in patriarchal sex-negativity have been notoriously reluctant to celebrate how God has created a variety of sexualities, and so there has been little respect for, much less delight found in, that exuberantly rich diversity within and among us. The fact of the matter is that some persons are heterosexual while others are gay, lesbian, bisexual, and transgender. Still others are asexual. All the while, each person deserves to love and be loved, gracefully and compassionately. Furthermore, we need an ethic that appreciates how celibacy and marriage are two options in which people can live faithful, responsible lives, but they do not exhaust the moral possibilities. Sexually active single persons, both older and younger, may exemplify moral integrity and spiritual maturity. Moreover, the ethical focus for gay and nongay alike, as well as for partnered and nonpartnered persons, should be the quality of respect and commitment in intimate relationships, the distribution and use of power, the maintenance of health, for heterosexual couples the avoidance of unintended pregnancy, and for everyone protection from abuse, exploitation, and neglect. Such an ethic will also hold the powerful accountable for their wrongdoing, including the batterer, the rapist, and sexually abusive clergy. Therefore, in order to fulfill their mandate to teach ethically good sex, faith communities will need to make a pivotal turn, no longer centering exclusively on marriage, heterosexuality, or pro-creative possibility as the only human good, but rather focusing on loving justice as the normative expectation for all intimate connections and embracing the diversity of human sexualities as divinely intended gifts for enriching life in community.

■ Cultural shifts are changing the meaning of sex

This contemporary reframing of Christian ethics resonates with three shifts taking place within contemporary culture regarding the meaning of sexuality. First, with the development of effective, affordable, and accessible means of birth control, including elective abortion as a backup, (heterosexual) sex has been radically decoupled from procreation. The normative practice for (fertile) male-female couples is no longer procreative sex, but rather contracepted sex. (Moreover, because many people are living longer and healthier lives, their sexual lives extend well beyond their fertile years, and women especially report enhanced sexual freedom and pleasure when they no longer fear unintended pregnancy.) In this context heterosexual couples make love for the same reasons that same-sex couples enjoy intimacy: to share pleasure and strengthen the bonds of intimacy and mutual affection. Second, with the global rise of feminism, patriarchal social and intimate relationships that disempower women and give men unearned advantages are giving way to egalitarian patterns in which gender is no longer the decisive factor in the distribution of roles, responsibilities, or power. The values of mutual respect, mutual care, and mutual responsibility for the safety and well-being of the persons-in-relation have displaced patriarchal presumptions that placed men's needs, including men's pleasure, at the center of attention. No longer are women willing to be in service to male interests apart from honoring their own needs, and no longer are they willing to sacrifice themselves "for others," often to their own severe disadvantage. Third, with greater appreciation for the complexity of human sexualities and a wider range of erotic possibilities, including heterosexuality, homosexuality, and bisexuality, a shift in focus is under way that evaluates *relational integrity* not by any particular gender configuration, but by the character of the exchange between persons and by the respect and care demonstrated for each other's well-being and for the well-being of their community.

These culture-shifting changes in the contemporary meaning of sex, as Dale Martin points out, are pressing us to rethink sexuality as well as the appropriate ethical norms for guiding intimate and other social interactions. While the challenge to "think anew" may be daunting and even disconcerting for some, the fact that a cultural shift in the meaning of sexuality is taking place is not a new phenomenon. During the first centuries of the Christian movement, Christian theologians associated sex with sin and death and strongly favored celibacy over marriage, but as Martin explains, "Sex doesn't 'mean' the same thing to us as it did to ancient people. . . . Most

Christians now believe that sex is basically good, that people are 'normally' happiest when they marry, have regular sexual relations with their spouse, produce children, and grow old surrounded by their family. Christians may think it is *acceptable* for some people to remain single, but it is certainly not preferable. Celibacy or singleness is seen, at least by most Protestants, but also in the dominant culture more generally, as second best if not downright tragic." However, as Martin observes, "this is a view that has been held in Christianity only since the seventeenth century."[40] Moreover, while Christian theologians during the Protestant Reformation elevated marriage above celibacy and made space for sexual intercourse at least for heterosexual couples, the marriage model they promoted was a patriarchal social pattern, emphasizing "Christlike" headship for men and for women the role of "good Christian wife," at once faithful, dutiful, and submissive. Only within the past few decades, with the rise of global feminism, has this patriarchal, male-supremacist ordering of gender and sexuality come under global scrutiny and been replaced, at least in some quarters, by a more egalitarian, women-friendly, and gay-affirming ethos. At the same time, it is fair to say that feminism, the so-called longest revolution, is also being met with fierce resistance, and the source of this resistance is often religion that has not yet forsaken its patriarchal past.

For most faith communities, the current problematic is that *conventional religious teaching has not yet caught up* with the emerging postmodern meanings of sex that have gained credence within the past four decades. Again, Martin is helpful in posing the following queries: "If sex isn't just for procreation anymore," he asks, "then why can't two men or two women have sex? If the meaning of sex is basically to express love or have fun, why can't two men or two women express their love by means of sex? If sex is best when it is between two people who treat one another equally and fairly and want to give themselves to one another, why limit that to only a male-female couple?"[41] These questions about homosexuality are being scrutinized with great intensity precisely because the inherited verities about *heterosexuality* can no longer be taken for granted. As Martin argues, "The debate that currently rages over homosexuality is not really about homosexuality. It is about sex itself."[42]

Religious discourse about human sexuality is further complicated by the frequent disregard of the most credible scientific perspectives currently available about these matters. Sexologist and American Baptist minister William Stayton points out that "in the last forty years, we have learned more about human sexual behavior and human sexual response than we have ever known," but the sad reality is that "almost all our new knowledge is in conflict with traditional religious beliefs about sexuality."[43] Examples include the scientific recognition that gender identities and expression are far more expansive than the conventional gender binary system recognizes, that there is a broad continuum of sexual orientations ranging from exclusively heterosexual to exclusively homosexual, and that masturbation is a "very healthy and natural practice for people of all ages."[44] In addition, there is more diversity among persons in terms of genetic and hormonal variations than often acknowledged. As

Stayton explains, "One out of every 2,000 live births is an intersex child, neither completely male nor female." Therefore, it is legitimate to ask the question about what a male is and what a female is, while admitting that these are questions for which "there is no simple answer."[45] However, religious perspectives about sex and sexuality miss the mark by skirting such ambiguities and by refusing to incorporate the best scientific wisdom of the day within their theological method. Stayton makes the argument this way: "Most of our traditional religious institutions have not adapted to all these differences in human development. Thus our religious institutions have been threatened and thus unable to be helpful and relevant to the sexual concerns of our time."[46]

■ Not youths' welfare but the calming of adult anxieties as the focus of abstinence-only education

In the midst of changing times, when long-standing cultural and religious attitudes about sex and sexuality are in flux, some respond by strengthening their grip on conventional wisdom and holding on tightly to the customary rules as if these are somehow fixed certitudes "fallen from heaven" without even a trace of an oppressive history or political agenda. Except for the most die-hard proponents of patriarchal Christianity, the dilemma that is surfacing for many people of faith is how to figure out what exactly to teach when the meanings of gender, sex, and sexual difference are being contested fast and furiously not only throughout the culture, but within faith communities as well. In my judgment our only good option as people of faith is to lean into change as we try to inculcate a progressive theological-ethical perspective that is sex-positive and focused on the gospel mandate to seek justice as right relation, both personally and communally. Insofar as "we ourselves, as sexual human beings, have changed," Martin summarizes, "our sexual ethics must change also." Once again, as has happened multiple times in the past, "the resiliency of Christianity" is being tested "in its ability to adapt its theology to the changes of history."[47]

This larger cultural context helps put faith-based debates about sexuality education into perspective and explain why anxious adults are inclined to return to the default position of offering youth an abstinence-only, "just say no" approach to sexuality. In surveying faith leaders across denominations, Clapp discovered that there is a general awareness "of the need for more to be done in this area" to educate and equip youth, but at the same time congregational leaders express considerable anxiety about how to proceed with sexuality education because of their "fear of directly confronting the topic."[48] Such anxiety indicates how patriarchal Christianity's sex-negativity continues to hold sway over people's moral imaginations. Along these lines, a denominational executive, speaking candidly about the politics of sexual education within the church, shared how things have become derailed. "We've produced some better materials than we had before," this person acknowledged, "but they've been written with the most conservative voices in our denomination in mind. The dominant question when these materials were reviewed was continually: 'Will this offend anyone?' rather than 'Does this meet the needs of young people?' We would have produced something very different if the second question had been the focus."[49]

Keeping the focus on doing whatever it takes not to offend adults has real consequences, including the displacement or outright neglect of youths' needs. When this happens, it is no longer youth and their developmental concerns that take center stage, but rather these are overridden by adult anxieties about sex and sexuality. One way to manage such fears, often unconsciously, is to project them onto youth by viewing them either as innocent "angels" requiring protection or as mischievous "devils" requiring discipline.[50] Either way, adult concerns and adult control set the agenda, typically resulting in a "just say no" message to young people.

The problem, once again, as the most credible research amply documents, is that abstinence-only education is remarkably ineffectual in preparing young people for moral agency with respect to their lives as sexual persons. Moreover, religiously affiliated youth have spoken out, loud and clear, that they are hungry for more information, more guidance, and more support from adults in learning how to navigate intimate relationships and thread their way through ethical dilemmas. However, if the unstated but compelling agenda in abstinence-only education is not to "offend" adults, then few adults will assume their appropriate responsibilities to mentor young people and share their moral wisdom. But then again, in a sexually illiterate culture, adults cannot share with youth what they themselves lack. Sadly, shielding adults from sexuality and, in particular, making adults feel safe and protected from having to deal with sexuality, in particular youth sexuality, become the overriding concerns.

If this is what is going on, then the leadership in faith communities is catering to the interests of the more powerful at the expense of the less powerful. That injustice does enormous harm to countless numbers of youth and, to be sure, adults as well. An alternative ethical frame is needed that will encourage the sexual health and moral development of younger (and older) persons while respecting them as persons rather than aiming to keep them under control and "merely" compliant. Young people deserve the kind of parenting and adult engagement that, on the one hand, offers consistent care and support and yet, on the other hand, increasingly lets go and offers less and less protection as adolescents, in their ongoing developmental process toward maturity, come more and more into their own strength, gain confidence and skills as interdependent moral agents, and assert themselves as the subjects of their own lives, including their sexual lives. As theologian Rita Brock maintains, "Innocence may be appropriate to babies, but innocence maintained in adults [and in developing young adults] is dangerous."[51]

■ Promoting responsible agency in a highly sexualized culture

Rather than focusing on children's so-called innocence (or their supposed devilishness) and thereby evading adult responsibility to prepare young people for the real world, it would be far more effective to equip young people for moral agency and to learn how to engage mindfully in what Brock calls "willful behavior," the self-awareness to make conscious choices along with a readiness to be held accountable for the consequences of those choices. Good parenting and, more generally, good adult mentoring nurtures this kind of willfulness in young people, not to be misunderstood as rebelliousness or stubbornness, but rather as "the capacity to gain the knowledge and self-confidence that enables her or him to assert her or his will in the world, sometimes in opposition to a parent's desires."[52] Teaching this kind of willfulness encourages personal responsibility and equips youth for informed decision making.

Education for ethical willfulness and responsible agency is urgently needed by young men and women alike who are bombarded by cultural messages that sex is best approached instinctively as if it is simply a matter of "doing what comes naturally," that intentionally planning for sex (as in preparing for contraceptive use) is immoral, and that true love means being "swept away" rather than consciously shaping one's intimate connections with another person by paying attention to what is good for oneself as well as the other. As a constructive alternative, we should be promoting principled sexuality education that encourages people to choose with eyes wide open whether, when, and how to engage in a sexual encounter, to take responsibility to do so safely with respect for oneself and the other person, to remain mindful of what is going on, and to pay attention to the likely consequences. All these are counter-cultural measures of resistance to a highly sexualized culture that encourages people to rely on alcohol, illicit drugs, and pornography to give them "permission" to be sexual. As John Stoltenberg wisely proposes, "If you can't take sober responsibility for your part in a sexual encounter, you probably shouldn't be having it—and you certainly shouldn't be zonked out of your mind *in order* to have it."[53]

As previously discussed, at least some religiously affiliated youth who are already sexually active are requesting faith-based education that addresses how to live and love responsibly as persons of faith, including knowing how to avoid the negative consequences of unintended pregnancy and sexually transmitted infection. In addition, all youth, both those who are sexually active and those not yet sexually active, are asking to be respected *as sexual persons* who are in the process of developing their sexual identities, including their habits of intimate relating that will inform them over a lifetime. Each and all of them stand in need of guidance about how their faith and values can inform and enrich their lives and their loving, including their loving themselves. Adult evasion of these realities leaves youth without adult support and mentoring, and the cost of such adult absenteeism weighs most heavily on the youth themselves who must navigate a complex world on their own as best they can.

■ How faith communities can play a constructive role

If the repeated requests of young people for better moral education and support go unanswered, many youth will "vote with their feet" and disconnect from their faith communities when they reach sexual maturation and find the church no longer helpful in making sense of their world. "For some young Christians," Sarah Park writes, "their decision to become sexually active coincides with their departure from the church. This may relate to outgrowing their child-like faith, or it may be prompted by a sense that their sexual life is not reconciled with their spiritual life and a sense of being judged."[54] To this I would add that because sexuality and spirituality are so intimately intertwined, self-respecting young people may also leave because the sexual theology offered by the church is either infantilizing or morally offensive, and sometimes both. Therefore, Park is right to suggest that "to take seriously the moral dilemmas young people face about their developing sexuality" may be one of the best avenues "to nurture the maturing of faith" in them and their peers.[55]

Accordingly, the Religious Institute's "Open Letter to Religious Leaders on Adolescent Sexuality" hits the nail on the head: "A new faith-based approach to adolescent sexuality grounded in developing the moral agency of teenagers is urgently needed."[56] At its best, sexual education is a lifelong process that involves acquiring scientifically accurate information about human sexuality as persons form their fundamental attitudes and values about sexual identities, intimate relationships, and ethical responsibility. Its primary goal is the promotion of sexual health and well-being of persons and the wider community. As Haffner and Ott explain, this open-ended educational process seeks to help young people as well as adults develop "a positive view of sexuality, provide them with information about taking care of their sexual health, and help them acquire skills to make sexual decisions now and in the future."[57] Educator Martha Kempner adds that curricula should communicate age-appropriate messages, including messages that can reassure adolescents that "they are sexual beings and that sexual feelings and fantasies are normal, even though young people do not need to act upon them." Educational programs should also avoid trying to "scare [teenagers] chaste" by relying on fear, gender-biased stereotypes, or what she calls "messages of shame" that imply that young people are incapable of being both sexually active and morally responsible.[58]

An example of a sex-positive, faith-based comprehensive sexuality education curriculum is the Our Whole Lives program developed collaboratively by the United Church of Christ and the Unitarian Universalist Association. Designed as a lifespan curriculum from preschool through adulthood, this program at the very outset makes explicit the value commitments that inform its entire approach to sexual health and well-being for persons of all ages: self-worth ("Each person is entitled to dignity and self-worth, and to his or her own attitudes and beliefs about sexuality"); sexual health ("Every individual has the right to accurate information about sexuality and to have her or his questions answered"); responsibility ("We are called to enrich our lives by expressing sexuality in ways that enhance human wholeness and fulfillment and express love, commitment, delight, and pleasure"); and justice and inclusivity ("Sexual relationships should never be coercive or exploitative").[59] Moreover, the OWL curriculum emphasizes that penis-in-vagina sex is "only one of many valid ways of expressing sexual feelings with a partner," thereby critiquing sexual fundamentalism that asserts that there is one and only one right way to be sexual or express sexual desire. The curriculum also underscores that while "all persons are sexual" and "sexuality is a good part of the human experience," it is "healthier for young adolescents to postpone sexual intercourse" until they are emotionally, physically, and spiritually ready to assume responsibility for their own and their partner's safety and well-being.[60]

This faith-based, sex-positive, and justice-centered educational program offers a welcome alternative to abstinence-only and "don't ask, don't tell" approaches to youth sexuality by proactively equipping young people with the tools and encouragement to develop their capacity for informed moral agency about sex and sexuality. It adopts the view that adolescents are both sexual persons and responsible persons who deserve to be supported as they develop skills and confidence for making appropriate decisions about their health and well-being. As Debra Haffner points out, a new paradigm of adolescent sexual health begins with the presumption that "adolescent sexual activity is not by definition dangerous, harmful, sinful, or painful." That presumption can be overridden, and in some circumstances, including coerced sex, it most certainly should be. At the same time, a progressive approach accepts the fact that teens will likely benefit from an education that informs them about how to share sexual pleasure as well as protect each other from harm, including from sexually transmitted infection, unintended pregnancy, and sexual violence.[61]

Similarly, the organization Advocates for Youth encourages both adults and youth to pay attention to the three core values of respect, rights, and responsibility. "Accurate, balanced sex education—including information about contraception and condoms—is a basic human right of youth," this group acknowledges. At the same time, this right is also a "core public health principle" that is strongly endorsed by mainstream medical associations, a wide range of educational organizations, and, perhaps most importantly, parents.[62] One sign that young people are empowered by such values-based comprehensive sexuality education comes from a 2010 United States survey of participants ranging from ages 14 to 94, which indicates that "condom use is becoming the norm for sexually active teenagers." As the report points out, "Indeed, [adolescents] are more responsible than adults about using condoms."[63] On some matters, it seems, young people are in a better position to teach sexuality education to adults than the reverse! Could it be, in fact, that one root of our troubles is our inability to trust young people because we have failed to meet our own adult responsibilities as ethical mentors and guides for sexual health and justice?

The Religious Institute's "Open Letter to Religious Leaders on Adolescent Sexuality" affirms that young people should be recognized and respected as the subjects of their own lives, not as objects to benignly "protect" and certainly not as objects to exploit. "All persons, including adolescents," the Open Letter emphasizes, "have the right and responsibility to lead lives that express love, justice, mutuality, commitment, consent, and pleasure."[64] The freedom to love and be loved is intrinsic to our personhood, although such loving takes a variety of forms, only some of which involve genital sex. To deny youth the freedom to explore their desire for intimate connections, in safety and with informed moral guidance from trusted adults, is not only to disempower them; it is also to infantilize them and undermine their spiritual integrity. Granted, youth will make mistakes, but the misuse of this sacred moral power for sharing respectful intimate touch does not rule out its proper—its ethically sound and delightfully pleasurable—use.

■ The issue is not actually sex, but rather power and relational integrity

The church's mandate is to educate people of all ages to be ethically astute lovers in their intimate and social, political, and economic connections. The church can play a constructive role in preparing people to enter into and sustain mature intimate relationships if and only if it relinquishes any inclination to play the role of "moral police" or code enforcer for Christian erotophobic patriarchalism. As an alternative, the church should promote what theologian Rosemary Ruether calls an "egalitarian ethic of mutual accountability," based on the assumption that "good sexuality is achieved through a process of learning and experience."[65] This process of maturation includes gaining self-awareness and acceptance of one's own sexual identity, coming to appreciate the range of gender/sexual identities and erotic possibilities represented among persons, and acquiring skills and confidence to become a self-directing moral agent who makes decisions that reflect one's best values and faith commitments. This process, Ruether reminds us, is not accomplished in "a single leap from virginity to marriage," but rather takes time and effort.[66] That insight should be kept alongside theologian Joan Timmerman's admonition that virtue is found "not in repressing but in cultivating the human capacity to respond sexually. . . . One does not come into life fully developed; one has an obligation to grow toward full adulthood."[67] And if faith communities are to remain relevant, they must find more constructive and creative ways to stand alongside people all along the way.

As young people engage in this process of personal maturation and sexual exploration, they should be encouraged to focus, first, on how to integrate *eros* and *philia* (pleasure and friendship) in intimate relationships. This includes learning how to give and receive sexual pleasure and how to use contraception effectively so that sex is possible without fear of unwanted pregnancy and without putting anyone's health at risk. This approach assumes, Ruether writes, that "young people can engage in sexual experimentation before they are ready for reproduction, perhaps 'going steady' with a partner, in a way that connects sexual pleasure and contraception with friendship: i.e. accountable, responsible relationships."[68]

As a second stage, couples can be encouraged to form a permanent bond with a life partner, but this commitment may or may not include parenting. However, it would presuppose that the parties were able to integrate *eros*, *philia*, and *agape* into their lives not only by honoring sexual pleasure in the context of friendship, but also by exhibiting a generous and loving care for others. "Is this so shocking, so hard to imagine?" Ruether asks. "I think this is what many young people are already doing. But they are doing it under a cloud of disapproval and hypocritical doublethink on the part of their parents, teachers, and pastors. [That] makes it very difficult for them to progress along the path to personal sexual maturity in a secure and self-confident way."[69]

In another proposal for developing a sexual ethic for youth and others, Marie Fortune argues in *Love Does No Harm* that we must appreciate "the complexity and ambiguity of [our moral] choices and [yet still] engage in the hard work of discerning the right thing to do. What I mean by 'right,' " she points out, is "the appropriate action, the just response, that causes least harm to self and others."[70] Accordingly, she proposes as a general guideline that, on the one hand, "it is right to share sexual intimacy in a context of choice and commitment" and, on the other hand, "it is wrong to coerce, force or take advantage of anyone sexually."[71] "Doing least harm," she proposes, "is a realistic and tangible goal to set for ourselves."[72]

Notice here that the age of the persons in relation, their gender or sexual orientation, and their marital or relational status do not by themselves determine whether sexual activity is morally good or not. What matters is whether the parties exercise care and mutual responsibility to use their erotic power in ways that avoid harm and, whenever possible, enhance pleasure and mutual well-being. Toward that end, Fortune strongly encourages us to enter into intimate association only with someone who is a peer, that is, "someone whose power is relatively equal to mine."[73] As she explains, "Seeking a peer relationship in which to find sexual intimacy is the best insurance there is for avoiding abuse and for finding trust and fulfillment in relationship. Look for a partner who is your equal, who is a grown-up, who knows how to take care of him/herself, earns his/her own living, and is not threatened by your strengths and capabilities."[74]

Erotic attraction between persons who are mutually caring and respectful friends (and who sometimes also become intimate life companions) breaks with the injurious patriarchal pattern of sexual exchange that eroticizes power and social role inequalities as "truly" sexy and regards sex as something one person "does" to another, the colliding of body parts rather than the meeting of persons. In contrast, an ethical eroticism asks that we stay alert to the person before us, as well as to our own needs and desires, and to seek a way of sharing intimate touch that is good for both. In doing so, we are wise to pay attention to how power plays out relationally between us, as well as to the ways in which the structural dynamics of racism, sexism, heterosexism, and economic inequality shape and misshape our lives, our desires, and our hopes and fears. "We deserve better than we have been given," Fortune writes, and with courage and perseverance "we can do this differently."[75]

In the early 1990s I coauthored a study for the Presbyterian Church (U.S.A.) entitled "Keeping Body and Soul Together: Sexuality, Spirituality, and Social Justice," which maps out, as an alternative to Christian patriarchalism, a justice-love ethic of "common decency." "One message the church must communicate," the report argues, "is that a Christian sexual ethic cannot be patriarchal and remain authentically Christian. Christianity and injustice are incompatible. A related message is this: A Christian sexual ethic must be a challenging, liberating, and gracious ethic of responsible justice-love."[76] Moving in this direction requires adopting justice-love as the appropriate norm for relationships, emphasizing mutual respect as well as an equitable sharing of power and resources, and affirming our common humanity across social differences. Finally, this ethic refuses to "condemn, out of hand, any sexual relations in which there are genuine equality and mutual respect. What is ruled out, from the start, are relations in which persons are abused, exploited, and violated. Moreover, an adequate sexual ethic . . . not only insist[s] that no harm be done, but more important, that people's well-being and self-respect be strengthened and deepened."[77]

In providing a vision of ethically good sex, this report invites people to consider the meaning of relational integrity for their own lives and reminds them that the shared task among us is to empower people "to make their own responsible choices [by] redirecting their ethical focus to the substance and quality of their relations whether they are heterosexual or homosexual, single or partnered."[78] Framed as affirmations rather than prohibitions, the value commitments that should inform sexual decision making include the following: (1) we value the goodness of our created sexuality, (2) we value sexual and spiritual wholeness, (3) we are committed to reclaiming eros and passion, (4) we value mutuality and consent, (5) we are committed to guaranteeing the bodily integrity and self-direction of every person, (6) we are committed to taking responsibility for our choices and actions, and (7) we are committed to fidelity in our relationships.[79] These affirmations are grounded in the conviction that the very human desire to connect with one another is the same desire that drives us to connect with God. Sexual desire is, therefore, a blessing, not a burden and not a curse. As a closing affirmation, this document underscores that "all persons, whether heterosexual or homosexual, while single or partnered, have a moral right to experience justice-love in their lives and to be sexual persons."[80] The church's leadership role is to promote and protect this right to sexual and relational integrity for all persons without distinction.

■ Advocating responsibility, not rules

Not long after the study document was released, a group of Presbyterian college students met to give their feedback. "You've failed us," they began, "because all you've provided is a set of broad principles, and then you expect us to figure out what to do. You're asking us to bear the responsibility, but that's asking too much of us. Besides, we need more guidance than that. We want rules, very clear rules, so that we can know without any doubt what's right and what's wrong." In reducing ethics and ethical inquiry to a set of rules, these young people also showed no hesitation in explaining that they were doubtful that they would actually obey the rules, so they expected the church to offer them forgiveness. Notice the setup: while the church's role is to enforce a restrictive and punitive code of patriarchal moralisms, it should also be willing to play the role of the lenient judge. However, this arrangement only keeps a sex-negative control system from ethical scrutiny and critique while it infantilizes people so that they never have to assume responsibility for their choices.

This chapter has mapped out a different approach to the moral life. While patriarchal Christianity has made it all about genital sex, male control, and adult policing of adolescent sexuality, a progressive Christian ethical eroticism makes it about intimate relationships of equality, the equitable sharing of power and pleasure, and how people of all ages learn how to extend mutual respect and care. The challenge and joy of coming of age, sexually and spiritually, involves the willingness to embrace one's moral freedom and decide for oneself how best to live and love in connection with others. Moreover, if more just and loving relationships were to reshape our intimate lives, can we not also imagine, with greater and greater anticipation, the spill-over effect that a justice-love ethic might have on our social, political, and economic connections as we take delight in raising expectations of what each one of us deserves, as well as what we owe others?

Shifting from a rule-based patriarchal moral framework to an egalitarian, justice-centered ethic also means redefining sexual sin. Most sexual sins are sinful not because they are sexual in nature, but because they involve the misuse of power by one party who feels entitled to take advantage of someone with less power. Examples include the rapist, the child molester, and the professional who sexualizes his or her relationship with a client, takes advantage of that person's vulnerability, and uses the relationship to meet the more powerful party's needs without regard for the needs or wishes of the other. Otherwise stated, sexual sin is sinful not because it involves sex, but because it involves the exploitation of persons. Exploitation also typically depends upon their objectification as "less than human" and upon rendering them voiceless and invisible as if "of no account."

The antidote to such sin is the graceful commitment to acknowledge the right of all persons *as sexual persons* to be treated with respect, dignity, and care and to create the social and cultural conditions that enhance the well-being of persons while building up community among them. For the less powerful, education for justice-love will aim at empowerment so that one may claim one's voice and take one's rightful place without reason to fear or need to apologize for being a sexual-spiritual person. For the more powerful, education will aim at letting go of a false sense of entitlement, learning how to share power with generosity and grace, and using one's resources to benefit others and not only oneself. Each of us, younger and older, female and male, single and partnered, should have the opportunity to learn—and benefit from—a sex-positive, justice-focused ethic that asks more for us and asks more from us. As

John Stoltenberg explains, we need to learn "as much as one can know about the values in the acts one has done and the acts one chooses to do and their full consequences for other people—as if everyone else is absolutely as real as oneself."[81] When such a justice-love ethic takes hold among us, we will have ample reason to give a resounding "three cheers" for a liberating Christian ethic of life and love.

How Far Can We Draw Outside the Lines and Still Be in the Picture?

*There can be little doubt that the [Christian tradition]
needs a new moral discourse on sex.*

CHRISTINE E. GUDORF[1]

Several assumptions have informed this examination of human sexuality and sexual ethics. First, the conventional Christian approach to sex and sexuality, most often negative and rule-oriented, is woefully inadequate. It has left people only further perplexed when it comes to sorting out these humanly significant, yet difficult questions about erotic power, gender and sexual difference, intimate relationships, and life together in community. Second, an alternative ethic is needed, one that is sex-positive, respectful of sexual diversity, and invested in challenging sexual oppression that informs other structures of social injustice. The preceding chapters have helped to explore the implications of such a contemporary, justice-centered social ethic of sexuality. Third, no doubt some readers will be asking themselves if this alternative ethic is "really" Christian.

If what counts as authentically Christian is allegiance to a fear-based, patriarchal paradigm of sexual and social control, then this study fails the test. However, the good news, as Daniel Maguire observes, is that "from the beginning there has never been just one Christianity."[2] The Christian movement is not a monolithic or fixed tradition, but rather a rich plurality of dynamic, often conflicting Christianities deeply divided over a host of issues, including sex, the role of women, and the diversity of family patterns.

Starkly divergent responses to the 2003 election of Gene Robinson as Episcopal bishop of New Hampshire illustrate this religious divide. Bishop Robinson is not only a divorced father of two adult children, but also an "out," that is, a publicly self-identified gay man who lives openly with his male partner. In response, Christian traditionalists are highly distressed that any church body would fail to underscore the incompatibility of Christian identity with "the gay lifestyle," much less give explicit approval to sexual immorality. With certitude they assert that homosexuality is intrinsically sinful, that only monogamous heterosexual marriage is biblically authorized, and that the marital family, the cornerstone of society, is undermined whenever church or state adopts a neutral stance toward non-normative sexualities or sanctions nontraditional families. In contrast, Christian progressives welcome nonheterosexuals into the life and leadership of the church, support their full civil, human, and ecclesiastical rights, including the freedom to marry and their eligibility to be ordained as church leaders, and press for a reformation of Christian theology and sexual ethics in light of the biblical mandate to pursue justice with and for those marginalized and oppressed, including those subjected to sexual injustice. The election of Bishop Robinson is a proud example of loyalty to gospel commitments.

This split over sexuality, sexual identity, and sexual justice within Christianity (and other religious traditions[3]) may be characterized in terms of a traditionalist-progressivist dichotomy. In *Christianity and the Making of the Modern Family,* theologian Rosemary Ruether points out that "no reconciliation is possible" between the two sides of this religious divide because their viewpoints are grounded in irreconcilably different presuppositions. Christian fundamentalists, operating with "fixed certainties" within an absolutist worldview, regard gay sex as morally objectionable "regardless of how loving or how committed is the relationship in which it takes place."[4] In contrast, Christian progressives show positive regard for a range of healthy and principled human sexualities, place the search for an inclusive, egalitarian justice at the heart of the moral-spiritual life, and regard diversity of cultures and religious perspectives as rich assets for community life rather than as threats to religious identity.

Because progressive Christians increasingly find that they have more in common, in terms of faith and values, with their liberal counterparts in other denominations and traditions than they have with their conservative co-religionists, a massive realignment within the religious landscape is taking place. This realignment may be described as a "new ecumenism,"[5] as the progressive wings of various denominations seek ways to link together in order to pursue justice advocacy in both church and society. Similar alignments are occurring among religious conservatives who are strategizing to forestall further change by reasserting heterosexual monogamy as the exclusive norm for intimate life.

In the midst of this religious and social ferment, progressive Christians will resonate with a question posed by Rabbi Yoel Kahn in his efforts to construct a contemporary Jewish ethic of sexuality based on gender and sexual equality, mutuality in sharing pleasure as well as taking responsibility for sexual health and well-being, and a strong commitment to bodily integrity and self-determination. Kahn asks, "How do we describe the logarithm of change that permits us simultaneously to dissent radically from received tradition while claiming to stand in and even represent the tradition from which it comes?"[6]

Every change movement faces a crisis in legitimacy when confronted with the task of justifying itself and demonstrating how its program of critique and reconstruction will strengthen rather than undermine the integrity of the tradition. That "proof" is not available in advance, of course, because the outcome of any proposed change is only known after the fact, when it is embodied. For progressive Christians interested in shifting from a patriarchal to a justice-centered, egalitarian paradigm with respect to sex and sexuality, "this [legitimacy challenge] is difficult," Christine Gudorf explains, "given that Jesus himself only indirectly mentioned sex or sexuality and the tradition has not only preferred celibacy to marriage but also degraded women such that they have only recently been seen as capable of true partnership with men."[7] For these reasons, the authority for reformulating Christian sexual ethics comes not so much from the past, either the Bible or tradition, but rather from diverse faith-filled witnesses in the present, including self-respecting women and LBGTQ persons of all colors and classes, who are rising up in protest of the suffering caused by status-quo arrangements and, further, are giving persuasive testimony to the transformative power of the Spirit stirring the waters and calling forth a "fresh word" to renew the people.

Progressive Christians accept the fact that a break with the past is necessary, especially in terms of repudiating Christian teachings that have been destructive and disrespectful of human dignity and caused enormous suffering to women, nonheterosexual persons, and many others. At the same time, *the impulse for change and ethical transformation is deeply rooted in core gospel values* of justice, compassion, liberation, and inclusive, egalitarian community. The challenge is to flesh out the implications of these gospel values for human sexuality. While theological renewal is always risky, the greater risk is found in refusing to critique outdated and highly questionable assumptions about women, sexual difference, and eroticism or in presuming that the past should somehow be exempt from ethical assessment.

While some would assert that fidelity requires us to hold on to—and transmit without question or amplification—a fixed and unchangeable truth that floats magically through history as "*the* Christian tradition," I stand with feminist, queer, and other liberation theologians who recognize that such claims are "pretentious nonsense." Theological insight and ethical wisdom must adapt and change in order for Christianity to remain a dynamic, living tradition that can address real life in a constructive rather than reactive manner. As Beverly Harrison observes, "Christian doctrine changes, and should do so, as the world changes and, with it, as human self-understanding changes. The lure and excitement of doing theology," she reminds us, "come from the call to revision the meaning of our faith."[8] Loyalty to the faith tradition does not require a slavish adherence to the past or "mere repetition" of dogma. Rather, we find continuity with the tradition whenever we join our forebears in faith by making our own spirited commitment to seek justice, compassion, and mutual respect alongside one other and in relation to the earth. As Harrison summarizes our mandate as educators and change agents, "Theologically, we must teach what we see from our struggle that deepens our relations in mutuality, even as we retell those stories that remind us that we have precursors and a living community in that struggle."[9]

While conflict, confusion, and struggle about sex and sexuality may be signs of trouble within communities, including faith communities, they may also be signs of hope. The effort to critique and transform Christian patriarchalism continues to be a protracted and difficult struggle in the United States and also globally. Alas, the resolution to this struggle will not likely come in our lifetimes. Therefore, we would be wise to take Daniel Maguire's counsel as we engage these issues in our congregations and communities, that whenever we address matters of human sexuality, cultural change, and Christian ethics we should "clarify [our] ideas and get friends."[10] In other words, if we stand a chance of sparking what Maguire calls "a moral revolution," then we will need to lift up a compelling moral vision while we also help organize vibrant social change movements to press the case for change and explore fresh ways to live with integrity and mutual care in richly diverse communities. For this reason I've dedicated this book to students at Bangor Theological Seminary who have invested in exploring the contours of justice, including sexual justice, for ministry and community life, and also to two local organizations in Maine that continue to offer remarkable leadership about these matters.

For those invested in pursuing a comprehensive social justice agenda as a spiritual discipline, it will be important, strategically and spiritually, not to become so preoccupied with the demands or costs of moral struggle that we fail to recognize the embodied pleasure that this sacred work can offer. Steve Clapp, a researcher who has long been interested in investigating how congregations reclaim spiritual vitality, has published *Taking a New Look: Why Congregations Need LBGT Members*, in which he outlines ten benefits that faith communities stand to gain if they intentionally confront sexual injustice and become more inclusive, welcoming, and respectful of a wide diversity of persons.[11] What Clapp and many others are discovering anew is that at the heart of Christian spirituality is a bold, life-changing, and life-enriching invitation to seek—and experience—justice as communal right-relatedness. The unexpected gift of joining this justice struggle is to find joy, as a contemporary hymn puts it, "in the midst of new dimensions."[12] Therefore, in closing it seems fitting to reaffirm a conviction that I've written about elsewhere: "Reverence for the body and delight in communal solidarity are the two marks of a genuinely liberating spirituality. . . . Embracing the body and pursuing erotic justice is an unexpected yet delightful pathway for spiritual renewal and replenishment."[13] For the gift of this good work, we should give thanks without ceasing.

▪ NOTES ▪

INTRODUCTION: WHERE DO WE DRAW OUR LINES, AND WHY?

1. Illustrated London News (May 5, 1928), from *The Collected Works of G. K. Chesterton* (San Francisco: Ignatius, 1986).

2. Stephanie Coontz, *Marriage: A History* (New York: Penguin, 2005), 282–83.

3. Dagmar Herzog, *Sex in Crisis: The New Sexual Revolution and the Future of American Politics* (New York: Basic Books, 2008), xi.

4. Anthony Weston, *A Practical Companion to Ethics* (New York: Oxford University Press, 1997), 1–2.

5. Ibid.

6. Christine E. Gudorf, *Body, Sex, and Pleasure: Reconstructing Christian Sexual Ethics* (Cleveland: Pilgrim, 1994), 2.

7. L. William Countryman, *Dirt, Greed, and Sex: Sexual Ethics in the New Testament and Their Implications for Today* (Philadelphia: Fortress Press, 1988 [rev. 2007]), 262.

8. Marvin M. Ellison, *Erotic Justice: A Liberating Ethic of Sexuality* (Louisville: Westminster John Knox, 1996).

9. Daniel C. Maguire, "The Shadow Side of the Homosexuality Debate," in *Homosexuality in the Priesthood and the Religious Life*, ed. Jeannine Gramick (New York: Crossroad, 1989), 38–39.

10. Luke Timothy Johnson, "A Disembodied 'Theology of the Body,'" in *Human Sexuality in the Catholic Tradition*, ed. Kieran Scott and Harold Daly Horell (New York: Rowman & Littlefield, 2007), 114.

CHAPTER 1: WHY DO WE HAVE TO KEEP TALKING ABOUT SEX ALL THE TIME?

1. Thomas Laqueur, "Orgasm, Generation, and the Politics of Reproductive Biology," in *The Making of the Modern Body: Sexuality and Society in the Nineteenth Century*, ed. Catherine Gallagher and Thomas Laqueur (Berkeley: University of California Press, 1987), 4.

2. Gayle Rubin, "Thinking Sex: Notes for a Radical Theory of the Politics of Sex," in *The Lesbian and Gay Studies Reader*, ed. Henry Abelove, Michele Aina Barale, and David M. Halperin (New York: Routledge, 1993), 11.

3. Peggy Brick, "Toward a Positive Approach to Adolescent Sexuality," *SIECUS Report* 17:5 (May–July 1989): 1.

4. James Davison Hunter, *Culture Wars: The Struggle to Define America* (New York: Basic Books, 1991), 52.

5. Rubin, "Thinking Sex," 3–4.

6. Walter Brueggemann, "Voices of the Night against Justice," in Walter Brueggemann, Sharon Parks, and Thomas H. Groome, *To Act Justly, Love Tenderly, Walk Humbly: An Agenda for Ministers* (New York: Paulist, 1986), 5.

7. Nelle Morton, *The Journey Is Home* (Boston: Beacon, 1985).

8. May Sarton, *At Seventy* (New York: W. W. Norton, 1984), 10.

9. Marvin M. Ellison, *Erotic Justice: A Liberating Ethic of Sexuality* (Louisville: Westminster John Knox, 1996), 2.

10. Thomas J. Gerschick, "The Body, Disability, and Sexuality," in *Introducing the New Sexuality Studies: Original Essays and Interviews*, ed. Steven Seidman, Nancy Fischer, and Chet Meeks (New York: Routledge, 2007), 255.

11. Ibid.

12. Delores S. Williams, *Sisters of the Wilderness* (Maryknoll: Orbis, 1993), 71.

13. Miguel De La Torre, *A Lily among the Thorns: Imagining a New Christian Sexuality* (San Francisco: John Wiley & Sons, 2007), 41 and 37.

14. John Boswell, "Homosexuality and Religious Life: A Historical Approach," in *Sexuality and the Sacred: Sources for Theological Reflection* (Louisville: Westminster John Knox, 1994), 362.

15. Ibid., 363.

16. Rosemary Radford Ruether, *Christianity and the Making of the Modern Family* (Boston: Beacon, 2000), 173.

17. Patricia Hill Collins, *Black Feminist Thought: Knowledge, Consciousness, and the Politics of Empowerment* (New York: Routledge and Kegan Paul, 1991), 198.

18. John B. Cobb Jr., *Matters of Life and Death* (Louisville: Westminster John Knox, 1991), 94.

19. James B. Nelson, *Embodiment: An Approach to Sexuality and Christian Theology* (Minneapolis: Augsburg Publishing House, 1978), esp. chapters 3–4.

20. Vern L. Bullough, "Christianity and Sexuality," in *Religion and Sexual Health: Ethical, Theological, and Clinical Perspectives*, ed. Ronald M. Green (Boston: Kluwer Academic, 1992), 15.

21. Mariana Valverde, *Sex, Power, and Pleasure* (Toronto: The Women's Press, 1985), 10.

22. Cobb, *Matters of Life and Death*, 97.

23. Rosemary Radford Ruether, "Homophobia, Heterosexism, and Pastoral Practice," in *Sexuality and the Sacred: Sources for Theological Reflection*, ed. James B. Nelson and Sandra P. Longfellow (Louisville: Westminster John Knox, 1994), 387–96.

24. Valverde, *Sex, Power, and Pleasure*, 19.

25. Christine E. Gudorf, *Body, Sex, and Pleasure: Reconstructing Christian Sexual Ethics* (Cleveland: Pilgrim, 1994), 1 and 2.

26. Susan Moller Okin, *Justice, Gender, and the Family* (New York: Basic Books, 1989), 135.

27. Thomas Laqueur, *Making Sex: Body and Gender from the Greeks to Freud* (Cambridge: Harvard University Press, 1990).

28. Anne Fausto-Sterling, *Sexing the Body: Gender Politics and the Construction of Sexuality* (New York: Basic, 2000).

29. Christine E. Gudorf, "The Erosion of Sexual Dimorphism: Challenges to Religion and Religious Ethics," *Journal of the American Academy of Religion* 69:4 (December 2001): 863–91.

30. Robert McAfee Brown, *Theology in a New Key: Responding to Liberation Themes* (Philadelphia: Westminster, 1978), 51.

31. De La Torre, *A Lily Among the Thorns*, 39.

CHAPTER 2: WHAT MAKES "GOOD SEX" GOOD?

1. Michael Warner, *The Trouble with Normal: Sex, Politics, and the Ethics of Queer Life* (New York: Free, 1999), 1.

2. Mark D. Jordan, *The Ethics of Sex* (Malden, MA: Blackwell, 2002), 156–57, 123, and 124.

3. Dagmar Herzog, *Sex in Crisis: The New Sexual Revolution and the Future of American Politics* (New York: Basic, 2008), 1.

4. Gayle S. Rubin, "Thinking Sex: Notes for a Radical Theory of the Politics of Sexuality," in *The Lesbian and Gay Studies Reader*, ed. Henry Abelove, Michele Aina Barale, and David M. Halperin (New York: Routledge, 1993), 11.

5. Beverly Wildung Harrison, *Making the Connections: Essays in Feminist Social Ethics*, ed. Carol S. Robb (Boston: Beacon, 1983), 146.

6. Dale B. Martin, "It's about Sex, Not Homosexuality," *Reflections: Sex and the Church* (New Haven: Yale Divinity School, 2006), 24.

7. Augustine, "The Good of Marriage," in *Theology and Sexuality: Classic and Contemporary Readings*, ed. Eugene F. Rogers Jr. (Malden, MA: Blackwell, 2002), 76.

8. Ibid., 73 and 80.

9. Ibid., 73.

10. Jordan, *Ethics of Sex*, 117.

11. Ibid., 113, my emphasis.

12. Rosemary Radford Ruether, *Christianity and the Making of the Modern Family* (Boston: Beacon, 2000), 78.

13. Rita Nakashima Brock, "Marriage Troubles," in *Body and Soul: Rethinking Sexuality as Justice-Love*, ed. Marvin M. Ellison and Sylvia Thorson-Smith (Cleveland: Pilgrim, 2003), 353.

14. Ibid., 74.

15. James B. Nelson, *Between Two Gardens: Reflections on Sexuality and Religious Experience* (Eugene, OR: Wipf & Stock, 2008), chapter 6, "Singleness and the Church," 96–109.

16. Jordan, *Ethics of Sex*, 119 and 120.

17. Ibid., 122.

18. Karen Armstrong, "Not So Holy Matrimony," *The Guardian*, June 30, 2003. Emphasis in the original.

19. Rubin, "Thinking Sex," 12.

20. Ibid., 14–15.

21. See Mark D. Jordan, *The Invention of Sodomy in Christian Theology* (Chicago: University of Chicago Press, 1997). Also, Mark D. Jordan, *Recruiting Young Love: How Christians Talk about Homosexuality* (Chicago: University of Chicago Press, 2011).

22. Nancy L. Fischer, "Purity and Pollution: Sex as a Moral Discourse," in *Introducing the New Sexuality Studies: Original Essays and Interviews*, ed. Steven Seidman, Nancy Fischer, and Chet Meeks (New York: Routledge, 2007), 52.

23. See Kelly Brown Douglas, *What's Faith Got to Do with It? Black Bodies/Christian Souls* (Maryknoll: Orbis, 2005), esp. part 1 (What Is It about Christianity?).

24. Karen L. Bloomquist, "The Politics of Sex and Power in the Churches" (unpublished paper, March 1993), 4, cited in Marvin M. Ellison, *Erotic Justice: A Liberating Ethic of Sexuality* (Louisville: Westminster John Knox, 1996), 56.

25. Fischer, "Purity and Pollution," 54.

26. Focus on the Family, "Colorado Statement on Biblical Sexual Morality," 1, www.citizenlink.com.

27. Ibid.

28. Ibid.

29. Ibid., 3.

30. Ibid.

31. Ruether, *Making of the Modern Family*, 175.

32. "Colorado Statement," 1.

33. Kathryn Joyce, "Arrows for the War," *The Nation* (November 27, 2006).

34. *Presbyterians and Human Sexuality 1991* (Louisville: Office of the General Assembly, Presbyterian Church USA, 1991), 7.

35. Ibid., 10.

36. Ibid.

37. Ibid., 20.

38. Ibid., 23.

39. Ibid.

40. Martin, "It's about Sex, Not Homosexuality," 27.

41. William R. Stayton, "Sexual Value Systems and Sexual Health," in *Sexual Health: Moral and Cultural Foundations*, vol. 3, ed. Mitchell S. Tepper and Annette Fuglsang Owens (Westport, CT: Praeger, 2007), 81.

42. Ibid., 82.

43. Ibid., 83.

44. Daniel C. Maguire, *A Moral Creed for All Christians* (Minneapolis: Fortress Press, 2005), 216.

45. Southern Baptist Convention, "Sexuality," www.sbc.net.

46. Southern Baptist Convention, "The Baptist Faith and Message," XVIII. The Family, www.sbc.net.

47. SBC, "Sexuality."

48. Southern Baptist Convention, Resolution on Homosexual Marriage (June 1996), www.sbc.net/resolutions.

49. SBC, "The Family."

50. United Church of Christ Synod 25 (2005), "In Support of Equal Marriage Rights for All," 1–2, www.ucc.org.

51. Ibid., 1.

52. Ibid., 2.

53. Ibid.

CHAPTER 3: IS IT STILL ADULTERY IF THE SPOUSE HAS ALZHEIMER'S?

1. Margaret A. Farley, *Just Love: A Framework for Christian Sexual Ethics* (New York: Continuum, 2006), 296–97.

2. Daniel C. Maguire, *Ethics: A Complete Method for Moral Choice* (Minneapolis: Fortress Press, 2010), 66.

3. "Obituaries: William A. Harkins," *The Times Record*, November 23, 2009, www .timesrecord.com.

4. Larry Rasmussen, quoted in Maguire, *Ethics*, 281.

5. Mark D. Jordan, *The Ethics of Sex* (Malden, MA: Blackwell, 2002), 5.

6. Maguire, *Ethics*, 72, 178.

7. Ibid., 18.

8. Ibid., xvi.

9. Ibid., 116.

10. Ibid., 74.

11. Richard Address, "Opinion: Is It Still Adultery If the Spouse Has Alzheimer's?" Forward.com, August 15, 2007, www.forward.com. My emphasis.

12. Ibid., 1.

13. See Kwame Anthony Appiah, *The Honor Code: How Moral Revolutions Happen* (New York: W. W. Norton, 2010), about killing violence aimed primarily at women for crimes of sex outside marriage.

14. Address, "Opinion."

15. Stephen Post, *The Moral Challenge of Alzheimer Disease* (Baltimore: Johns Hopkins University Press, 2000).

16. Ibid., 1–2.

17. Ibid., 37.

18. Helen D. Davies et al., " 'Til Death Do Us Part': Intimacy and Sexuality in the Marriages of Alzheimer's Patients," *Journal of Psychosocial Nursing* 30:11 (1992), 5.

19. Post, *Moral Challenge*, 33–34.

20. Ibid., 27 and 34.

21. Ibid., 39.

22. Ibid., 40.

23. Ibid., 34.

24. Ibid., 40.

25. Davies, "Til Death Do Us Part," 5.

26. Ibid., 6.

27. Societal myths about the sexuality of older persons, including older persons living with disability, include the following: older disabled persons are not interested in sex; older disabled persons should learn to adjust to a life of celibacy, especially after they reach the age of sixty; older disabled women do not experience orgasm; older people who abstain from sex are healthier than their sexually active peers; and sexual activity for older persons is immoral. See Stephen A. Rollin and Wallace S. Woodard, "Sexuality and the Elderly," *Journal of Rehabilitation* 47:4 (October 1981): 64–68.

28. Farley, *Just Love*, 301.

29. Ibid., 301–2.

30. Tammy Nelson, "The New Monogamy," *Networker* (July–August 2010): 22.

31. Ibid., 304–5.

32. Ibid., 305.

33. Ibid., 2.

34. Stephanie Coontz, *Marriage: A History* (New York: Penguin, 2005), 10.

35. Ibid.

36. Augustine, "From 'The Good of Marriage,'" in *Theology and Sexuality: Classic and Contemporary Readings*, ed. Eugene F. Rogers Jr. (Malden, MA: Blackwell, 2002), 82. See also Jordan, *Ethics of Sex*, chapter 5, "Marriage Acts," 108–14.

37. Coontz, *Marriage: A History*, 124.

38. Cited in Cheshire Calhoun, "Who's Afraid of Polygamous Marriage? Lessons for Same-Sex Marriage Advocacy from the History of Polygamy," *San Diego Law Review* (Summer 2005): 1028 and footnote 32.

39. Farley, *Just Love*, 87.

40. Ibid., 263–64.

41. Scott Anderson, "Polygamy in America," *National Geographic* (February 2010).

42. Ibid., 57.

43. In *The New Jim Crow: Mass Incarceration in the Age of Colorblindness* (New York: The New Press, 2010), Michelle Alexander notes that the United States rate of incarceration (750 per 100,000) is about eight times that of Germany (93 per 100,000), but even more striking is the racial dimension of this phenomenon. "In Washington, D.C., our nation's capitol," she notes, "it is estimated that three out of four young black men (and nearly all those in the poorest neighborhood) can expect to serve time in prison. Similar rates of incarceration can be found in black communities across America" (6–7).

44. Debra Mubashshir Majeed, " 'The Battle Has Been Joined': Gay and Polygynous Marriages Are Out of the Closet and in Search of Legitimacy," *Crosscurrents* 54:2 (Summer 2004): 5, www.crosscurrents.org.

45. Ibid., 4.

46. Nelson, "New Monogamy," 23.

47. Scott Haldeman, "A Queer Fidelity," in *Sexuality and the Sacred: Sources for Theological Reflection*, ed. Marvin M. Ellison and Kelly Brown Douglas (Louisville: Westminster John Knox, 2010), 312, 313, and 314.

48. James B. Nelson, *Embodiment: An Approach to Sexuality and Christian Theology* (Minneapolis: Augsburg Publishing House, 1978), 140.

49. Ibid.

50. Ibid., 144.

51. Ibid.

52. Ibid., 144–46.

53. Marie M. Fortune, *Violence against Women: The Sin Revisited* (Cleveland: Pilgrim, 2005), 52–55 and 101–3.

54. Farley, *Just Love*, 266.

55. Ibid., 309.

56. Ibid., 264.

57. Fortune, *Love Does No Harm*, 133.

58. Ibid.

59. Eric Mount Jr., *Covenant, Community, and the Common Good: An Interpretation of Christian Ethics* (Cleveland: Pilgrim, 1999), 9 and 21.

60. Mary Hobgood, "Marriage, Market Values, and Social Justice: Toward an Examination of Compulsory Monogamy," in *Redefining Sexual Ethics: A Sourcebook of Essays, Stories, and Poems*, ed. Susan E. Davies and Eleanor H. Haney (Cleveland: Pilgrim, 1991).

61. Mount, *Covenant, Community, and the Common Good*, 64.

62. John D'Emilio, "Capitalism and Gay Identity," in *Sexuality: A Reader*, ed. Karen Lebacqz with David Sinacore-Guinn (Cleveland: Pilgrim, 1999), 198.

63. William Walsh, "Polyamory, Polyandry, Polygyny, Polygamy: Oh, My!" (unpublished paper), 3.

64. Ibid., 4.

65. Valerie White, "Polyamory Is a Feasible Alternative to Monogamous Marriage," in *Sex: Opposing Viewpoints*, ed. Mary E. Williams (Farmington Hills, MI: Greenhaven, 2006), 18.

66. J. N. Ferrer, "Monogamy, Polyamory, and Beyond," *Tikkun* 22:1: 40.

67. Gary Kennedy, M.D., quoted in "Love in the World of Alzheimer's," *Washington Post*, December 10, 2007.

68. Robert Goss, "Proleptic Sexual Love," 57.

69. Ibid., 61.

70. Ibid., 62–63.

71. Mark D. Jordan, *Blessing Same-Sex Unions: The Perils of Queer Romance and the Confusions of Christian Marriage* (Chicago: University of Chicago Press, 2005), 165.

72. Marvin M. Ellison, *Erotic Justice: A Liberating Ethic of Sexuality* (Louisville: Westminster John Knox, 1996), 86.

73. Anthony Weston, *A Practical Companion to Ethics* (New York: Oxford University Press, 1997), 51–56.

74. Nelson, *Embodiment*, 151.

CHAPTER 4: IS SAME-SEX MARRIAGE A "MUST" OR A "BUST"?

1. Paula Ettlebrick, "Since When Is Marriage a Path to Liberation?" *Out/Look* 2:2 (Fall 1989): 14.

2. Daniel C. Maguire, *Ethics: A Complete Method for Moral Choice* (Minneapolis: Fortress Press, 2010), 212 and 213.

3. Lisa Leff, "Same-Sex Marriage Vote Down to Wire," *Maine Sunday Telegram*, Sunday, November 2, 2008, A18.

4. Glenn T. Stanton, "Is Marriage in Jeopardy?" www.ankerberg.com.

5. Ibid.

6. United Church of Christ Synod 25 (2005), "In Support of Equal Marriage Rights for All," 2, www.ucc.org. Subsequent page references are to this document.

7. Andrew Sullivan, introduction to *Same-Sex Marriage: Pro and Con; A Reader*, ed. Andrew Sullivan (New York: Vintage, 2004), xxvi.

8. Ibid., xx.

9. Andrew Sullivan, *Virtually Normal: An Argument about Homosexuality* (New York: Vintage, 1996), 185.

10. John D'Emilio, "The Marriage Fight Is Setting Us Back," *The Gay and Lesbian Review* (November–December 2006).

11. Martha Ackelsberg and Judith Plaskow, "Response," *Journal of Feminist Studies in Religion* 20:2 (Fall 2004): 107 and 108.

12. Mary Hunt, "Roundtable Discussion: Same-Sex Marriage," *JFSR* 20:2 (Fall 2004): 83.

13. Daniel Maguire, "The Morality of Homosexual Marriage," in *Same-Sex Marriage: The Moral and Legal Debate*, ed. Robert M. Baird and Stuart E. Rosenbaum (Amherst: Prometheus, 1997), 62.

14. Richard D. Mohr, *A Moral Perfect Union: Why Straight America Must Stand Up for Gay Rights* (Boston: Beacon, 1994), 41. Mohr notes that historically, the institution of civil marriage has been marked by "major gender-based differences," including the obligation of a husband to provide for his wife's material needs, his control of her property (with or without her consent), and his entitlement to sex (a husband by legal definition could not rape his own wife). These and other gender-based differences have been reevaluated as unjust and, therefore, discarded by either judicial or legislative means. He concludes that "now that gender distinctions have all but vanished from the legal *content* of marriage, there is no basis for the requirement that the legal *form* of marriage unite members of different sexes. The legal definition of marriage—'union of one man and one woman'—though

doggedly enforced in the courts, is a dead husk that has been cast off by marriage as a living legal institution" (37).

15. Carlos A. Ball, *The Morality of Gay Rights: An Exploration in Political Philosophy* (New York: Routledge, 2003), 104–5.

16. Ibid., 57.

17. *Baker v. Vermont* (filed December 20, 1999), 6. Cited on the web page of Gay and Lesbian Advocates and Defenders, www.glad.org.

18. *Perez v. Sharp*, www.freedomtomarry.org.

19. Ibid.

20. Maguire, "Morality of Homosexual Marriage," 59.

21. William Sloan Coffin, *A Passion for the Possible*, 2nd ed. (Louisville: Westminster John Knox, 2004), 63 and 65.

22. Cited in Marie M. Fortune, *Love Does No Harm: Sexual Ethics for the Rest of Us* (New York: Continuum, 1995), 55.

23. For a progressive interfaith statement in support of marriage equality, see the 2004 "Open Letter to Religious Leaders on Marriage Equality" on the website of the Religious Institute for Sexual Morality, Justice, and Healing (www.religiousinstitute.org). For suggestions on how religious leaders can promote marriage equality, see the Action Kit prepared by the Freedom to Marry Project (www.freedomtomarry.org/take_action.asp). For progressive yet divergent perspectives, see Marvin M. Ellison, *Same-Sex Marriage? A Christian Ethical Analysis* (Cleveland: Pilgrim, 2004); Mark D. Jordan, *Blessing Same-Sex Unions: The Perils of Queer Romance and the Confusions of Christian Marriage* (Chicago: University of Chicago Press, 2005); and David G. Myers and Letha Dawson Scanzoni, *What God Has Joined Together? A Christian Case for Gay Marriage* (New York: HarperCollins, 2005).

24. Beverly Wildung Harrison, *Justice in the Making: Feminist Social Ethics*, ed. Elizabeth M. Bounds et al. (Louisville: Westminster John Knox, 2004), 55.

25. Kelly Brown Douglas, using the term *platonized Christianity* to describe the dualistic distortions that have plagued western Christianity, analyzes how an oppressive Christian tradition, in demonizing sexuality, has entered into alliance with state power to punish non-normative people as "sexual deviants" and, therefore, enemies of God. See her *What's Faith Got to Do with It? Black Bodies/Christian Souls* (Maryknoll: Orbis, 2005), esp. part 1.

26. See note 12 above.

27. William N. Eskridge Jr., *The Case for Same-Sex Marriage: From Sexual Liberty to Civilized Commitment* (New York: Free Press, 1996), 9.

28. Ibid., 58.

29. Ibid., 84.

30. On friendship and sexuality, see Carter Heyward, *Touching Our Strength: The Erotic as Power and the Love of God* (San Francisco: Harper & Row, 1989); Mary E. Hunt, *Fierce Tenderness: A Feminist Theology of Friendship* (Minneapolis: Augsburg Fortress, 2009); Elizabeth Stuart, *Just Good Friends: Towards a Lesbian and Gay Theology of Relationships* (London: Mowbray, 1994); and J. Michael Clark, *Doing the Work of Love: Men and Commitment in Same-Sex Relationships* (Harriman, TN: Men's Studies Press, 1999).

31. Michael Bronski, *The Pleasure Principle: Sex, Backlash, and the Struggle for Gay Freedom* (New York: St. Martin's, 1998), 242–43 and 249.

32. Alison Solomon, "Get Married? Yes, but Not by the State," *Village Voice*, January 9, 1996, 29.

33. Stephanie Coontz, "Too Close for Comfort," *New York Times*, November 7, 2006.

34. Ibid. See also "Study: Gain a Spouse, Lose Your Friends," *Portland Press Herald,* May 29, 2007, A4.

35. Carter Heyward, *Touching Our Strength: The Erotic as Power and the Love of God* (San Francisco: Harper & Row, 1989), 13.

36. Ibid.

37. See Mary E. Hobgood, *Dismantling Privilege: An Ethics of Accountability*, 2nd ed., esp. chapter 3, "An Economic Ethics of Right Relationship" (Cleveland: Pilgrim, 2009).

CHAPTER 5: WHY DON'T BATTERERS JUST LEAVE AND RAPISTS JUST CEASE AND DESIST?

1. Laura Stivers, *Disrupting Homelessness: Alternative Christian Approaches* (Minneapolis: Fortress Press, 2011), 19.

2. Carol J. Adams, *Woman-Battering* (Minneapolis: Fortress Press, 1994), 11.

3. Karen Lebacqz, "Love Your Enemy: Sex, Power, and Christian Ethics," *The Annual of the Society of Christian Ethics 1990*, ed. D. M. Jeager (Washington, DC: Georgetown University Press, 1990), 9.

4. The Yogyakarta Principles are available at www.yogyakartaprinciples.org.

5. Carol J. Adams and Marie M. Fortune, preface in *Violence against Women and Children: A Christian Theological Sourcebook*, ed. Carol J. Adams and Marie M. Fortune (New York: Continuum, 1995), 12.

6. Women's violence is also directed at children, other women, and men with less privilege and standing. Therefore, a comprehensive ethical assessment of intimate violence must expand beyond a gender analysis and critically examine race, class, and other dynamics, including intimate violence between same-sex partners. On the latter, see *Violence in Gay and Lesbian Domestic Partnerships*, ed. Claire M. Renzetti and Charles Harvey Miley (New York: Harrington Park Press, 1996), and *Naming the Violence: Speaking Out about Lesbian Battering*, ed. Kerry Lobel (Seattle: Seal, 1986).

7. James Newton Poling, *Understanding Male Violence: Pastoral Care Issues* (St. Louis: Chalice, 2003), 10 and 11.

8. Adams, *Woman-Battering*, 7.

9. Philosopher Kwame Anthony Appiah in *The Honor Code: How Moral Revolutions Happen* (New York: W. W. Norton, 2010) argues that societies utilize codes of honor to maintain a cohesive identity and sense of personal and social integrity. However, a moral revolution that has yet to happen is one in which men's violence against women is publicly acknowledged as dishonorable and morally wrong. "Every society needs to sustain codes," Appiah writes, "in which assaulting a woman—assaulting anyone—in your own family is a source of dishonor, a cause of shame" (169).

10. National Coalition Against Domestic Violence (NCADV), *Domestic Violence Facts*, www.ncadv.org.

11. Maine Coalition Against Sexual Assault, www.mecasa.org.

12. Gloria Steinem, foreword to *Women Respond to the Men's Movement*, ed. Kay Leigh Hagan (San Francisco: HarperSanFrancisco, 1992), v.

13. Carol J. Adams, "Toward a Feminist Theology of Religion and the State," in Adams and Fortune, *Violence against Women and Children*, 15.

14. NCADV, *Domestic Violence Facts*.

15. Steinem, foreword, vi.

16. Karen Lebacqz, "Love Your Enemy," 4–5.

17. Adrian Thatcher, *Marriage after Modernity: Christian Marriage in Postmodern Times* (Sheffield: Sheffield Academic, 1999), chapter 3, "The Biblical Models of Marriage," 95.

18. Christine E. Gudorf, "Western Religion and the Patriarchal Family," in *Perspectives on Marriage: A Reader*, ed. Kieran Scott and Michael Warren (New York: Oxford University Press, 2001), 296.

19. Ibid.

20. Lebacqz, "Love Your Enemy," 3–4.

21. Ginny Nicarthy, *Getting Free: You Can End Abuse and Take Back Your Life* (Seattle: Seal, 1982), 286.

22. Lebacqz, "Love Your Enemy," 11 and 12.

23. Ibid., 17–18.

24. Ibid., 19.

25. The term is used by R. Emerson Dobash and Russell Dobash in their classic study, *Violence against Wives: A Case against Patriarchy* (New York: Free Press, 1979).

26. Adams, *Woman-Battering*, 43.

27. Diana Scully, *Understanding Sexual Violence: A Study of Convicted Rapists* (Boston: Unwin Hyman, 1990), 4.

28. Ibid., 169. See also Danielle L. McGuire, *At the Dark End of the Street: Black Women, Rape, and Resistance—A New History of the Civil Rights Movement from Rosa Parks to the Rise of Black Power* (New York: Alfred A. Knopf, 2010).

29. Ibid., 4.

30. Ibid., 141.

31. Ibid., 149.

32. Ibid., 150.

33. Ibid., 74.

34. Ibid., 158.

35. Ibid., 155.

36. Ibid., 97.

37. Ibid., 98.

38. Ibid., 165.

39. Ibid.

40. Ibid., 166.

41. Ibid., 110.

42. Susan Schechter, *Women and Male Violence: The Visions and Struggles of the Battered Women's Movement* (Boston: South End Press, 1982), 238.

43. Lebacqz, "Love Your Enemy," 7.

44. Adams, "Toward a Feminist Theology," 23.

45. Ellyn Kaschak, *Engendered Lives* (New York: Basic Books, 1992), 183–84, quoted in Marie M. Fortune, *Love Does No Harm: Sexual Ethics for the Rest of Us* (New York: Continuum, 1995), 60.

46. Barbara Hart, "Lesbian Battering: An Examination," in *Naming the Violence: Speaking Out about Lesbian Battering*, ed. Kerry Lobel (Seattle: Seal, 1986), 182–83.

47. Adams, *Woman-Battering*, 16.

48. Ibid., 20.

49. Poling, *Understanding Male Violence*, 90.

50. Adams, *Woman-Battering*, 8.

51. Traci C. West, *Wounds of the Spirit: Black Women, Violence, and Resistance Ethics* (New York: New York University Press, 1999), 15.

52. Ibid., 14 and 15.

53. Ibid., 183.

54. Ibid., 120.

55. See Kelly Brown Douglas, *Sexuality and the Black Church: A Womanist Perspective*, esp. chapter 2, "Stereotypes, False Images, Terrorism: The White Assault upon Black Sexuality," 31–59.

56. West, *Wounds of the Spirit*, 86.

57. Ibid., 147.

58. Ibid., 187 and 192.

59. Donna J. Cecere, "The Second Closet: Battered Lesbians," *Open Hands* 3:2 (Fall 1987): 12. Emphasis added.

60. Jim Wallis, *The Soul of Politics: A Practical and Prophetic Vision for Change* (Maryknoll: Orbis and The New Press, 1994), 97.

61. Karen Lebacqz, *Justice in an Unjust World: Foundations for a Christian Approach* (Minneapolis: Fortress Press, 1987 [rev. 2007]), 149.

62. John Stoltenberg, "A Coupla Things I've Been Meaning to Say about Really Confronting Male Power," *Changing Men* 22 (Winter–Spring 1991): 8.

63. Paul Kivel, *Men's Work: How to Stop the Violence That Tears Our Lives Apart* (New York: Ballantine, 1992), xiii–xiv.

CHAPTER 6: IS "PRO-CHOICE" WHAT WE MEAN TO SAY?

1. Gloria H. Albrecht, "Contraception and Abortion within Protestant Christianity," in *Sacred Rights: The Case for Contraception and Abortion in World Religions*, ed. Daniel C. Maguire (New York: Oxford University Press, 2003), 96.

2. Beverly Wildung Harrison, *Our Right to Choose: Toward a New Ethic of Abortion* (Boston: Beacon, 1983), 251.

3. The Alan Guttmacher Institute, "In the Know: Questions and Answers about Pregnancy, Contraception, and Abortion" (New York: Alan Guttmacher Institute, 2004), A.1–A.3.

4. The Boston Women's Health Book Collective, *Our Bodies, Ourselves: For the New Century* (New York: Simon & Schuster, 1998), 413.

5. Guttmacher, "In the Know," K.1.

6. Ibid., E.2.

7. Harrison, *Our Right to Choose*, 244–45.

8. Guttmacher, "In the Know," F.1.

9. Ibid.

10. Rachel Atkins, executive director of the Vermont Women's Health Center, puts the matter this way: "There aren't 'women who have abortions' and 'women who have babies.' Those are the same women at different points in their lives." Cited on the website of the Mabel Wadsworth Health Center in Bangor, Maine, www.mabelwadsworth.org. Nancy Foss of Maine's Abortion Access Project provides a "mental picture" by asking people to visualize thirty women they know gathered in a room and to include their mothers, sisters, wives, aunts, cousins, and friends. As Foss then explains, at least ten of these women have had an abortion, but because of the weight of the abortion stigma, it is unlikely that the person doing this visualization is aware of these terminations. "Sometimes this visual/mental exercise," Foss suggests, "helps contextualize for folks who think this [issue] isn't connected to them in any way." Personal correspondence, July 26, 2011.

11. See Christine E. Gudorf, "Contraception and Abortion in Roman Catholicism," in *Sacred Rights: The Case for Contraception and Abortion in World Religions*, ed. Daniel C. Maguire (New York: Oxford University Press, 2003), esp. 55–60.

12. Boston Collective, *Our Bodies, Ourselves*, 388.

13. This social justice argument is developed by Beverly Harrison in *Our Right to Choose*.

14. Frances Kissling, "Should Abortion Be Prevented?" *Conscience* 27:4 (Winter 2006–7): 16.

15. For example, see Exhale: An After-Abortion Counseling Hotline, with service available at www.4exhale.org or 1-866-439-4253. Exhale serves women who have abortions, as well as their partners, friends, and family, with a commitment to maintain confidentiality and also respect the cultural, social, and religious beliefs of all callers. See also Backline, a similar online service available to women and men seeking confidential support to talk about pregnancy, parenting, abortion, and adoption, at www.yourbackline.org or 888-493-0092. In the current cultural and political climate, Nancy Foss observes that space has been created for women to express regret about abortion decisions, but hardly any room has been opened up for women to say that they regret having a child. "We are barely able to leave room for women who don't want any kids, much less support women who have the courage to say out loud that they regret being a mother" (see note 10 above).

16. Frances Kissling, "Can We Ever Say a Woman Can't Choose?" Salon.com (June 21, 2009): 2, www.salon.com.

17. Guttmacher, "In the Know," F.1.

18. Harrison, *Our Right to Choose*, 2.

19. Frances Kissling, "Should Abortion Be Prevented?" 16.

20. Harrison, *Our Right to Choose*, 183.

21. Mary Gordon, "A Moral Choice," *Conscience* 11:2 (March–April 1990): 13.

22. Public Religion Research Institute, "What the Millennial Generation Tells Us about the Future of the Abortion Debate and the Culture Wars," June 9, 2011, www.public religion.org. Also, "'Pro-Choice' or 'Pro-Life,' Sure, but Both?" *The Portland Press Herald*, Friday, June 10, 2011, A2.

23. See Ellen Messer and Kathryn E. May, *Back Rooms: Voices from the Illegal Abortion Era* (New York: St. Martin's, 1988).

24. Frances Kissling, "Ending the Abortion War: A Modest Proposal," *Christian Century* 107:6 (February 21, 1990): 181.

25. Beverly Wildung Harrison, "Theology and Morality of Procreative Choice," in *Making the Connections: Essays in Feminist Social Ethics*, ed. Carol S. Robb (Boston: Beacon, 1985), 128–29.

26. For the story of a couple who discovered at the twentieth week of pregnancy that their fetus had a fatal birth defect and chose to carry the pregnancy to term even though "babies with acrania [the skull is not fully formed] have a fairly good chance at living to full term and even some chance of being born alive, but they usually don't live more than a few days after birth" (11), see Dayna Olson-Getty, "Life Expectancy: On Not Praying for a Miracle," *Christian Century* (September 22, 2009): 11–12.

27. Harrison, *Our Right to Choose*, 18.

28. Daniel C. Maguire, "Visit to an Abortion Clinic," in *The Moral Revolution: A Christian Humanist Vision* (San Francisco: Harper & Row, 1986), 164.

29. Jael Silliman, Marlene Gerber Fried, Loretta Ross, and Elena R. Guttierrez, *Undivided Rights: Women of Color Organize for Reproductive Justice* (Cambridge: South End Press, 2004), 5.

30. Ibid.

31. Guttmacher, "In the Know," B.1.

32. See, for example, Ed Wheat, M.D., and Gaye Wheat, *Intended for Pleasure: Sex Technique and Sexual Fulfillment in Christian Marriage* (Grand Rapids: Fleming H. Revell, 1977, 1981, 1997, and 2010). While sexual pleasure is affirmed as good, the norm for "Christian sex" remains exclusively heterosexual and marital.

33. Christine E. Gudorf, *Body, Sex, and Pleasure: Reconstructing Christian Sexual Ethics* (Cleveland: Pilgrim, 1994), 31.

34. Marie M. Fortune in *Love Does No Harm: Sexual Ethics for the Rest of Us* (New York: Continuum, 1995) discusses procreative responsibility under the rubric of stewardship. "The choice to terminate a pregnancy," she writes, "can be a choice to do least harm. Being able to take responsibility to protect oneself against disease or unwanted pregnancy requires a sense of self that is worth protecting *and* a partner who is trustworthy" (108). Emphasis in the original.

35. Gordon, "A Moral Choice," 13 and 14.

36. Kissling, "Is There Life After 'Roe'? How to Think about the Fetus," *Conscience* (Winter 2004–5): 3.

37. Sylvia Thorson-Smith, "What Does 'Pro-Choice' Really Mean?" *Horizons* (May–June 2006): 2.

38. Boston Collective, *Our Bodies, Ourselves*, 413.

39. Ibid., 389.

40. Harrison, *Making the Connections*, 87.

41. Emily Erwin Culpepper, "She Who Creates Values," *Conscience* 13:2 (Summer 1992): 16.

42. Christine E. Gudorf, "To Make a Seamless Garment, Use a Single Piece of Cloth," in *Abortion and Catholicism: The American Debate*, ed. Patricia Beattie Jung and Thomas A. Shannon (New York: Crossroad, 1988), 281.

43. Harrison, *Making the Connections*, 118–19.

44. For a historical perspective on white male exploitation of African American women and how women of color have organized to resist and strategized to support victims and call for communal justice, see Danielle L. McGuire, *At the Dark Edge of the Street: Black Women, Rape, and Resistance: A New History of the Civil Rights Movement from Rosa Parks to the Rise of Black Power* (New York: Alfred A. Knopf, 2010).

45. Nelle Morton, *The Journey Is Home* (Boston: Beacon, 1985).

CHAPTER 7: WHAT DO WE HAVE TO LEARN FROM, AS WELL AS TEACH, YOUNG PEOPLE ABOUT SEX?

1. Quoted in Steve Clapp, Kristen Leverton Helbert, and Angela Zizak, *Faith Matters: Teenagers, Religion, and Sexuality* (Fort Wayne: Lifequest, 2003), 29.

2. Ibid., 27.

3. James B. Nelson, preface to Marie M. Fortune, *Love Does No Harm: Sexual Ethics for the Rest of Us* (New York: Continuum, 1995), 12.

4. Mark D. Jordan, *The Ethics of Sex* (Malden, MA: Blackwell, 2002), 16.

5. Beverly Wildung Harrison, *Justice in the Making: Feminist Social Ethics* (Louisville: Westminster John Knox, 2004), 69.

6. Clapp, *Faith Matters*, 14. Emphasis added.

7. Fortune, *Love Does No Harm*, 15.

8. Religious Institute on Sexual Morality, Justice, and Healing, "An Open Letter to Religious Leaders on Adolescent Sexuality" (Norwalk, CT: The Religious Institute, 2007), 1.

9. Debra W. Haffer and Kate M. Ott, *A Time to Speak Faith Communities and Sexuality Education*, 2nd ed. (Norwalk, CT: The Religious Institute, 2005), 11.

10. Ibid., 11–12.

11. Sarah G. Park, "Love God, Love Neighbour, Love Self: A Christian Approach to Adolescent Sexual Ethics" (unpublished paper, August 1, 2008).

12. Religious Institute, "Open Letter to Religious Leaders on Adolescent Sexuality," 1.

13. Advocates for Youth, "The Truth about Abstinence-Only Programs" (2007), 2.

14. Ibid.

15. Ibid., citing C. Trenholm et al., *Impacts of Four Title V, Section 510 Abstinence Education Programs Final Report* (Princeton: Mathematic Policy Research, 2007). Emphasis added. See also Donald Kirby, *Do Abstinence Only Programs Delay the Initiation of Sex among Young People and Reduce Teen Pregnancy?* (Washington, DC: National Campaign to Prevent Teen Pregnancy, 2002).

16. Clapp, *Faith Matters*, 22–23.

17. Ibid., 35.

18. Ibid., 60.

19. Ibid., 44.

20. Ibid.

21. Haffner and Ott, *A Time to Speak*, 12.

22. Clapp, *Faith Matters*, 42.

23. Ibid., 43.

24. Marie Fortune in *Love Does No Harm* cites statistics that indicate "at least one-third of all females are introduced to sex by being molested by a 'trusted' family member" (95) and that "some 74 percent of women who had intercourse before age 14 and 60 percent of those who had sex before age 15 report having had sex involuntarily" (122).

25. Clapp, *Faith Matters*, 86.

26. Ibid., 87–90.

27. Fortune, *Love Does No Harm*, 112.

28. Clapp, *Faith Matters*, 103.

29. Ibid., 95.

30. Ibid., 97 and 98.

31. Kelly Brown Douglas, *What's Faith Got to Do with It? Black Bodies/Christian Souls* (Maryknoll: Orbis, 2005), 196.

32. Clapp, *Faith Matters*, 59.

33. Ibid., 118.

34. Ibid., 124.

35. Ibid., 121.

36. Ibid.

37. Claire Greslé-Favier, *"Raising Sexually Pure Kids": Sexual Abstinence, Conservative Christians, and American Politics* (New York: Rodopi, 2009), xv.

38. Peggy Brick, "Toward a Positive Approach to Adolescent Sexuality," *SIECUS Report* 17:5 (May–July 1989): 1.

39. Marie M. Fortune, *Sexual Violence: The Sin Revisited* (Cleveland: Pilgrim, 2005), 76. Emphasis in original.

40. Dale B. Martin, "It's about Sex, Not Homosexuality," in *Reflections: Sex and the Church* (New Haven: Yale Divinity School, 2006), 26. Emphasis in original.

41. Ibid., 27.

42. Ibid.

43. William R. Stayton, "Sexual Value Systems and Sexual Health," in *Sexual Health:*

Moral and Cultural Foundations, vol. 3, ed. Mitchell S. Tepper and Annette Fuglsang Owens (Westport, CT: Praeger, 2007), 79.

44. Ibid.

45. Ibid., 85.

46. Ibid., 79–80.

47. Ibid., 28.

48. Clapp, *Faith Matters*, 113.

49. Ibid.

50. Kate M. Ott, "Searching for an Ethic: Sexuality, Children, and Moral Agency," in *New Feminist Christianity: Many Voices, Many Views*, ed. Mary E. Hunt and Diann L. Neu (Woodstock, VT: Skylight Paths, 2010), 160.

51. Rita Nakashima Brock, "Ending Innocence and Nurturing Willfulness," in *Violence against Women and Children: A Christian Theological Sourcebook* (New York: Continuum, 1995), 78.

52. Ibid., 82.

53. John Stoltenberg, *Refusing to Be a Man: Essays on Sex and Justice* (New York: Penguin, 1989), 39. Emphasis in original.

54. Park, "Love God, Love Neighbour, Love Self," 6.

55. Ibid.

56. Religious Institute, "Open Letter to Religious Leaders on Adolescent Sexuality," 1.

57. Haffer and Ott, *A Time to Speak*, 25.

58. Martha E. Kempner, *Toward a Sexually Healthy America: Abstinence-Only-Until-Marriage Programs That Try to Keep Our Youth "Scared Chaste"* (New York: Sexuality Information and Education Council of the United States (SIECUS), 2001), 12 and 60–61.

59. "Our Whole Lives Program Values and Assumptions," in *Our Whole Lives: Advocacy Training*, 23.

60. Ibid., 23 and 24.

61. Debra W. Haffner, "Toward a New Paradigm on Adolescent Sexual Health," *SIECUS Report* (December 1992–January 1993): 26.

62. Advocates for Youth, "The Facts: The Truth about Abstinence-Only Programs" (2007), www.advocatesforyouth.org.

63. Roni Caryn Rabin, "Condom Use Is Highest for Young, Study Finds," *New York Times*, October 4, 2010.

64. Religious Institute, "Open Letter to Religious Leaders on Adolescent Sexuality," 2.

65. Rosemary Radford Ruether, "Sexual Illiteracy," in *Conscience* (Summer 2003): 2, www.catholicsforchoice.org.

66. Rosemary Radford Ruether, *Christianity and the Making of the Modern Family* (Boston: Beacon, 2000), 219.

67. Joan Timmerman is quoted in Kate M. Ott, "Searching for an Ethic: Sexuality, Children, and Moral Agency," in Hunt and Neu, *New Feminist Christianity*, 164.

68. Ruether, *Christianity and the Making of the Modern Family*, 219.

69. Ibid.

70. Fortune, *Love Does No Harm*, 16.

71. Ibid., 19.

72. Ibid., 34.

73. Ibid., 38.

74. Ibid., 84.

75. Ibid., 139 and 142.

76. *Presbyterians and Human Sexuality 1991* (Louisville: Office of the General Assembly, Presbyterian Church USA, 1991), 20.

77. Ibid.

78. Ibid.

79. Ibid., 20–23.

90. Ibid. 23.

81. Stoltenberg, *Refusing to Be a Man*, 5.

EPILOGUE: HOW FAR CAN WE DRAW OUTSIDE THE LINES AND STILL BE IN THE PICTURE?

1. Christine E. Gudorf, "A New Moral Discourse on Sexuality," in *Human Sexuality in the Catholic Tradition*, ed. Kieran Scott and Harold Daly Horell (Lanham, MD: Rowman & Littlefield, 2007), 51.

2. Daniel C. Maguire, *A Moral Creed for All Christians* (Minneapolis: Fortress Press, 2005), 216.

3. See Marvin M. Ellison and Judith Plaskow, eds., *Heterosexism in Contemporary World Religion: Problem and Prospect* (Cleveland: Pilgrim, 2007).

4. Rosemary Radford Ruether, *Christianity and the Making of the Modern Family* (Boston: Beacon, 2000), 223, 173.

5. Ibid., 224.

6. Yoel H. Kahn, "Making Love as Making Justice: Towards a New Jewish Ethic of Sexuality," in *Sexuality and the Sacred: Sources for Theological Reflection*, 2nd ed., ed. Marvin M. Ellison and Kelly Brown Douglas (Louisville: Westminster John Knox, 2010), 262.

7. Gudorf, "New Moral Discourse on Sexuality," 64.

8. Beverly W. Harrison, *Our Right to Choose: Toward a New Ethic of Abortion* (Boston: Beacon, 1983), 117.

9. Ibid.

10. Maguire, *Moral Creed for All Christians*, 29.

11. Steve Clapp, *Taking a New Look: Why Congregations Need LGBT Members* (Fort Wayne: Lifequest, 2008).

12. Julian Rush, "In the Midst of New Dimenions," Hymn #391 in *The New Century Hymnal* (Cleveland: Pilgrim, 1995).

13. Marvin M. Ellison, *Erotic Justice: A Liberating Ethic of Sexuality* (Louisville: Westminster John Knox, 1996), 120 and 122.

▪ INDEX ▪